# PORTRAIT OF SURREY

# *Portrait of*
# SURREY

BASIL E. CRACKNELL

ILLUSTRATED
AND WITH MAPS

ROBERT HALE · LONDON

© Basil E. Cracknell 1970 and 1974
First published in Great Britain 1970
Second edition 1974

ISBN 0 7091 4527 6


Robert Hale & Company
63 Old Brompton Road
London S.W.7

PRINTED IN GREAT BRITAIN BY
LOWE AND BRYDONE (PRINTERS) LTD, THETFORD, NORFOLK

# CONTENTS

6 CONTENTS

PART THREE

# SURREY SOUTH OF THE CHALK

# ILLUSTRATIONS

*Photographs by the author*

MAPS

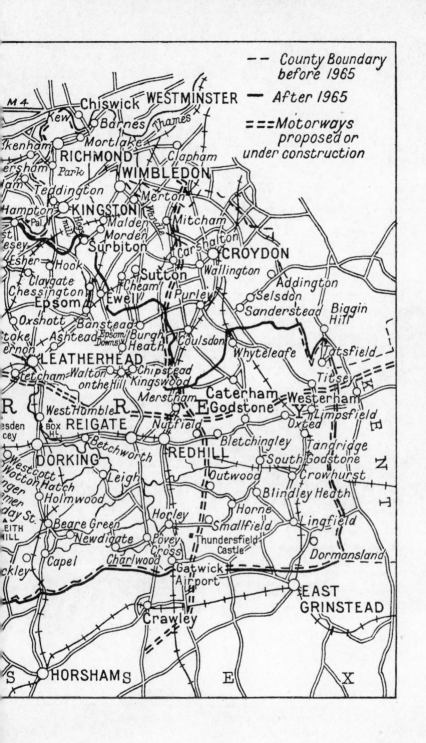

M 4

- - County Boundary
before 1965
— After 1965
=== Motorways
proposed or
under construction

Chiswick WESTMINSTER
Kew
Barnes Thames
ckenham Mortlake
ersham RICHMOND Clapham
am Park
Teddington WIMBLEDON
Hampton Merton
Pal KINGSTON Mitcham
mill Malden Carshalton
esey Morden CROYDON
st Surbiton Wallington
Esher Hook Addington
Claygate Sutton Selsdon
Chessington Cheam Sanderstead Biggin
Epsom Ewell Purley Hill
Oxshott Banstead
toke Ashtead Epsom Burgh Coulsdon Tatsfield
ernon Downs Heath Whyteleafe
LEATHERHEAD Chipstead Titsey
fetcham Walton Kingswood
on the Hill Merstham Caterham Westerham
West Humble R E Godstone Limpsfield
cey BOX REIGATE Nutfield Oxted
HL Bletchingley Tandridge
DORKING Betchworth REDHILL South Godstone
Westcott Leigh Outwood Crowhurst
Wotton Hatch Blindley Heath
nger Holmwood Horne
mer Horley Lingfield
day St. Beare Green Smallfield
EITH Newdigate Povey Thundersfield
HILL Cross Castle Dormansland
Capel Charlwood Gatwick
ckley Airport EAST
GRINSTEAD
Crawley

HORSHAM S E X

# I

# DAVID AND GOLIATH

Surrey is a county in mortal danger. It lies in an exposed position athwart the Capital's natural path of expansion in the south-westerly direction. Ever since the Great Wen first began to expand outwards, and especially since vehicular traffic became common-place in about the late seventeenth century, Surrey, along with the other Home Counties, has been subject to a ceaseless invasion from across its north-eastern frontier. It is over a hundred years now since Charles Dickens wrote in *Household Words* of: "Suburban open spaces being entombed in brick and mortar mausoleums for the suffocation, as well as for the accommodation, of an increasing population"—and still the process goes on inexorably. At first the impact was felt only in the immediate environs of London, but with improved communications and a rapidly growing population the trickle became a flood. Today this David and Goliath relationship overshadows every other aspect of Surrey's development and indeed threatens the very existence of Surrey as a distinctive entity, not merely administratively (the Royal Commission on Local Government's proposal to split the county in two has been dropped, but the danger still exists), but visually as well.

Surrey today finds herself in the position Middlesex was in a hundred years ago—being swallowed by Goliath morsel by morsel, her identity being gradually extinguished in London's urban sprawl. Less than a hundred years ago Surrey's eastward border joined the Thames at Deptford; and when Evelyn moved from Sayes Court, Rotherhithe, to Wotton near Dorking, in the seventeenth century, he was moving from one part of Surrey to another. To this day the only dock system south of the river is known as Surrey Commercial Docks, and still the Oval is Surrey's main cricket ground. When a Thamesman talks of the 'Surrey' side he means the whole length of riverside between Greenwich and Teddington. But in 1888 London took its first great bite of Surrey's territory, and from that time onwards Surrey's border ended at Putney. Then in 1965 the Capital took another great gulp and the new border joined the Thames at Surbiton. Will Surrey, by the end of the century, become the Middlesex of the south bank—merely a vast suburb of London? The name 'Surrey' signifies the 'people of the southern region', i.e. in contradistinction to the Middle-Saxons of Middlesex who lived on the other side of the river. Will the commuter-culture so penetrate into Surrey that it will become merely the people 'of B.R. Southern Region'? Surrey shares with Hertfordshire the unenviable distinction of being the most threatened of the Home Counties. Haslemere, the town in Surrey furthermost from London, lies forty-two miles from Charing Cross. and Royston, the furthermost town in Hertfordshire, is exactly the same distance to the north: compare these for instance with Harwich and Margate, the furthermost towns in Essex and Kent, both of which lie seventy-three miles from London. Even before Cobbett coined the phrase 'Jews and Jobbers', Surrey was popular as a residential area for London's businessmen, and today the term 'Stockbroker Belt' (sometimes rather unkindly called the 'Gin and Sin Belt') is nationally known. Attractive as many of these out-of-town homes undoubtedly are, and worthy citizens though many of their inhabitants may be, their very existence poses a serious threat to the survival of Surrey as a genuine entity. These people, with their big cars and their desire for large houses in extensive grounds on Surrey's heaths and hills, are the advance guard of an urban invasion. They are 'homesteaders' settling the countryside and thus paving the way, all unwittingly perhaps, for the townsfolk who will follow in their wake and 'metropolitanize' the land.

Meanwhile the less affluent Londoners seek to enjoy spasmodically what the stock-brokers enjoy permanently, by climbing into their cars at weekends and exploring "the highways and byways of Surrey". When the well-known Surrey naturalist and author, Eric Parker, wrote his book of that title in 1908 he was writing as a walker for fellow-walkers. In his preface he wrote: "Those

who believe that the best way to see any country is to walk
through it will find that as a general rule the book and its chapters
are divided ... into the compass of a day's walking," and he adds:
"my own plan has been simple enough: it has been to set out in
the morning and walk till it was dark, and then take the train back
to where I came from." Today, regrettable as it may seem, few
people walk any distance for pleasure. The pace of life, and the
sheer convenience of the motor car, has changed our ways. Why
wait on a draughty station platform when one can ride in heated
comfort in a car and come and go just as you please? In fact why
walk at all when one can ride? So a quiet, or rather a noisy,
revolution has been taking place. The footpaths are largely
deserted, the roads are overcrowded; more people see more and
more of Surrey, and know less and less of what they see. They
know the exteriors of a hundred Surrey churches and have been
inside perhaps a dozen. They know all the best Surrey beauty
spots and hills—provided a good road goes within a hundred
yards. They hear the birds but no longer recognize their songs,
they enjoy the general landscape effect of the trees and flowers but
can no longer identify the species, for, as Katherine Kenyon once
wrote: "Country people always see more than mere 'trees'; they
see oak or elm, larch or beech." The weekend motorists see
Surrey through a glass screen; not quite the glass screen of a
museum, but something equally unnatural, the windscreen of
their motor cars. Indeed, one wonders whether they ever really
see at all, for, to quote General Smuts, "Nothing is seen when the
viewer does not know what he is looking at."

Happily there are signs that this revolution may almost have
spent itself. In Britain, as in the United States (where the newly
discovered pleasures of adventure-walking, or 'backpacking' as
they call it, are all the vogue just now), people are increasingly
getting out of their cars and rediscovering for themselves what the
countryside has to offer at close quarters. This is not to say that
the old walking days will ever fully return—the car has altogether
too many advantages to be discarded. But we are now searching
for a *modus vivendi* with it. The car is inexorably part of our lives
today. My instinct is to use it, as naturally as Eric Parker's was to
reject it. My book is built round the assumption that we are all
motorists today. Yet I shall also assume that the reader is prepared

to use his car as a means to an end—that end being the fuller enjoyment of all that Surrey has to offer. And that may mean sometimes
forsaking the roadside and plunging into the quieter remoter
places accessible only on foot. The time may not be far distant,
indeed, when only those who are prepared to leave their cars and
walk will be able to find the peace and seclusion that the countryside still has to offer. Long before the advent of the motor car the
poet Cowper wrote: "They love the country, and none else, who
seek for their own sake its silence and its shade." The motor car
constitutes the greatest immediate threat to rural Surrey, lying, as
it does, at the very doorstep, or rather garage gates, of London.
How can Surrey absorb the tens of thousands of motorists who
swarm its narrow lanes and byways each fine weekend without
the very peace and beauty they seek being itself destroyed? This is
the problem of problems for rural Surrey, and it will occupy our
attention many times during this Portrait.

Perhaps I have allowed anxiety for the future to cause me to
adopt too pessimistic an attitude. Anyone writing in the 1930s
might have been fully justified in forecasting, as at least one author
did, that by the end of the century, if things continued as they
were then, Surrey would be one vast suburb of London. In fact
the war intervened, and after it came the Town and Country
Planning legislation which saved Surrey from such a fate. The
Green Belt policy (which began life as a 'Green Girdle' policy
until someone decided that this was altogether too effeminate a
title) was reinforced and indiscriminate residential development
halted. No new towns were built in Surrey and only two L.C.C.
out-county estates (Sheerwater and Merstham), so that Surrey
took a smaller share of London's outgrowth in the post-war period
than the other home counties. The threat to Surrey comes not so
much from planned large-scale development of this kind but from
a continuation of scattered residential development and from the
steady expansion of villages and small towns which ultimately
coalesce and form large urban areas, such as has already occurred
along Thames-side, between Guildford and Godalming, at
Reigate and Redhill, and between Horley and Crawley.

On the whole Surrey has good reason to be grateful for the
various Town Planning Acts which have protected so much of
her countryside. This achievement is the more remarkable when

one considers that a substantial part of Surrey has poor soils which are of little value for agriculture. The Bagshot Sands and the ill-drained heavy clays of the plains and the Weald are poor farming country—"rascally commons" as William Cobbett called them—and thus unlikely to come under the protective umbrella of the Ministry of Agriculture. The choice of Bracknell in Berkshire for a new town probably saved the Surrey heathlands from extensive large-scale urban development, whilst Crawley just over the border in Sussex probably saved the Surrey Weald. The town planners have long been interested in the poor agricultural land of south-west Surrey as a potential area for what they call in ugly planners' jargon 'overspill' population, but so far its relative remoteness and indifferent communications have saved it from such a fate, and lovers of rural Surrey will hope that it may long remain so. However if one threat has been averted the other still remains—the abrasive effect of crowded roads at weekends, and congestion at the accessible beauty spots. The new Countryside Act, with its encouragement for the creation of "country parks" to help accommodate these pressures, is of great significance for Surrey, probably more than for any other part of Great Britain. Surrey has always had its many great parks. As I write I have before me a copy of John Speed's map of Surrey dated 1610 in which no less than thirty-six great parks are shown, covering perhaps 10 per cent of the whole area of Surrey; and two centuries later a writer commented: "It is a common observation that this county contains a larger proportion of gentlemen's seats than any other district of England of the like extent." In a sense these were the original 'homesteaders' before the stockbrokers—they were the Lord Mayors of London, the Chancellors and bankers, and the Directors of the East India Company, who lived in Surrey and visited the capital when business took them there. It is a strange reversal of events that has now brought these parks, and others like them, to serve the people who live in London and only visit Surrey for pleasure. Already Surrey's stately homes are magnets drawing many thousands of Londoners every year, and if the new Countryside Act achieves its objectives, Surrey of tomorrow will have many more extensive open-air recreation parks specially planned for the needs of her populous neighbour, whilst at the same time siphoning off some of the pressures from Surrey's

2

village greens, rural verges and commons. It is in every way fitting that Surrey was the first county in Britain to open a picnic site (at Burford Bridge near Box Hill), provided with permanent refreshment facilities, under the new Countryside Act. The mid-twentieth century has at last made a start with the vital task of striking a balance between the needs of an urban population and the responsibility for preserving intact a diminishing rural heritage. Surrey is in the front line of this struggle. On its successful outcome depends the survival of much that is most worth preserving in the county.

This Portrait follows a mainly geographical pattern, although two or three chapters depart from the strict geographical sequence, such as Chapter 9, Piercing the Chalk Wall. The county indeed lends itself to this treatment since it falls so neatly into a three-fold natural division. The North Downs (G. K. Chesterton's "colossal contours"), that great ridge of chalk which runs through the centre of the county and which was the ancient route from Salisbury Plain to the Kent Coast, divides Surrey into three parts. Thus everyone who lives in Surrey lives either on the Chalk itself

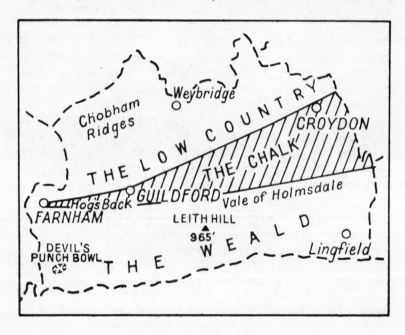

(as I have done all the years I have lived in the county), or to the north or south of it. Other writers have perhaps used different terms, but all have bowed to the 1,000-foot inevitability of that wall of chalk. Whilst I would not go so far as the author I read recently who wrote off the whole of Surrey north of the chalk as "suburban", in contrast to the area south of the chalk which he called "essential Surrey", yet I cannot deny that there is a great deal that is unlovely, and even plain ugly, about the Surrey Plain. However, as we shall see shortly, it has its merits, and in particular it has its rivers. The rivers of Surrey flow mostly northwards to join the Thames, which flows parallel with the Chalk Wall. Thus we have a grid pattern, comprising the Thames, its tributaries and the Chalk. The Plain with its rivers, the Chalk with its views, and the Weald with its remote villages at the end of winding roads; they represent the threefold division of Surrey, and they ensure that the county will always have that wonderful variety of scenery that makes it one of the loveliest in Britain.

# PART ONE

# SURREY NORTH OF THE CHALK

# THE SPIRIT OF THE LOW COUNTRY

Almost all of Surrey between the Thames and the Chalk Wall is low-lying and merits the title I once came across in relation to this part of Surrey—the 'Low-Country'. Of course there are isolated hilly knolls like Wimbledon Common, Telegraph Hill, St George's Hill and St Anne's Hill; and there are extensive areas of higher ground in the west along the border country. But for the rest the Low Country is coterminous with the land coloured bright green on the relief map as being less than 100 feet above sea level. This is the country of meandering and dividing rivers, of willows and weirs, of railway embankments, obtrusive to the eye because they cannot be hidden in cuttings, of towns and suburbs sprawling across the unresisting terrain as shapeless as splodges of jelly on a plate—and above all it is the country of the River Thames, which forms part of its northern border and which dominates a large swathe of land on either side.

The Low Country is a fan-shaped area, with the narrowest part in the east, and the widest part in the west along the Blackwater River. The most easterly section belongs to London itself—and the central section to the London Clay, that sticky bottomless slough that gave London its Underground Railway and the Low Country its heavy crawler tractors battling with the mud. The westerly section is sandy heathland, the Bagshot Sands, a very different kind of terrain, scarcely qualifying for inclusion as part of the Low Country, save for its lying north of the Chalk. This is a country of sudden ridges which provide a welcome contrast to the prevailing flatness elsewhere; even the chalk country to the south does not present an obvious feature because it dips gradually northwards until it disappears beneath the London Clay. The

Man of the Weald knows every line and wrinkle of the profile of the Chalk Downs, but the people of the Low Country see no profile there at all—except for the Hog's Back, of course. For this reason the Ridges of Chobham, Bagshot and Oxshott are doubly precious to the people of the Surrey Plain.

It is one of the curious features of the Low Country that it has only one really important road—the historic Portsmouth Road. A glance at the map shows that only this road seems to know exactly where it is going and makes direct towards its destination. Apart from a hiccup at Church Cobham, the Portsmouth Road goes straight as a die from London to Guildford. As for all the other roads they just seem to wander around, linking together the villages and towns just as they happen to lie. I have several times driven from Caterham to Windsor, and even now I still manage to lose my way in the labyrinth of roads around Hersham, Weybridge and Addlestone. It is curious that no major route came into being along the south bank of the River Thames, but possibly this was because the Great West Road on the opposite bank served all traffic heading westwards from London. Thus the Low Country is in effect a single corridor with many lesser passages but only the one important one. It is noteworthy that the old Portsmouth Road follows the higher ground wherever it can, thus it goes via Putney Heath, Kingston Hill, Esher Common, Painshill and Ockham Common—and even so this was a notoriously difficult and sticky road. The cluster of seven antique shops in the tiny village of Ripley on the Portsmouth Road, strategically placed to attract the traveller, aptly symbolize the 'corridor' character of the Low Country.

Flatness, which means more than the mere absence of hills, is part of the spirit of the Low Country. Flatness that has an immediate and positive impact on the observer—like the flatness of the Beddington Marshes, or the lower flood plain of the Mole, or of the gravel-pit country on either side of the Thames. Flatness that makes it possible to create a shallow lake a mile long near Weybridge just by damming a tiny stream; flatness that makes a tree an event and an aerodrome an eventuality; flatness that carries with it the ever-present threat of flooding; flatness that provides the local art teachers with ready-made lessons in perspective; flatness that calls to mind Victorian paintings of cattle lying in riverside pastures. Where else in Surrey is there such flatness?

Water is also part of the spirit of the Low Country. Not because of its absence, as on the Chalk, or because of its abundance in a multitude of swift-flowing streams or stagnant ponds as in the Weald, but because the streams that were born in other parts of the county, or indeed in other counties, have here reached their maturity. The Low Country is the land of wide mature and meandering rivers, of which, of course, the River Thames is the most important. In the Low Country water means above all "messing about in boats". No one lives far from a navigable river—or from the sight, sound or smell of boats. It was the Thames that caused the Low Country to have only one major through road—and the Mole gave that road its hiccup. It is the rivers that have given the Low Country a measure of scenic beauty that it so sadly lacks otherwise: the quiet meanderings of the lower Mole, the ponds of the Wandle, the string of villages along the Lower Wey, the meadows of the Bourne—how much poorer the whole region would be without these. And then there is the River Thames itself —now more truly a Surrey river than ever before since the re-drawing of Surrey's northern boundary. Bridges, towpaths, weirs and locks, swans on placid waters, the wake of an outboard motor, the peacefulness of yachts at anchor, white sails on a worked-out gravel pit—these are part of the essence of the Low Country.

Suburbia is now an integral part of the Low Country—but not of its spirit. There is indeed something deadening and destructive about suburbia—it has precious little spirit of its own. However, there is undeniably an attraction about that outer ring of suburbia that lies beyond the fifteen houses-to-the-acre belt. The beautiful modern homes around Claygate and Esher, on St George's Hill or along the banks of the Thames from Maids of Honour Row to Windsor—these represent a segment of society that can best be described as 'County'. The Bentleys and Rovers parked outside the outer suburban stations, the children in their jodhpurs riding ponies across the sandy heaths where the stockbrokers live, the ladies driving to the shops and talking in high strident tones over their coffee in olde worlde tea shoppes; I suppose these must now be counted part of the spirit of the Low Country. They are to be found, of course, on the Chalk and in the Weald, but nowhere are they in such profusion as among the sandy heathlands interspersed among the claylands of the Low Country.

Villages as such are not characteristic of the Low Country. One can think of isolated attractive villages north of the Chalk, such as Chobham, Ripley or Ockham. But, even so, the Low Country has nothing comparable with the string of beautiful villages along the Tillingbourne or in the Fold Country of the Weald. Unhappily, it is not the village that is part of the spirit of the Low Country as it is today but the upstart town. Woking rather than Wanborough, Camberley rather than Church Cobham, and Surbiton rather than Stoke D'Abernon—these must now be counted part of the spirit of the Low Country. With few physical barriers to impede them the upstart towns of the Plain have engulfed huge areas of flat land around them, so that Weybridge has overflowed into Byfleet, and Byfleet into Woking, and Woking into Bisley, and Bisley into Pirbright and Camberley—and so the dismal game of tag goes on, each trying to grab the tail of the town in front. The time has surely come to call a halt to this dangerous game, for there are indeed no winners, only losers. The town planners must devise a scheme for the Low Country that preserves a balance between town and country; not artificial 'garden' corridors between one town and the next, but genuine belts of countryside that provide a real visual and aesthetic break. If they do not succeed in this, even the upstart town (which for all its brashness and ugliness often has a certain vitality and vigour of its own) will eventually be itself submerged in the anonymous and faceless sea of suburbanity of its own creating. No one exactly loves the upstart towns of the Low Country ('upstart' because they have had no historical importance, and have grown faster in the last hundred years than any other towns of Surrey), but at least they have a recognizable personality and entity of their own, and it is worth trying to prevent them from sliding ignominiously into anonymity; however small their contribution to the spirit of the Low Country, it is yet worth preserving.

The history of the past is a more vital part of the spirit of the Low Country than it is of any other part of Surrey. Because of the extreme difficulties of travelling across the Weald, and the pre-emption of the chalk lands for sheep grazing and agriculture, the great homes and royal parks of Surrey were mostly concentrated

north of the Chalk. The Low Country is the Royal part of Surrey.
Kings won their crowns at Kingston, and a king lost his dictatorial
power at Runnymede, whilst successive kings built their great
palaces at Richmond, Hampton Court, Oatlands and Windsor.
Abbeys, too, contributed richly to the history of the Low Country, the two great abbeys of Chertsey and Merton extending their
influence into every part of the Low Country and far beyond.
Many of the churches of the Low Country date from Norman
times and before, whilst in the Weald it is rare indeed to find a
church as old as this. The illustrated leaflets published by the
Ministry of Works and Public Buildings (custodians of our ancient
monuments), the 1,000-year-old stones of Chertsey Abbey set in
the midst of recently planted turf, the latest initials carved on a
Norman archway—these are all part of the spirit of the Low
Country.

The Low Country is associated with the Capital in a more integral way than are the Chalk and the Weald. With its unlimited
reserves of flat land, combined with the direct means of access
along the River Thames, the Low Country inevitably attracted
the major share of London's expansion in the south-westerly direction. In addition to the growth of suburbs and upstart towns there
was a burgeoning of those various facilities that a capital city needs
and which require considerable land. The Brooklands Race Track
near Weybridge (now part of the British Aircraft Corporation
factory), Chessington Zoo, Bisley Rifle Ranges, the Farnborough
Air Show, the great water reservoirs of Littleton and Walton, the
race courses of Kempton Park and Sandown, Wisley Gardens,
and a host of golf courses—these all symbolize the Low Country's
role in satisfying the Capital's insatiable urge for *lebensraum*;
they are part of the spirit of the Low Country.

# SURREY-IN-LONDON,

## AND KINGSTON UPON THAMES

There was a time when the two small rivers, the Beverley Brook and the Graveney, marked not only the eastward boundary of Surrey but also the westward edge of London's expansion. But not for long. There was no containing the Great Wen in the Victorian era of unrestricted growth, and certainly these two rivulets were not going to stand in its way. So it was that Barnes, Mortlake and Richmond spread southwards to the edge of Richmond Park, whilst Wimbledon and the four 'Ms' (Merton, Malden, Morden and Mitcham, or five if we include Motspur Park) spread westwards to meet the eastward growth of Kingston upon Thames and Surbiton. By the beginning of the Second World War the process was complete; the only green spaces left were the parks and commons that had been saved from the hand of the developers. When, after 1963, the various urban districts and boroughs in the area were absorbed into the three new London Boroughs of Richmond, Kingston upon Thames and Merton, this was merely the inevitable consequence of that process. Yet the Surrey County Hall is still at Kingston upon Thames, whilst it is difficult to think of places like Chessington and Mitcham as otherwise than in Surrey, and no doubt the captain of the boat-race crew that wins the toss will continue for many years yet to choose 'the Surrey Station'. Even the Post Office continues to regard many of these newly Londonized boroughs as still in Surrey. For a while, therefore, at least until they wear their new bowler hats a little less self-consciously, we may be excused for regarding them as still part of Surrey—'Surrey-in-London'.

There is no denying that much of Surrey-in-London is dull and drab; either old-drab like the monotonous rows of Victorian villas in parts of Wimbledon and Merton, or new-dull like the semi-detacheds of Morden or Tolworth. However, one soon learns how to sort the wheat from the chaff. There is no point in searching, like an ageing lady trying to recapture her youth, for the odd scraps of original countryside that still remain. The countryside has gone past recall; its scattered remnants, like caged animals, can only sadden and hurt. William Cowper long ago wrote this bitter epitaph for suburban Surrey's lost countryside:

> Suburban villas, highway-side retreats,
> That dread the encroachment of our growing streets,
> Tight boxes, neatly sash'd, and in a blaze
> With all a July sun's collected rays,
> Delight the citizen, who, standing there,
> Breathes clouds of dust, and calls it country air.

The fields and meadows of suburban Surrey we cannot now restore. Instead we must look for the ribs of the old skeleton that still stick up above the mundane soil in which they are all but buried. There are many exciting discoveries to be made, as exciting in their way as finding a Roman vase on an old rubbish heap. Here is an old village pond and a little group of weatherboarded cottages, there is a village green and a Tudor inn, or a little row of Georgian houses, or a medieval bridge . . . the list is endless. Because so many people go around with their eyes shut to these things they see only the dull and the drab and miss the thrill of discovering for oneself these miraculous survivals from the past. To enjoy Surrey-in-London one needs the photographer's skill in seizing upon a detail and enlarging it, touching out the irrelevancies and touching in, with the help of the imagination, a more appropriate background; we must learn to 'zoom in' on the many fascinating and often beautiful cameos with which Surrey-in-London abounds, sparing no regrets for what has gone and acquiring an ever deeper sense of gratitude for what remains.

There is no better place in which to practise our newly acquired skill than Mitcham. For here the ribs of the past stick out more obviously than in many other places. Who can be unmoved by the tranquil setting of the green, vying with Hambledon for the distinction of being the oldest cricket green in the world, surrounded by ancient inns like the 'Old Cricketers', the 'Buck's Head', the 'Swan', and oldest of all, the 'King's Head', where people had been coming to watch the cricket for nearly a century before Lord Nelson and Lady Hamilton used to drive over from Merton to watch the sport. Or who can remain oblivious of its stately Georgian houses, dating from the time when Mitcham became a fashionable suburb, thanks to its proximity to London, a place "noted for its grand air and choice company"; or its noble church occupying a site dating back to the thirteenth century and linked by a tunnel to the old 'King's Head', the existence of which was proved in a sad manner some time ago when a child went exploring down there, became trapped and was dead when discovered. To drive down the relatively modern Church Road, with its rows of mean little brick houses, their doors abutting directly onto the pavement and their inhabitants breathing permanently the sickly smell from the adjacent paint works, into Old Mitcham, is to pass from death into life. But only if you have a lively imagination and can people the old village with the Dolliffes, Bonds and Barrons being driven to their London offices in their carriages, or the lesser gentry driving off to their local factories, the Ruckers and Fennings going off to their calico factory on the Wandle, the Rutters going off to their snuff mill down by the same river, or the Paines going off to their new fireworks factory. Or the village people working as domestics in the great houses, and as labourers in the market gardens and lavender farms (Surrey's famous 'flower farms') for which Mitcham had long been renowned and in the mills and factories down by the Wandle; and finding their pleasures watching the cricket—or once a year at Mitcham Fair. I do not find it hard to imagine the peasantry of a bygone age enjoying Mitcham Fair, for it was part of my own childhood. So great was the reputation of Mitcham Fair in my youth that as soon as my brother and I were allowed to go any distance by ourselves we set off to walk from Streatham to Mitcham Fair, with five shillings in our pockets and a meal in our haversacks. The thrill of hearing the sounds from a distance, and then seeing for the first time that miniature city of caravans and amusements of all kinds is with me still, and even today the sound of fairground music transports me in a flash to Mitcham Green and the permanently sunny days of the 1930s. Mitcham Fair is still one of the oldest and largest fairs in and about London.

As Mitcham grew in population during the nineteenth century so it lost its attractiveness to the local gentry, and at the same time improved transport facilitated rapid travel to the capital from places farther afield. One by one the big houses were sold and were generally pulled down and replaced by housing estates. Only the village centre, and, of course, the green, survived. But on a fine summer's evening, when the last pair are batting and you are beginning to think about that pint at the 'Old Cricketers', it is not difficult even today to zoom in on the Mitcham of the Dolliffes, Bonds and Barrons.

Unfortunately, not many of the other suburbs have retained their village character to anything like the same extent as Mitcham, probably because they never had such a highly developed village life. After all, Mitcham already had a population of 4,387 as early as 1831, at a time when Merton, Morden and Malden were small villages with populations in the hundreds. Thus one searches in vain for anything like Mitcham Green and must be satisfied with lesser cameos. Merton, of course, is associated chiefly with Lord Nelson and Lady Hamilton, but now that the rows of villas built on the site of Nelson's home, Merton Place, each road having a name commemorating the connection, have themselves fallen to the developers' bulldozers, there is very little of the Nelson Touch left at Merton. With incredible disregard of the site's historical significance they have named the block of flats built on the foundations of Nelson's home 'High Path Estate'—did the admiral ever sail in such a ship or win such a sea battle? Now that Nelson's memory is fading at Merton, we must fall back on the town's older and even more important association—Merton Priory. Happily there is more visible evidence of this connection. In the churchyard of Merton Parish Church has been re-erected the twelfth-century gateway to Merton Priory, and one can still walk in the garden by the Wandle and see the foundations of the priory that in 1221 owned the whole of Merton as well as huge estates elsewhere, and which gave its name to the oldest of collegiate institutions, Merton College, Oxford. But Henry VIII put down the priory and put up his palace at Nonsuch—using the same stones. The estate was broken up and Merton lost its historic connection with a great royal foundation. Henry I gave, in 1114, and Henry VIII took away. That presumably is the prerogative of kings.

Morden today is primarily a tube station. It is the terminus of the Northern Line, the only underground line that penetrates any distance south of London and as such is of great importance to many people living in a wide arc around it. On those rare occasions when a real pea-soup fog descends upon London—happily now few and far between if indeed they will ever recur in this age of smokeless fuels—anyone who lives within walking distance of an underground station forsakes his accustomed method of travel and goes to ground—or rather underground. It was on one such occasion in the early 1950s, when many elderly people died of smog, that I decided to take the underground to Morden and to walk from there to my home at Banstead. I arrived at Morden without difficulty, but once I left the station trouble began. The fog was unbelievably thick; I literally could not see my hand in front of my face. I set off to walk the three miles to Banstead, but after half an hour's walking I found myself back at Morden underground station—I had walked in a complete circle! Several hours and many lungs-full of fog later, I arrived at Banstead. They don't make fogs like that today.

My other image of Morden is equally uncomplimentary. It concerns that most soulless of huge estates, itself the direct consequence of the construction of the underground railway—the St Helier Estate. They tried in vain to soften its deadly uniformity by naming the roads after British abbeys, as if even the planners were horrified at what they had done and tried, too late, to make amends. But it defies mollification, just as the 150 Sunday-school children I once tried to teach there defied my modest attempts to inculcate some sense of Divine beauty. It was altogether too great a gap compared with their present reality.

However Morden, too, has its cameos; the stately Morden Park House, for instance, with its attractive park and its rare remnant of 'crinkle crankle' (serpentine) wall in the stable yard, or Ravensbury Park where the children can go boating on the Wandle, or the modern Crown House development opposite the tube station, an impressive multi-storey building that soars boldly above the surrounding mediocrity and gives exactly that visual fillip the district so badly needs.

*The Pagoda, Kew Gardens*

Malden, the fourth of the cluster of 'M' suburbs, shares with its initial-sakes the same dreadful suburbanity that clings to them like a cloud to a mountain top. Yet here, too, there are cameos to reward the diligent zoomer, especially Old Malden with its pond and green, its seventeenth-century red-brick manor house, and its weatherboarded cottages more reminiscent of Essex than Surrey (at nearby Coombe Hill Road there is indeed a typical Essex weatherboarded cottage brought all the way from Colchester).

Moving northwards we now approach the segment of Surrey-in-London, bordered by the Beverley in the east and a great loop of the Thames on the north and west. This is very different country from the flat clayland of the Surrey Plain over which we have been passing hitherto and which lay utterly exposed and defenceless in the face of London's all devouring expansion. On the plain there were no great commons or Royal Parks like Wimbledon or Richmond to stay the urban tide—it flowed across the flat country unimpeded until people eventually realized what was happening and cried, "Enough—no more". But in the country of the great loop, the commons and parks, and the River Thames itself, broke the impact of the onrush and split it into various lesser streams so that it changed the landscape but did not obliterate it. It is perhaps significant that no traces of Roman occupation have been discovered at Wimbledon—they skirted round this awkward knoll of high country tucked into the loop of the river. So we have here a succession of Mitchams. Places like Barnes, Petersham, Ham and Wimbledon have all retained their old village atmosphere to a surprising degree; whilst Richmond has never lost that air of a fashionable just-out-of-town resort that seems almost synonymous with its name.

Wimbledon was for me the gateway to adventure. As a child I would take a train from Streatham to Wimbledon Station with my brother, and we would climb the hill to the common with eager steps. On arrival at the common we would fling ourselves onto the turf, like bathers running into the surf, and with such a sense of freedom and release that could probably only be known by two boys who had spent their childhood deep in the country and had then suddenly found themselves immured in a city. Before us lay miles of seemingly unexplored countryside, with a windmill where we could refill our water bottles before again

3

*The Windmill on Wimbledon Common*
*Cricket on Mitcham Green*

plunging into the jungle, and a mysterious encampment named Caesar's Camp (actually a Neolithic earthwork) and a brook named the Beverley which was for us a river—an insurmountable barrier beyond which lay the limitless landscape of Richmond Park. They said you could see deer roaming about freely in the Park, but we never saw them as it was always time to run back to catch the train home. Eric Parker was surely right when he said that Wimbledon Common can transport the traveller the longest distance in the shortest time: "you may step aside from an asphalt highway 50 yards and you are in deep country." Does Wimbledon Common still unlock the doors of adventure to the youth of the 1970s? I like to think so, and would fight tooth and nail to prevent its being built upon should such sacrilege ever be proposed.

If familiarity breeds contempt, then I am glad that I have seldom had occasion to visit Barnes, for the acute sense of surprise and delight I had when first I saw Barnes Village is with me still. You have to turn off the Lower Richmond Road to enjoy the Barnes of the village pond, the weatherboarded cottages and the little groups of Georgian houses at Barnes Terrace overlooking the River Thames. I have rowed past these on many occasions, and the contrast they present to the negative aspect of the river bank along the reservoir-dominated Hammersmith Reach delights me afresh each time—although not so much, I am sure, as it does the crew of the lagging boat in the Oxford and Cambridge Boat Race, for Barnes Terrace means that Mortlake Brewery is only half a mile away. It is a great pity that the ugly railway bridge at Barnes spoils what could be one of the prettiest reaches of the river; and that Mortlake is now only renowned for its ugly brewery, whilst the tapestry industry, for which it was once nationally famous, is now altogether forgotten.

Kew retains even more of its village atmosphere than does Barnes. Kew Green, with its church and its Georgian houses, many of them owned at one time by people connected in some way with the gardens, makes as perfect an entrance to the Royal Botanical Gardens as one could wish. It is difficult to convey to the stranger the affection which every Londoner, and every 'Surrey-in-Londoner', has for Kew Gardens. This is not some remote stately park to be observed through iron railings, or from the window of a car, but gardens in the true sense—an extension of one's own suburban plot. You hear people talking about the magnolias being 'out' as if they were talking about the apple blossom in their own back garden, and with the same sense of personal pride. Even the Pagoda, the most striking example of chinoiserie in Britain (you can see it from the Chiswick Flyover, dominating the horizon); and the great glass Palm House, forerunner of the Crystal Palace; or the famous flagstaff of Douglas Fir 225 feet high; or the various exotic temples; cannot take away the intimacy of the gardens. Londoners have made Kew Gardens their own; parents take their young children there, the old people stroll there and talk knowingly about the plants and shrubs whilst they watch the other people out of the corner of their eye, and lovers meet there on a fine afternoon and soon lose interest in things horticultural until dusk falls and a patrolling groundsman cycles round flushing them out before the great iron gates clang to. Kew Gardens are to London what the Skansen Gardens are to Stockholm, only infinitely more gracious and charming. Yes, Kew Gardens is still a microcosm of London life, still as attractive as ever—but no longer, I am afraid, are they as peaceful as they once were. They now lie immediately below one of the flight-paths for planes landing at Heathrow, and giant airliners roar ceaselessly overhead—no sooner has one passed than the next is arriving. The gardens are now menaced by a foe more dangerous and more difficult to cope with, than any that may have been envisaged years ago when they built the high brick wall round the perimeter —noise!

And so, as Pepys would say, to Richmond—and there is no place more redolent of Pepysian charm and *joie de vivre*. Richmond is the capital and doyen of the country of the great loop; it is as deeply imbued with the aura of aristocracy as a Roman Catholic church with the aroma of incense. Richmond, of course, is not its original name. Up to the fifteenth century it was called Shene. Henry VII rebuilt Shene Palace after it had been destroyed in a great fire in 1497 and gave it the name of his earldom in Yorkshire. So Richmond Palace, already for several centuries the home of England's kings and queens, resumed its royal progress under its new name. The Palace vied for magnificence with Hampton Court across the river, the most splendid of Tudor palaces, and it remained in use as a royal residence until the time of George II. Richmond still preserves its royal connections through H.R.H. Princess Alexandra and the Hon. Angus Ogilvie, who live at Thatched House Lodge in Richmond Park. Only a Tudor gateway and some lesser buildings remain of the original Richmond Palace by the Green, but many of the other buildings that were attracted to its vicinity over the centuries still remain, such as the delightful 'Maids of Honour Row', 'Old Friars', Old Palace Place and Asgill House. Another group of period houses occupies the slope of Richmond Hill with its famous view, and the hill is capped by the huge Star and Garter Home for Disabled War Veterans. This is rather too large and dominating for my taste, but at least one can derive much satisfaction from the fact that the disabled servicemen can enjoy so beautiful a view of the England they fought to preserve. The view they enjoy today is virtually the same as that which so entranced Jeanie Deans in *The Heart of Midlothian*:

> The Thames, here turretted with villas and there garlanded with forests, moved on slowly and placidly, like the mighty monarch of the scene, to whom all its other beauties were but accessories, and bore on his bosom an hundred barks and skiffs whose white sails and gaily fluttering pennons gave life to the whole.

Richmond Hill brings us to Capability Brown's magnificent entrance to Richmond Park. It is the existence of the park with its 2,400 acres, together with Hampton Court, Bushey Park and Kew Gardens, that enables the Borough of Richmond to make the astonishing and proud boast that no less than half its total area of 14,000 acres is permanent open space. What other London Borough could match this? Richmond Park is surrounded by a wall, as other parks are, and it has its by-laws and regulations, as other parks do, but to most people who go there it is far more than just another man-made park—it is rather a miraculously surviving piece of primeval Surrey. The deer are wild stags to be hunted, the mounds are mountains, the plantations are dense forests and the ponds are great lakes that might be the source of the Nile if one's eye did not catch sight of the tower blocks of flats at Roehampton. True there are roads through the park, but even the Kruger National Park has its tracks.

But Richmond Park can be homely too, and I like particularly these verses from a poem by Patrick Chalmers:

### Richmond Park

Oh, have you been to Richmond of a windy April morning,
When the loose white clouds are flying and the blue is washed and
    clean,
When the beeches on the hill-top don a diffident adorning
And the river twines its silver through the shimmer of the green,
When the cuckoo flings his notes
And the thrushes crack their throats
And the boatmen at the eyot start a-varnishing their boats?

Have you seen its gallant vistas in the splendour of a June day,
Oh, the rhododendron thickets and the water and the wood!
When the stags are still in velvet and across the hush of noon-day
Comes the throbbing of the motors past the Gate of Robin Hood,
When the bracken by the ponds
First unfolds its crinkled fronds
And the dragon-flies are dancing round the slender willow wands?

Have you been to Royal Richmond when the year is growing
    mellow,
And October, mild and fruitful, on its woodland sets her mark,
When the footpath—of her bounty—has a carpet red and yellow
And the great harts roar a challenge as the twilight meets the dark,
And at half past five or so
There are lights that flash and glow,
Thrilling upward in the quiet out of Kingston down below?

Oh, have you been to Richmond when the days are short and chilly,
When a red December sunset has been swallowed in the fog,
When the wanderer, belated in the frosty air and stilly,
Sees the tree-tunks full of goblins, and he whistles up his dog,
And turns to look again
At the firelight on the pane,
In the keeper's cottage window, going home by Clarence Lane?

(From "Green Days and Blue Days")

Happily the Park does not end suddenly at its ten-mile wall, otherwise the illusion might be impossible to sustain even in the imagination. Instead it merges into open spaces at Palewell,

Petersham and Sheen Commons on the north, and into the riverside meadows at Ham Common. I find it a most satisfying thought
that because sovereigns in times past zealously guarded their hunting preserves like Richmond Park millions today can enjoy them
without let or hindrance.

Although Richmond is still the most aristocratic of boroughs,
it is Kingston upon Thames (so called to distinguish it from
Kingston upon Hull) that is called the Royal Borough, a distinction it shares with only three other boroughs in the country,
Windsor, Kensington and Chelsea, and Caernarvon. This is
entirely because of a piece of weathered grey sandstone which now
rests outside the Guildhall—the ancient coronation stone on which
at least seven Anglo-Saxon kings were crowned during the century and a half before the Norman Conquest. Although its career
as a royal seat came to an early end, 'King's Town' continued for
another six centuries to enjoy the special importance it derived
from being the lowest bridge (apart from London Bridge) on the
River Thames. It became a remarkable nexus of routes focusing
on the bridge and fanning out from it in all directions; it was
probably this centricity that made it, in the words of Leland the
Tudor historian, "the beste market towne in all Southerey". And
Kingston today is still a great shopping, cultural and administrative centre. Everyone in Surrey knows Bentalls the famous
Kingston department store that seems to keep ahead of its other
Surrey rivals, Shinners of Sutton, Grants Allders and Debenhams
of Croydon, or Harveys and Plummers of Guildford. Kingston's
Market Place, where the kings were crowned centuries ago, is still
there right in the centre of the town, gay with coloured stalls and
as animated as a market place should be (it has been much improved following its face-lift from the Civic Trust a few years
ago).

Kingston upon Thames's location at the bridgehead made it an
important coaching town, but for some curious reason this very
commercially prosperous community dug its heels in when the
first proposals were made to bring a railway to Kingston and
refused to let it enter the town. So it was that the first station was
built at Surbiton, which grew rapidly as a result of this windfall.

Kingston upon Thames is not really a town for the visitor to
linger in. It is a port of call for shopping, or to catch a river

steamer, or to visit the cinema, or to see some official at the County Hall (although now a London Borough, Kingston still houses the administrative offices of the Surrey County Council). However, like the other urbanized parts of Surrey-in-London, it has its cameos: the busy waterfront by the bridge and the riverside gardens; the period houses in the High Street, especially the 'Griffin'; the never-noticed medieval Clattern Bridge by the Market Place, where the ducking stool stood in times gone by; the chain of Tudor conduit houses erected by Cardinal Wolsey; the seventeenth-century Cleaves Almhouses in London Road; and, just beyond them, the sixteenth-century Lovekyn Chapel.

The Royal London Borough of Kingston upon Thames, an amalgam of the former municipalities of Kingston, Surbiton and Malden and Combe, is a true riverside borough, and few parts are more than a hundred feet above sea level. If you want to climb to the highest point in the borough you have a choice; you can either go to Telegraph Hill in the extreme southern tip, or you can climb the twenty-one storeys of Tolworth Tower—both rise to about 250 feet. The latter is either a triumph or a disaster according to your point of view. I was discussing it with an architect friend of mine recently, and he told me that it is a classic building of its kind and figures prominently in the professional literature. I cannot comment on its technical merits, but I like it for several reasons: because it is so uncompromisingly a product of its times, because of the daring way in which the architect has perched his massive pile on such spindly legs, and above all because it gives that urgently needed third dimension in an otherwise flat and featureless landscape.

Another high point in the borough is Combe Hill. It always used to puzzle me that this high ground should bear a low-sounding name, until I discovered recently that it is derived from the Celtic word 'cwm' meaning a hilltop. Combe is renowned as the place from which Cardinal Wolsey obtained his water supply for Hampton Court Palace, taking it there through a 3½-mile conduit that crossed the River Thames, but for me it will always be Robin Hill, the name John Galsworthy (who was brought up here) chose for it in the Forsyte Saga.

The Royal Borough pokes a long finger southwards to embrace Chessington Zoo, the largest privately owned zoo in England.

If you are motoring westwards from Epsom you suddenly find yourself crossing the border of 'London', and after a mile or so you are back in Surrey again. Chessington has sadly changed since Eric Parker, described it as surrounded by "quiet empty countryside". First came the huge mental hospitals of Horton, complete with their own private railway connections, then the zoological gardens and amusement park, and finally the sprawling Ordnance Survey Department, transferred recently to new offices in Southampton. Chessington Hall, where Fanny Burney first heard that her novel *Evelina* was a success, is now no more and Chessington Church, is no longer "deep in the fields" but deep in a modern housing estate. No one visits Chessington for peace and quiet these days, but to see the zoo. I have myself taken several parties of children there, and it makes a very satisfying venue for a day's outing; whilst the children are enjoying themselves in Pets Corner, or on the miniature railway that circumnavigates the zoo, you can hide yourself away in the old mansion called Burnt Stubbs and try to imagine the Cromwellian troops sacking the fourteenth-century house that once stood on this site, leaving it a 'burnt stub'.

When the reshuffle of boroughs within Greater London was taking place in 1965, probably the decision which caused more heart-searching than any other was the abandonment of the River Thames as an administrative boundary. Apart from a tiny outlying part of Woolwich on the north bank, the Thames had divided Surrey and Kent from Middlesex and Essex since before the Norman Conquest. However the imperative of numbers prevailed over ten centuries of history. Administrative economies demanded boroughs of about 200,000 people, and the only way to achieve this was by ignoring the Thames. So ignored it was—and probably rightly so. For the river is no longer the divisive influence it once was. Today it is fast becoming a unifying influence, as people seek to enjoy its recreational and amenity facilities to the full. The need today is for comprehensive planning of these facilities, and an authority that controls both banks and not one only is more likely to produce a sensible comprehensive plan for the optimum use of the river. So it came about that Twickenham found itself part of the London Borough of Richmond, and Sunbury-on-Thames and Staines became part of the

Administrative County of Surrey. It is no longer true that Surrey is the home of the people who live 'south of the river'.

Twickenham brings to the Borough of Richmond two great glories; its own bank of the River Thames and the great Palace of Hampton Court. It also brings a few more inimitable gifts, such as Strawberry Hill, for ever associated with the Gothic Revival and with Horace Walpole, who loved to watch the "barges as solemn as barons of the Exchequer"; Sion Row and Montpelier Row and their association with Walter de la Mare; and Marble Hill House and its associations with George II, who built it for his mistress Henrietta Howard and so helped to preserve the magnificent view from Richmond Hill. Twickenham's other contributions include Peg Woffington's Cottage at Teddington, one of an attractive row; the Georgian houses at Hampton Court Green; and the village of Hampton, still remarkably preserving both its village atmosphere and an unusually high proportion of its seventeenth and eighteenth-century houses, the village that Anthony Trolloppe liked so much better than Hampton Court, "that well-loved resort of Cockneydom".

But all these fade into insignificance beside the great uplifting work of Man's genius that is Hampton Court Palace. It was altogether too grand and magnificent to outlast a monarch's envy, and Cardinal Wolsey found himself obliged to offer it to Henry VIII only a few years after it was finished—although even this did not save him from disgrace. The palace as we know it today is not the palace that Wolsey built; several English kings added bits and pieces. Henry VIII himself built the Great Hall, and William of Orange added the Fountain Court. The landscaping of Bushey Park and Home Park—with Diana securely chaste in the middle of her large pond—completed the transformation of a sumptuous home into a royal palace, the English 'Versailles'. Yet such is human nature that we love Hampton Court as much for its vine (the oldest in England) and its maze, as for its architectural glories. I spoke to my son recently after he had been on a school visit to Hampton Court and evoked little or no response until I mentioned the vine. Immediately his eyes lit up as he reported what he had heard about the hundreds of bunches of grapes that are produced from this one vine every year. A few years ago I arranged for a young French couple who were staying with us to visit Hampton

Court, and the only thing they wanted to talk about on their return was getting lost in the maze—which might have been less surprising if they had not been brother and sister. Whilst visiting Paris recently I stopped to gaze in awe and a deep sense of personal insignificance, at the magnificent exterior of the Louvre as seen from the Tuileries Gardens. After a while, however, I found my-self studying intently the statue of a nude figure in the immediate foreground; the sculptor had cleverly placed her in such a position that if she moved an inch she would surely fall right off her pedestal—just as General Smuts, in Parliament Square, is depicted in the very act of striding forward at the point when one is most off balance. One could almost see this poor lady's muscles tensed in the effort of keeping herself on that block of stone—and that, I am afraid, remains as vivid a memory for me as the Louvre itself.

# THAMES-SIDE SURREY
## FROM EAST MOLESEY TO EGHAM

Thames-side Surrey is a district of many striking contrasts. St Anne's Hill, Chertsey, rises sheer from the flat river valley and makes 250 feet seem more like 750; the monotonous Moleseys give place to the superb residential districts of Esher and Claygate; ancient buildings and sites like the 1470 gateway to Bishop Wayneflete's Palace (better known as Wolsey's Tower), Walton's parish church, parts of which date back to Saxon times, and historic Runnymede, exist side by side with ultra modern structures like the fine new Urban District Council offices of Walton and Weybridge, Walton's new swimming pool opened in 1965, the new Roman Catholic church at Thames Ditton—circular and with a central spire—and Sir Edward Maufe's fine Air Forces Memorial at Runnymede. And through the centre of it all flows the River Thames, unchanged and unchanging—magnificently aloof to the novelties of today that are tomorrow's yesterdays. Yet even Old Father Thames has had a little rejuvenation treatment; the half-tide lock at Richmond, built in 1894, conceals the lines of old age by preventing the retreating tide from exposing ugly mudflats in the tidal parts of the upper river; whilst here and there a little discreet surgery has removed a wrinkle or two, as in the Desborough Channel at Shepperton.

Surrey's northern frontier has always belonged intimately to the river that served for centuries to divide it from its neighbours, and now that Sunbury and Staines have been incorporated into the Administrative County of Surrey the Thames from Hampton Court Bridge to Staines Bridge is wholly a Surrey river. Although there are all too few opportunities for the motorist to enjoy the river, many stretches of which are totally inaccessible to the private motorist and remain largely the preserve of the fortunate few who own holiday homes on the banks or have boats of their own, the Thames is nevertheless the principal playground for the people of north Surrey. It is to them what Hampstead Heath is to the north Londoner, what the sea is to the people of Brighton or Hove, or what the mountains are to the people of a Welsh mountain village. They talk endlessly of boats and buoys, tides and tackle, moorings and masts, along a hundred creeks and aits from Taggs Island to the Hythe. And now they are spilling out from the river itself into the nearby disused flooded gravel pits, so that it is a not uncommon experience in Thames-side Surrey, when motoring along a road a mile or two distant from the river, to see a fleet of sailing dinghies weaving in and out among the derelict jibs and bucket excavators of a disused gravel pit. There is in fact a desperate shortage of water for sailing, and as soon as the gravel operators have finished with a pit and Nature has reclaimed its own, if not before, the sailing clubs of the district are there in the queue. What fun there can be in going round and round a flooded gravel pit, with usually the noise and dust of a still-working pit as your neighbour, I cannot tell, but the urge to sail makes the devotees oblivious of their environment—just the water and the boat and a little wind is enough. Happily for them a recent report by the Surrey County Council's Town Planning Committee says that the rate of gravel extraction will be increased in the years ahead, as reserves nearer London are exhausted; but even now the writing is on the wall, for the North Surrey reserves will themselves be exhausted by about 1984. By that time there will probably be more boats on disused gravel pits than on the Thames itself. A few years ago, the Metropolitan Water Board announced that they were prepared to allow sailing on some of their reservoirs for the first time. In Surrey the Walton-on-Thames Sailing Club has been allowed to use the Island Barn Reservoir at East Molesey. A few years before this I flew over this reservoir and its huge neighbours the Queen Elizabeth II Reservoir, and, biggest of them all—and the largest in the world when it was built in 1925—the Queen Mary Reservoir, and I was moved by the oddity of these vast sheets of empty water set in the midst of a teeming water-hungry population. Now at last they are empty no more. Now they are frequently speckled with myriads of white sails, and we have to cast our eyes skyward to see them, for the water level of these great reservoirs is far above the level of the adjacent rooftops. These will never compare with natural lakes: they are severely geometrical in shape, there are seldom any trees: on the banks, and the winds blow across them with devastating force, so much so that they can generate sizeable and destructive waves even in such a confined space—a breakwater three quarters of a mile in length had to be built almost across the Queen Mary Reservoir to reduce the impact of these waves.

Sunbury-on-Thames, like nearly all the Thames-side villages (but, as we shall see, unlike virtually all the Wealden ones), is an ancient village dating back to Saxon times. Today it is still a river-side town of great character. The mellowed brown-bricked houses, made of local clay, cluster round the eighteenth-century church on the river bank, its distinctive cupola set against a back-ground of trees a familiar landmark to Thames yachtsmen. Lower Halliford and Shepperton complete the trio of villages on Surrey's north bank. Again the local-made brown bricks are much in evidence, and they lend a characteristic mellowed air to the older buildings. St Nicholas Church at Shepperton occupies an attrac-tive position on the little backwater known as the Silent Pool, the second of that name in Surrey.

Surrey north of the Thames has suffered heavily from indis-criminate modern development, yet there remain many reward-ing cameos for the patient searcher. Church Square, Shepperton, for instance has two interesting inns: the 'Anchor' (a true anchor in this instance—elsewhere in Surrey where one finds an inn bear-ing the name Anchor, for instance the 'Blue Anchor' at Blindley Heath, it is probably a corruption of 'anker', a measure of wine and spirits once in common use), and the 'Kings Head' with its associations with Nell Gwynne. The 'Kings Head', one of the tiniest—and busiest—of riverside pubs, lies immediately opposite the church, and on a fine Sunday evening the customers, often still wearing their yellow PVC windcheaters, spill out into the lane outside and hum the hymn tunes coming from across the way. The manor house has beautiful lawns sweeping down to the riverside; the Old Rectory is old enough to have given shelter to Richard III before the battle of Bosworth Field; and at War Close are tumuli said to have been connected with the Roman crossing of the Thames at the time of Julius Caesar. For centuries historians have speculated as to where the 'Cowey Stakes', where Julius Caesar wrote of forcing the passage of the river against the British, were situated, but the most common opinion is that they were in fact here at Shepperton, and the tumuli at War Close lend tangible support. Lower Halliford has an attractive village green and a 300-years-old inn, the 'Ship Hotel'. Nearby is 'Vine Cottage', the early home of George Meredith, which links the lowest part of Surrey with one of its highest parts since Meredith later moved to a cottage at Box Hill where he spent the greater part of his life. He found his wife in the Thames-side meadows, but his literary inspiration in the hills. Littleton Church, like so many other churches and older buildings in the flat marshy riverside area, shows evidence of subsidence in its leaning arches, whilst the wonderful profusion of building materials used in its construction, chalk, flints, local-made bricks and even Reigate Stone, reflects the paucity of suitable materials close to hand.

We now recross the river to the historic Surrey of the people who lived on the 'south' side of the river. At first it seems a distinction without a difference; the same rather monotonous and tasteless urbanization has taken place throughout the wide arc of country between Long Ditton and Walton; apart from the river itself, which never fails to delight, it is a depressing area. Its cardinal sin is that it is mainly dead flat. Its venial sins are many and various. The reservoirs, those towering green ramparts up to 100 feet high, make the nearby houses seem puny and irrelevant and effectively block whatever view there may once have been, so that the road between Molesey and Walton amply merits the description I once saw applied to it: "The ugliest road in Surrey". The streets are laid out in a particularly aimless and shapeless fashion as if the absence of hills and valleys left the town planners, or estate developers, at a loss as to how to shape their roads. They have built first a race-course, and now houses, on Molesey Hurst, one of the earliest and best-known of Surrey cricket-grounds and holy ground to lovers of the sport: cricket was being played here in the 1730s, when it was customary to use only two stumps set two feet apart and only 12 inches high—although it was not long before the endless complaints of the bowlers that their balls had gone right through the wicket caused the third stump to be introduced! And the last of the venial sins—that every ten years or so the whole district is subject to disastrous floods.

People still talk of the Black Monday morning of 15th September 1968, when 8,000 families in the Molesey and Ditton areas were flooded out. Each family has its own poignant flood story, just as we all had our personal 'bomb' stories during the war: how they saw their pet goldfish floating past the mantelpiece, how they moored boats to the tops of the garden gates, how twin rainbows spanned the Thames Valley on the day the floods abated as if to signal the Almighty's relenting. Yet within a week or two of the disaster there was no visible sign of it. I toured the area looking for evidence of the waters' destruction and desecration, but I found nothing, not even the giant hot-air driers they used to dry out the basements. The real aftermath of a flood lies in the minds of the people who experience it. Whilst such floods occur they can never forget the dangers of living at the confluence (and on the flood plains) of two rivers, the Thames and the Mole. Nor does the future hold much hope of relief. A recent expert report to the General Parliamentary and Scientific Committee on Flood Studies and Flood Prevention forecasts that the climate of the second half of the twentieth century will be wetter and colder and that floods will become more frequent.

Walton is as pleasing as the Moleseys are depressing, and it is difficult to see why this should be so since they each occupy a similar position on flat land by the river. Walton, however, seems to have been adopted by the wealthy, perhaps because of the excellent recreational facilities offered by the river in the vicinity, but possibly because they could not hope to match the opulence and elegance of Hampton Court across the river from the Moleseys and so chose a neighbourhood where the competition was less fierce! Whatever the reason, Walton is a pleasant residential area with a magnificent new town centre and town hall and an older High Street with a pleasing country-town atmosphere; old and new have been made to blend together exceptionally well at Walton. The town's principal asset, apart of course from its location by the river, is the ancient church of St Marys, one of the very few churches in Britain that has stone work dating back to Saxon times (the Saxons built most of their churches in timber and very few of them have survived), with its massive tower well buttressed, in the fashion of Thames-side churches, to prevent the soft sub-soil from claiming yet another victim. Walton Church contains an oak cabinet in which is a scold's bridle bearing the inscription dated 1632:

> Chester presents Walton with a bridle
> To curb women's tongues that talk too idle.

This was the Parthian Shot of a man who had lost his estate through the malicious gossip of a lying woman. There would have been more visible assets of Walton's past glories in the days before the lovely eighteenth-century bridge, beautiful enough to be chosen by Turner as the subject of one of his paintings, had been destroyed in a great storm (the present iron girder bridge is so ugly that no one but a contractor would wish to paint it); or the Tudor mansion of Ashley Park had been demolished in the 1920s; or, going further back into history, before Oliver Cromwell had razed to the ground the royal palace of Oatlands.

Located between Walton and Weybridge, Oatlands was one of the many palaces built by Henry VIII either to accommodate his many wives (in this case Anne of Cleves) or just to accommodate his whim. The name survives in various forms, as a Drive, a Road, a Close, a Park, an Avenue, and even, because this is a riverside district, as a Mere! In the 1830s, Oatlands Park, in the words of Fanny Kemble the famous actress who once lived at Weybridge; was "cut up into small villa residences and rascally inclined citizens' boxes". As for the stones of the old palace they had long since gone further afield—you must look for them embedded in the locks and weirs of the Wey Navigation. Cromwell probably thought he was doing the nation a great service by demolishing the palace and deforesting the park which had been reserved for the royal hunting. But not so! It is an irony of history that if Oatlands had been zealously preserved for the exclusive use of the Crown, as Richmond Park was for instance, it might today remain as a valuable open space. Surrey's south bank hereabouts badly needs its Hampton Court Park, or its Bushey Park, and Oatlands today might be performing that role if Cromwell hadn't "knocked it about a bit".

*The Entrance to Hampton Court Palace*
*The new Council offices. Walton*

Weybridge possesses that most priceless of all assets in flat country—height. Monument Hill for me is the making of Weybridge; and if I had to choose which of the Thames-side towns I would like to live in, it would be Weybridge. Descending Monument Hill gives me the same twinge of pleasure as does the descent of the hill into Dover, or Broadstairs or Folkestone—or indeed any hill which has water at the bottom. The water at Weybridge is a little distant from the town, for Weybridge's bridge is over the Wey and not the Thames (there is no bridge over the Thames between Walton and Chertsey), but when you reach the Thames you are rewarded with one of the loveliest stretches of riverside in Surrey. The cutting of the Desborough Channel not only provided a fine stretch of water for rowing and punting races but left a wide meander of the river available for sailing or just lazing and quiet relaxation. Near Weybridge, perhaps because it is joined at this point by Surrey's largest river, the Wey, the Thames has an unusually large number of islands, aits or eyots as they are variously described, including D'Oyly Carte Island, on which stands the house formerly owned by the family of that name.

Water at Weybridge implies not only two rivers but a lake— the attractive Broadwater, a lake about a mile long running parallel with the Desborough Channel and created by the Earl of Lincoln, owner of Oatlands Park. When frozen, this lake provides excellent skating and the scene resembles something out of Breughel.

Weybridge town was a natural and important settlement from early times, although, because of its low-lying situation, it was probably not occupied by the Iron Age people who preferred the high country of nearby St George's Hill, where one of their encampments has been discovered. Iron Age Man was not alone in appreciating the attractions of St George's Hill; today some of the leading celebrities of the entertainment world live there. Until very recently two of the Beatles, Ringo Starr and John Lennon, lived on the exclusive St George's Hill estate (they moved when it seemed to be becoming too popular), and their neighbours included Tommy Trinder, Eric Sykes, Dick Emery, Angela Browne, Englebert Humperdinck and Tom Jones—no wonder the locals call it England's 'Beverley Hills'! A £100,000 house, a private swimming pool, and a place in the exclusive golf club, are as

4

*The River Thames near Lower Halliford*

necessary to one's peace of mind as the most modern of radar-operated burglar alarms, the pack of guard dogs and the regular subscription to the estate's private Securicor patrol. There is said to be a three-year queue to join the golf club, but if you are desperate enough there is a back way in—you merely have to buy a house that carries with it a covenant allowing the purchaser to join the golf club—where else could such a thing exist but in Britain's Sunset Boulevard?

The event which began Weybridge's rise to importance as a commercial and industrial centre was the construction of the Wey Navigation by Sir Richard Weston in 1651, and a further boost was given in 1796 by the construction of the Basingstoke Canal linking that town with Weybridge. The full story of these two canals must await a later chapter, but Weybridge is probably unique amongst towns in the south of England in standing near the entrance not only of one canal but two.

The parish church of Weybridge is unusual in that it has a soaring spire rather than a squat tower, and it is a familiar landmark for miles around. The town also boasts a monument with a curious history. It used to stand at Seven Dials near London's Soho District but was pulled down in the eighteenth century; it was mistakenly supposed to have treasure buried underneath, and this was apparently believed to be worth more than the monument itself which eventually found its way to a Weybridge stonemason's yard. After some years it was refurbished and re-erected in its present site in memory of the Duchess of York. The Duchess seems to have won the affection of the people of Weybridge for her concern for the dead—she personally tended the little cemetery of seventy tombstones near Oatlands, each one bearing the name of one of her favourite dogs! What happened to her collection of favourite monkeys, each of which had its own pole with a little house on top, history does not relate.

Of all the Thames-side towns and villages, except perhaps Esher, which lies a little inland and in higher country, Chertsey has been the most successful in retaining much of its original charm. Perhaps this is due to its location off the main roads and railways out of London, or simply to the few extra miles it lies from the capital. "Chertsey, the stillest of country towns", observed Matthew Arnold, "leads nowhere but to the heaths and pines of Surrey." Or it may somehow have been due to its long association with Chertsey Abbey, the most influential of all the religious houses of Surrey, not excluding Waverley or Merton. Chertsey Abbey may be no more now than a few stones in a garden, but to the local historian it still extends its influence and sway over a large part of Surrey and the adjacent counties. The main religious houses of Surrey were each established on low-lying marshland by a river: Waverley by the Wey, Merton by the Wandle, and Chertsey by the Thames. Being one of the earliest foundations to be established after the conversion of Britain to Christianity (it dates from A.D. 666), Chertsey Abbey received generous grants of land in and around Surrey. The abbey was suppressed in 1537, and when it came to be demolished its stones, so precious in this stoneless country, began a two-stage journey that took them first to the new palace at Oatlands that Henry VIII was building and then, as we have seen, to the works of the Wey Navigation. If a schoolboy in Chertsey were asked to write an essay on the subject "If I were a stone of Chertsey Abbey", he should have no difficulty in composing a fascinating story.

Chertsey, like Weybridge, has a bridge and a hill. Chertsey's Bridge, however, is over the Thames itself, a beautiful seven-arched bridge dating from 1785. With its nearby boatyards and tea rooms and the adjacent lock, it makes an attractive place in which to deposit the family whilst you go off to potter about the abbey grounds just a short walk away, or take a look at Hardwick Court Farm, reputedly the birthplace of Henry VI, with its magnificent tithe barn dating from 1325 and one of the largest in England. Then if they tire of the river, you can take them to Chertsey's hill, St Anne's Hill, with its panoramic views across the flat country of the Thames stretching away to Runnymede and Windsor Castle in the distance, and its old chapel ruins which, as Aubrey remarks, "look like a place apt for pilgrims to visit", although he adds with disarming honesty, "but I could hear no account of that". Unhappily the view has been largely spoiled in recent years by the building of the giant intersection of two motorways below the hill.

Like the Shambles of York, or the Royal Mile of Edinburgh, Egham lies in the lee of a great building—Windsor Castle, and it shares a little of the lustre of its great neighbour. Although the visitor is probably unaware that the one-time little hamlets of Egham, Hythe, Thorpe, Englefield Green and Stroude, were in times past part of Windsor Great Park, yet he cannot but be aware of the influence of the royal castle on the whole area from the first time he sees its noble profile on the distant horizon. There is even something park-like about these hamlets, scattered, like parkland trees, in the green and blue meadow that lies between St Anne's Hill and the river (blue because so many have been excavated for gravel and are now flooded).

Egham, as a name, has nothing to do with ham or eggs—but the town certainly has. For many years Egham was an important coaching station on the road to the south-west, and it still retains a vestige of the atmosphere of the coaching days, although not of course on a par with Guildford, the other coaching station roughly equidistant from London on the Portsmouth road. At one time there was stabling for eighty horses at Egham's 'Red Lion'; it was wiser, if you were heading westwards and the day was drawing on, to spend the night here and face the dangers of Bagshot Heath and its highwaymen in the daylight hours.

A line drawn vertically through the centre of the Egham Urban District roughly divides it into two distinct parts, the flat riverside meadows to the east, and the undulating sandy district of Windsor Great Park and Virginia Water to the west. The riverside has been rather intensively developed both residentially and industrially, but there are still some interesting corners. There is the village of Thorpe with its beautiful Norman church of St Mary's, squat and four-square with a low battlemented tower, almost the arch-type of Thames-side churches; or the great Elizabethan mansion of Great Fosters (now a hotel) with its chalk mullioned windows, its carved fireplaces, its moat and its sculptured box hedges, one of the foremost examples of Tudor architecture in the county; or the quiet open meadows of Thorpe Green; or the most famous of all meadows in England—Runnymede.

One should approach Runnymede from the north, for there is no more impressive entrance to the county of Surrey. The road keeps close to the river for a mile or two after crossing the county boundary and then suddenly the river does a dog-leg turn away to the north-east leaving the road to continue straight on across the famous meadows of Runnymede. The entrance to Runnymede is

marked by a memorial gateway erected to commemorate the gift
of the historic meadow to the nation by Lady Fairhaven in 1929.
As few people these days pass through the gateway on foot the
inscription on it is seldom read, which is a pity for it prepares the
visitor for what lies ahead:

In these meads, on 15th June 1215, King John, at the instance of
deputies from the whole community of the realm, granted the
Great Charter, the earliest of constitutional documents, where under
ancient and cherished customs were confirmed, abuses redressed, the
administration of justice facilitated, new provision formulated for
the preservation of peace and every individual perpetually secured in
the free enjoyment of his life and property.

Noble words for a noble occasion—and how supremely fitting it
is that the people of England's green and pleasant land should have
secured their freedom, not at a Bastille, a church door at Witten-
berg, a Boston quayside, or a Vice-regal Palace in New Delhi—
but in a meadow.

Across the river from Egham lies the busy town of Staines. I
find it as difficult to realize that Staines is now part of Surrey as to
realize that Sheen, Sutton and St Helier are in Surrey no longer.
Staines was, after all, the north bank's bridgehead town *par
excellence*; it was the place where the historic Imperial Way leapt
across the Thames to continue its journey to the South-west. And
still today the old Roman Road, now the A 30, heads past London
Airport straight as an arrow to the point where the *'pontes'* were
located which gave Staines its ancient name of Ad Pontes. Roman
directness still has its virtues, for who would wish to linger among
the horizon-killing embankments of the huge water reservoirs
which surround Staines so that it has to stand permanently on its
toes to keep its head above water. Not that many people are
aware of Staines' struggle for survival these days. Most through
travellers take the bypass and congratulate themselves on avoiding
the busy High Street. But just now and again, especially on a quiet
Sunday morning, or on a summer's evening, they should remind
themselves that Staines has a beautiful stone bridge built by
Rennie, a town hall at least as impressive as its double at Ipswich,
and in St Mary's an impressive Georgian church occupying a site
that had already been in religious use for 400 years when William

the Conqueror's enumerators came round and noted the vine-
yards that flourished in the locality at that time.

The other half of the Egham District looks down, like the silent
cloister of the Air Forces Memorial on Cooper's Hill with its
20,456 names, upon the flat riverine country below. Behind
Cooper's Hill lies Englefield Green, the home of so many families
who were wealthy enough to enjoy having royalty as near neighbours, among them the donors of Runnymede itself. Indeed the
people of Englefield seem to have had an eye for an attractive open
space for they managed to keep their green inviolate when so
many other open spaces elsewhere in Surrey were being developed.
Some of the houses surrounding the green still carry ownership of
grazing rights for cattle and sheep on the green, although what use
these are today I am not sure. The largest part of the 'high' country is occupied by Virginia Water—not the lake of that name of
course but the rapidly growing community that has attached itself
in the last fifty years as much to the vital railway station as to the
other amenities of the district. Although many of its houses are
luxurious and very well designed in themselves, there is a rather
depressing absence of a sense of community about the whole
district—at least so far as the casual visitor is concerned. Where is
the town centre? Is it at Virginia Water Station, or on the London
Road, or where? One sees a district of lovely homes, but each one
is an island, part of an archipelago of affluence. Only the 8.15 a.m.
to London unites this community, and then only for the fifty
minute journey twice a day; unless it be the Wentworth Golf
Club, symbol of social success—the Queen of the Islands. Yet
Virginia Water is worth visiting for the Water. There is something unique about the great lake in its greater park, with its
planted ruins, transplanted from the ruins of Leptis Magna near
Tripoli in North Africa, like some discarded film set (even the lake
itself is artificial having been created by the damming of several
streams), and its massive overflow cascade visible near the London
Road. Even the high fence that surrounds the park reminds one
that this is the Royal Demesne and that kings and queens, as well
as commoners, had their rights protected for all time on the
meadow of Runnymede.

# 5

# THE RIVERS OF THE PLAIN:
# THE WANDLE, MOLE AND WEY

There is only one river worthy of the name that belongs exclusively to the Surrey Plain, and that is the River Wandle. There are brooks like the Beverley and the Windle, several streams that all seem to call themselves 'The Bourne', rivers that are really rivulets, like the Hogsmill and the Graveney, and glorified ditches like the Tolworth 'Watercourse', which all flow wholly, or almost wholly, across the plain, but none of these is truly a river. Of course the Mole and the Wey are more important, but they rise outside the county and belong as much to the Surrey Weald and the Chalk as they do to the plain. So we will give pride of place to the plain's own offspring—that unruly tomboy of a river that so ill matches its languid-sounding name—the Wandle.

Probably most people would say that of all the rivers that flow through Greater London only the Thames itself has retained any personality of its own. The others, such as the Lea, Brent, Ravensbourne—and the Wandle, have been robbed of their character by the spread of urban London during the last century and a half. Few roads or footpaths follow the courses of these rivers, and it often happens that one of the most important functions they now perform is the negative one of acting as a convenient boundary line between one local authority and another. The traveller is usually unaware of their existence except when he happens to cross them, and even then he will seldom know the name of the river unless he lives in the neighbourhood. This is understandable because the valleys through which these town-rivers flow have been so intensely developed with bricks and mortar that the physical contours have become obscured—one is vaguely conscious of going downhill and then up again without being aware of the valley as a whole—and often even without being aware of having crossed a river. In the countryside this same valley would form a pleasant rural landscape with the river as its focal point of interest. Not so long ago the Wandle was just such a river.

The Wandle is only some 11 miles long, but in that short distance it falls about 150 feet, or 14 feet every mile. It rises among the springs that emerge from below the Chalk near Croydon and joins the Thames near Wandsworth Bridge. Because of its rapid flow (it has been described as a 'cataract') the Wandle has never been important for navigation, save in its lower reaches, but on the other hand it has been ideally suited as a source of power since the rapid fall facilitates the construction of weirs and dams. As early as Domesday times there were as many as thirteen water mills on the Wandle grinding corn. In the heyday of the river's industrial career, during the early eighteenth century, there were no less than sixty-eight water wheels working on the Wandle, an average of one every 300 yards! At that time the Wandle was one of the busiest rivers in the world.

With the introduction of steam engines and electric power the old water wheels gradually fell out of use, but a few are still maintained in working order, more or less for sentimental reasons, just as some farmers still keep a few farm horses. Some years ago when I called at the Mitcham Fibre Mills to have a look round the old water mill I was shown one of these old water wheels that is kept in full working order and is sometimes run, mainly for the benefit of visitors like myself; I was allowed to photograph the wheel and to inspect the labyrinth of sluices and mill races which surrounds the property. The river's course has been altered artificially so many times that it is impossible now to see where the original channel was.

The Wandle is a river with many headwaters but few tributaries. The main series of springs are at Haling Park in Croydon, and the secondary headwaters rise at Carshalton; the two branches joining at Hackbridge. Thence onwards the river receives only one natural tributary, the little Graveney, which enters near Tooting Graveney, but it also receives the unnatural but quantitatively very significant flow of water from the Beddington sewage farm. This is the last piece of recognizable countryside the railway traveller from Sutton sees before he plunges into London proper; and often he will see huge black and horned cattle from far-off parts of the country fattening on the lush grass before they too make a journey, their last, to the abattoirs of London. Here too he can sometimes see strange and exotic birds enjoying the safety and seclusion of this flat wilderness so curiously sandwiched between Croydon, Sutton and Mitcham. It is worth twenty minutes standing in a commuter train to see such a sight.

The Wandle is not entirely urbanized. There is a short stretch, through Beddington Park, where it has retained something of its erstwhile beauty. Here can still be seen the "cleare rivulet Wandle . . . so full of the best trouts" described by Camden in 1607, and the scene cannot have changed greatly since the Carews of Pembrokeshire settled here in Tudor times and built their great house on the banks of the river so conveniently near to London and the Court. Beddington Hall is now used by the Borough of Croydon as a Special School for the education of sub-normal children (Carew Manor School), but before being converted to this use it was an orphanage—the oldest girls orphanage in the world. Here, centuries ago, were planted the first potatoes in England, and here also may still be seen the orangery wall honeycombed with heating ducts, a relic of the great orangery said to have been planted by Sir Francis Carew from seed imported by Sir Walter Raleigh from Florida. This was the first orangery planted in England, and in its prime it produced 10,000 oranges in a season; but the hard frost of 1739 killed the trees. Also worth seeing at Beddington is the old red-brick dove-cote in the grounds of the house which has 960 nesting holes for about 2,000 birds. Through the park flows the Wandle, still following the sinuous course it has followed over the centuries, and still with the weirs that once made it so famous as a workhorse among rivers.

Below Mitcham the Wandle has one last saunter among the green fields of Merton, dividing briefly to enclose the island on which Merton Abbey once stood, before it enters the dark defile formed by the cardboard mills of north Merton, plunges under the main road at Colliers Wood (at the point where the Roman Stane Street crossed the river), and then feels its way through the gloomy urban labyrinth of Haydons Road, Summerstown and

Earlsfield to its confluence with the Thames at Wandsworth. The river took its present name from the town at its mouth around 1586 (before that it was called "Hlida Burnam" or the loud brook) and in return it made possible the borough's early industrial prosperity. But Wandsworth robbed the lower Wandle of its rural beauty, turning it into the gutter of a stream which Tennyson could only describe as "foul and dank, foul and dank, by wharf and sewer and slimy bank". It is difficult to believe that this can still be the river that Isaac Walton praised for the excellence of its trout, that Pope called "blue transparent vandalis", and that John Evelyn in 1675 called "the most crystal stream we have in our country".

The Mole is more aptly named than the Wandle, for it has much in common with that friendly furry burrowing creature. In fact there appears to be no etymological connection between the two. The experts are still unsure of the origins of the name, but at least they are certain that it was nothing to do with the mole. Their latest theory is that the word is derived from the name of an Anglo-Saxon family owning land near the lower part of the river (hence 'Mole-sey'), but there are still some who cling to the older theory that the name is derived from the Latin word for mill, *molina*, and they point out that on old maps the Mole is called "Emlyn River" which is the Celtic word for mill. Whatever its origins, however, it is an apt enough name for a river whose curious burrowing habits (described in a later chapter) have attracted the attention of travellers down the ages.

In all its forty-two miles the River Mole scarcely passes through any important towns or villages, although it narrowly misses a good number. It seems to have an uncanny knack of turning aside just as it seems about to pass through a town, whether it be Horley, Dorking, Leatherhead, Church Cobham, Esher or East Molesey. Perhaps this characteristic, as much as its tendency to 'go to ground', explains why it has been called by various poets: "sullen", "silent" and "sulky". And the shyness is mutual for the Mole is avoided as much as it avoids. Not many rivers of its length have so few churches located on its banks, and only one of them, Stoke D'Abernon, is actually built right on the side of the river. Also in character is the fact that the river has no tow-path. Unlike the Wey, it has never been much used for navigation, although as early as 1664 an Act was passed (but never executed) granting permission for the River Mole to be made navigable from Reigate to the Thames, and it is thus relatively unknown for much of its course. For many miles between Leatherhead and Esher the river wanders far from inhabited parts, much of its course lying through private grounds. Perhaps Pope was thinking of these lower reaches when he wrote in "Windsor Forest" of "sullen Mole that hides his diving flood".

Although only a mile separates the Mole and the Wey at Church Cobham the two rivers have little more than their Wealden origins in common. Whereas the Wey was for centuries an important artery of commerce, and was directly responsible for the growth and prosperity of several large towns and important industrial centres, the Mole can claim none of these things, yet it possesses something that most readers would rate higher in order of importance—it has great natural beauty and, in its passage through the North Downs, has carved out a landscape as beautiful as any in Surrey or indeed in the South of England.

Below Leatherhead the Mole enters the Surrey Plain. Its great feat of breaking through the chalk wall accomplished, it can now meander quietly among flat meadows towards the Thames. There is no place which better epitomizes its change of mood than Stoke D'Abernon. Here is the one church that the Mole can call her own, and it is the oldest church in Surrey. What a superb situation it enjoys. The river flows in a wide arc enclosing a flat expanse of meadow on which cattle peacefully graze, whilst on the north bank, occupying a low bluff by the river, is the church with an imposing mansion alongside. The juxtaposition of these two buildings, the one ancient and humble, the other relatively modern and proud, in a scene of such splendid rural seclusion makes one of Surrey's most impressive sights. What a pity that only the few, the very few, who heed the modest little signpost "To Stoke D'Abernon Church" on the main road will ever see it—or perhaps that is as well or they would soon have to build tarmac car parks and refreshment booths, and the whole effect would be destroyed. The mansion was for some time a residential selection centre for the Civil Service, where many an aspirant for the Administrative Class cooked his goose by shovelling his peas onto his fork; it is now owned by the Inner London Education Authority.

At Church Cobham the Mole makes one of its characteristic

feints towards the village—and gets near enough to enable a picturesque mill to be sited by the road—but then it sheers off and by-passes the village altogether. Just beyond Street Cobham the river is crossed by the main London to Portsmouth Road, but hardly one in a hundred of the motorists who speed along this wide main road are aware of having crossed the Mole, flowing here in a deeply incised valley. Even fewer have seen the river at this point from its banks because "Trespassers will be Prosecuted" notices are depressingly abundant. Since no one walks to Portsmouth these days, probably the plaque set in the side of the parapet of the bridge is hardly ever read—which is a pity for it takes us back in a flash to the time, 850 years ago, when crossing the River Mole was something of an adventure, and one not easily forgotten:

> The first bridge on this site was built about the year 1100 by Queen Matilda, wife of King Henry I, as an Act of Charity in consequence of the drowning of one of her maidens at the ford. This bridge was built by the County under an Act of Parliament in 1783, and was widened on the north side by the County Council of Surrey in the year 1914.

Near the river, just westward of the bridge, lies Painshill Cottage, where Matthew Arnold, who styled himself in a letter to a friend: "The hermit of the Mole", spent his last days; and Painshill Park with its magnificent cedars, as fine as any in England, and its gardens with a lake fed by waters lifted artificially from the River Mole. A major road improvement took place here some years ago to improve the junction between the Portsmouth Road and the Byfleet Road, and to take some of the pain out of Painshill.

The Mole neatly traces the edge of the high country on which Esher stands, and the view northwards from the bridge over the Mole at the foot of Lammas Hill, with Wolsey's Tower rising above the trees in the distance, has always greatly intrigued me— not so much because it is beautiful but because it highlights the important influence that natural features have on the pattern of settlement. On one side of the river the rising land is occupied by houses, and on the other side the flat meadows extend as far as the eye can see with hardly a building on them. Just a short distance on from the bridge is one of the very few places where the road runs alongside the River Mole for a few yards, and the intelligent way in which the opportunity thus presented has been utilized makes one wish that more such opportunities could be created where they do not already exist. I once tried to find some way of getting by car down to the banks of the Mole between this spot and Church Cobham, and I found it utterly impossible—the river still remains the least accessible of Surrey's assets—more a frozen asset than a liquid one.

Esher is one of the most attractive of the several attractive villages near the Mole. It has a wonderfully well-preserved air of quiet prosperity and semi-urban gracefulness, especially around the Green, and an equally well preserved church, St George's, dating from 1540. Nearby is Claremont, the magnificent stately home designed by Capability Brown for Clive of India. The house is now a girls' boarding school, and the estate is largely owned by the National Trust.

Skirting Esher, the Mole enters the flat flood-plain of its larger sister the Thames. The two are united at East Molesey near Hampton Court. As the poet Drayton wrote:"'Gainst Hampton Court he (the Thames) meets the soft and gentle Mole." It would perhaps have been more appropriate if he had reversed the order for, as another poet has reminded us, the Thames scarcely notices the addition to its large family of waters of such a minor relative. The Mole, after all, has traversed only one county and part of another, and has brought wealth and prosperity to none of the towns and villages on its course; yet the little Mole has given great pleasure to many people and has turned many a mundane scene into one of utter enchantment. And the Mole has brought wealth of another kind, for, as Robert Bloomfield wrote: "Where the Mole still silent glides, dwells peace, and peace is wealth to me." Thanks to this unassuming river, there are many people living along or near its banks who will echo the words of Keats after a walk along the Mole Valley near Box Hill: "O, thou would'st joy to live in such a place."

The third river of the Surrey Plain, and undeniably the most important river in Surrey, is the Wey. The River Wey has for centuries been navigable for the twenty miles as far as Godalming, and it has thus been a major factor in the development of the

Surrey Weald and particularly of Guildford, the County Town. It is worth remembering that 75 per cent of the river's catchment area lies south of Guildford; in this chapter, however, we are concerned only with the river's role in the life of the Surrey Plain.

The River Wey, unlike the shy and retiring Mole, is by nature extrovert; it goes out of its way not to avoid towns but to pay a social (and often a business) call on as many as possible as it meanders its way leisurely towards the Thames. When it meets a large historic house like Sutton Place it cannot resist embracing it in a huge affectionate loop. It is continually linking hands with its canalized cousins, and in sheer exuberance breaking into several channels so that you frequently have to cross not only one but sometimes four or five bridges when you cross 'The Wey', and you are never quite sure which is the river proper and which are lesser branches of the family. At Byfleet, as we have seen, it makes friendly overtures towards its sister the Mole, but she isn't having any and sheers shyly off to creep unnoticed into the Thames through a gap between East Molesey and Thames Ditton (although via Walton would have been a much shorter route), whilst the Wey strikes boldly northwards, bisecting Byfleet and Weybridge and finally falling on the Thames as if greeting a long-lost friend. They are both Surrey rivers—but so different!

The first of the string of Weyside villages below Guildford is Burpham on the south bank, little more than a school, a church, a dangerous 'S' bend, and an old inn where one can imagine the bargees having a last drink before continuing on to Guildford. The next meander embraces Sutton Place, now the home of millionaire Paul Getty. It was built in 1523 by Sir Richard Weston, one of the Sutton Westons (hence the name). The house has an honoured place in Surrey's history and is generally best known as one of the earliest mansions in Britain that was not fortified in any way. It had no battlements or moat, but a glance at its situation may suggest one reason for this—with the Wey protecting it on three sides artificial protection was hardly necessary. Another reason may be that, as a Roman Catholic family, the Westons preferred not to have to seek the permission of the Sovereign to fortify their home. The house is a fine example of an early truly indigenous style of architecture; no attempt was made to copy the classical style, or to ape the architectural styles of other countries.

◦ Below Sutton Place lie the two important villages of Send and Old Woking. This whole area has been rather spoiled in recent decades by tasteless residential development, but sufficient still remains of these old villages to give some impression of what life was like in the great days of canal navigation before the railway came to rob the villages of their beauty and to give, in compensation, a new town as barren as the heath on which it was built— Woking. Both villages, and Horsell a near-neighbour, have churches over six centuries old, and the antiquity of these churches, as of so many others on or near the Wey, is some indication of the river's importance as a routeway in times past. However they lay slightly off the main radial roads from London and were therefore rather remote. Although Defoe in 1724 described Old Woking as "a country market town", he added that it was "so out of the way that 'tis very little heard of in England". The Basingstoke Canal was constructed in 1796, but although it passed between Horsell and Old Woking the curious thing is that it does not appear to have stimulated the development of either village. However, when the London and South-West Railway Company decided in 1838 to build a station, and later a junction, on a heath between Horsell and Old Woking, shown on the old maps as "Woking Heath", the district suddenly found itself no longer between the radial routes to London but slap in the middle of the newest and most important rail link in this part of Surrey. For a short time the new station of 'Horsell for Woking', like Godstone Road (later Purley) station south of Croydon built at about the same time, found itself almost the only building on the landscape. But it was not long before people began to realize the benefits of living near the railway, and Woking was launched on the road of expansion—probably the most rapid expansion of any town in Surrey. During the period 1811 to 1851 the town's population doubled, and it continued to increase in geometric progression so that today the borough has a total population of some 70,000 people, and it is still growing by about 2,000 per annum, about the size of Old Woking! Yet I find Woking a depressing place. It is still, in my eyes, a barren heath with no natural features to justify the existence of the town at all—just the railway itself. And the railway at Woking lords it over the whole town; it bisects, or rather trisects the town, and isolates the northern half and the town centre from the southern half; they have even built a major parade of shops right facing the railway line—every traveller to Portsmouth or the South-West must be familiar with it. The surrounding heaths and pinewoods must appeal to many people, or presumably they would not be so keen to live there, but the absence of any natural feature save the River Wey (which really belongs to Old Woking) makes Woking in my opinion the least attractive town of its size in Surrey. If Woking had a hill it would be more interesting—but then it would be Weybridge!; if it had a range of hills it might even be beautiful—but then it would be Guildford!

My favourite stretch of the Wey is that between Pyrford and Newark Priory (not Newark Abbey as so many people persist in calling it). The river valley at this point is very wide, and the Wey divides into no less than seven streams. The very flatness of the valley floor is emphasized by the knob on which Pyrford Church stands, and lends added stature to the ivy-clad ruins of the priory which, standing on a slight rise in the midst of water meadows, totally dominate the landscape. Yet what a price the monks had to pay here, as at Waverley further up this same river, for the absence of near neighbours; it needs little imagination to realize that every time the river was in flood the monks were up to their knees in water. The builders of Pyrford Church, a chapel of the priory and built soon afterwards, were really more practical; they chose a beautiful site and built there a church wholly worthy of it. It stands intact today when most of the stones of Newark have been spread around the district for the repair of the roads. Pyrford Church seems to grow out of the very hill itself, as do the elms that surround the church. In this reach of the river, and for another three or four miles as far as Wisley Church, a carbon copy of Pyrford in style if not in situation, the Wey puts on her best clothes —but unhappily it is for a funeral. For soon the river enters the urbanized lower reaches of Byfleet and Weybridge before it loses itself in the waters of the Thames. During the early years of this century, Eric Parker watched, from his home above the river, the rape of the beautiful Lower Wey, the building of Brooklands Race Track, the sewage works and later the aircraft factories, and no lines more poignantly express the sadness of beauty lost than these he wrote at the time:

> From pine and stream to steam and stone
> From peace to din and pain
> From old unused to new unuse
> But never Wey again!

# 6

# ALONG THE SPRING LINE
# FROM CARSHALTON TO THE CLANDONS

The Chalk is like a sponge lying on a sloping plate: it absorbs the rain water in its deep cavities and in due course the moisture collects on the clay 'floor' at the base of the chalk (the 'plate') and flows northwards, emerging eventually at the edge of the Chalk in a line of springs. From earliest times this line of springs has given rise to a succession of villages, called by John Toland in 1711 "a perpetual chain of villages within a mile or less of each other", each well endowed with its own supply of water that never failed. Fresh clean cold water it was, fresh and clean from its passage through hundreds of feet of chalk filter, and cold from its long sojurn deep in the bowels of the earth. The water rising in the springs in the very centre of Ewell are said to be the coldest in England.

Wherever there was a natural routeway southwards across the chalk country these villages grew into little country towns that in recent years have become boroughs and suburbs. Croydon, by the springs that feed the Wandle, is the principal example, but others are Sutton, near the headwaters of the Beverley Brook, Epsom and Ewell near the headwaters of the Hogsmill, and Leatherhead at the northern end of the Mole Gap. Between them lay lesser villages that slumbered peacefully from century to century, their population hardly changing, until they suddenly found themselves in the path of London's outward expansion and changed almost overnight from hamlets into suburbs like Beddington, Carshalton, Cheam and Ashtead. Westwards of Leatherhead the spring-line villages retained their innocence rather longer, but after the railway came they too succumbed.

The Bookhams, the Horsleys and the Clandons are about as closely spaced as the villages of the Tillingbourne on the other side of the Chalk—and for the same reason, the spring line. No part of Surrey has changed more in a single lifetime than the northern edge of the Chalk from Croydon to the Clandons. Between the penny-farthing and the family Ford, in one great frenzy of building, this huge slice of Surrey was largely covered with bricks and mortar. For all practical purposes that part of Surrey lying between Croydon and Cheam died as a distinctive part of the county, and the absorption of these districts into the Greater London Council (they belong now to the London Borough of Sutton) in 1965 was but a delayed recognition of something that had happened some decades before.

Most typical of the water-line villages nearer London is Carshalton (the name means the farm on the spring where cress is grown), still the most picturesque of them all, although it seems a far cry now from Ruskin's description:

> Twenty years ago [he writes in 1870] there was no lovelier piece of lowland scenery in South England, nor any more pathetic, in the world, by its expression of sweet human character and life, than that immediately bordering on the sources of the Wandle, and including the low moors of Addington, and the villages of Beddington and Carshalton, with all their pools and streams.

That was Carshalton just before the penny farthing was invented, and it had hardly changed since the seventeenth century when Dryden wrote:

> The Wandle cometh in, the Mole's loved mate,
> So amiable, so fair, so pure, so delicate.

and John Evelyn in 1658 had written of the village: "It is excellently watered, being on the sweet Downs, and a champagne about it full planted with wall-nut and cherry trees, the ponds by the church are brimming with clear cool water."

The Wandle, as we saw in an earlier chapter, was a busy work-a-day river from quite early times, but from the following old couplet it would seem that the presence of mills on the river did not prevent Carshalton from being a very attractive place:

> A neat little village surrounded by hills,
> It supports itself chiefly by snuff and corn mills.

Seen on a misty day, with the sun trying to break through, the ponds of Carshalton (which have seldom been known to freeze) have a delicate Japanese-print quality about them. Old Carshalton Church lies immediately opposite the ponds, occupying the same central position it has enjoyed for centuries and will no doubt continue to enjoy long after the furore a few years ago—over the curate who was accused of Romanish practices and removed by the Bishop from his parish—has been forgotten. The weather-boarded old inn 'The Greyhound' completes this charming scene. Just round the corner from the church is Carshalton village, still recognizably a village with more rural atmosphere than most of the other spring line villages between Croydon and Leatherhead possess. In the other direction lies Carshalton House, built by Dr Radcliffe, founder of the Radcliffe Library at Oxford about 1670, but now St Philomena's Convent School, and protected by the usual high wall that makes convents, like mental hospitals, places of mystery and imagination.

Sutton lost its village innocence earlier than the others thanks to its situation on the road to Banstead Downs where the racing fraternity of London gathered, and thanks also to the construction of one of the first turnpikes, the London to Brighton road via Sutton and Reigate, built in 1755. The Old Cock Inn with its sign stretching right across the road and its three toll gates, symbolized Sutton's status as a staging post on the most important road southwards from London.

Familiarity with the Downs, and the desire to live near them, brought several wealthy families to live in Sutton, and during the latter part of the seventeenth century the village became a notable centre of society. Great houses built at this time included Sutton Manor, Sutton Court, Sutton Hall and Cheam Manor House. Probably it was the arrival of these wealthy families, who wanted to live in the higher parts of the parish on the lower slopes of the chalk downs, that accounts for the fact that Sutton, alone among the spring-line villages, developed mostly on the chalk rather than on the low country where the springs emerged.

Sutton is changing its character more rapidly than any other part of Metropolitan Surrey except Croydon. The central area will be entirely redeveloped, the High Street pedestrianised, and traffic routed along parallel by-pass roads. There will be huge car parks on the periphery (one completed already). Tower buildings rising to 280 feet will dominate the skyline around the rebuilt station and many new stores will revitalise the shopping facilities as appropriate to a borough of about 200,000 people. The Civic Centre being built will in due course include a new central library, public hall, theatre and Liberal Arts College.

One day in 1526 King Henry VIII went hunting on Banstead Downs, and he was so delighted with the district, and no doubt with the view of his capital in the distance, that he decided there and then to demolish the village of Cuddington (then called Codyngtone) and to build a magnificent palace, of which it might truly be said that there was 'nonsuch' in Christendom. Day after day loads of stone were carted to the site (much of it coming from the old abbey at Merton), 3,050 in five months according to a contemporary account, whilst 600,000 bricks were burnt in clamps near the site. Eventually it was complete, a palace unequalled anywhere in splendour and extravagance. Leland called it "a structure so beautiful, so elegant and so splendid, that in whatsoever direction the lover of florid architecture turns his eyes he will say that it easily bears off the prize". The key word is "florid", and opinions vary as to whether it could really be called beautiful. F. J. C. Hearnshaw in *The Place of Surrey in the History of England* calls it "a hideous abnormity", but it undoubtedly seems to have captured the imagination and admiration of its contemporaries. However, its very size may have been its undoing. Like Brunel's great ship *The Great Eastern*, it was too big for normal use; in short, it was a white elephant. After a relatively short life of 140 years, during which it was rather severely damaged in the Civil War, Charles II gave it to the notorious Barbara Villiers, Countess of Castlemaine and Baroness Nonsuch, as a consolation prize for being passed over in favour of Nell Gwynne. The countess soon decided that this semi-ruin would be the ruin of her, so expensive was it to repair and maintain, and she had it demolished and sold the material for building. So it happened that the stones of old Merton Abbey were once more carted off, this time to help build the great houses that were springing up at this time around the newly fashionable Epsom: houses like Durdans, home of the Earl of Berkeley; Pitt Place, home of Lord Lyttleton; and Woodcote Grove, home of Josiah Diston, in the entrance hall of which one of the elegant marble fireplaces from Nonsuch Palace found a new home. Later another and more modest mansion was built in Nonsuch Park, and that one still survives. In 1935, in one of those rare acts of civic vision, Sutton and Cheam and Epsom and Ewell local authorities, and the Surrey and London County Councils, purchased Nonsuch Park for the use of local residents. In so doing they went a long way to redeem Henry VIII's rape of Cuddington Village—out of evil comes goodness. Mr Chuter Ede, that great Surrey man, said on the Twenty-First Anniversary of the purchase of Nonsuch Park: "What Henry VIII did to Cuddington enabled Surrey County Council to deal with Nonsuch, hundreds of years later, as a piece of 'No Man's Land' to be awarded to the best candidate." He added; "Surrey is a very pretty county, but do you know, I think this is the prettiest spot in it." So we have a lot to thank Henry VIII for after all.

The next village on the spring line is Ewell, or 'By-the-Spring', where what is known as the 'Long Spring' rises in the centre of the village, gives its name to the Spring Hotel, and its water to both the horse pond and the lake in the grounds of Bourne Hall, and then joins the Hogsmill *en route* to the Thames. Apart from the fine new Bourne Hall, Old Ewell village has few buildings memorable in themselves, but its ancient Tudor cottages and its graceful Georgian houses, dating from the time when Ewell was a fashionable satellite of Epsom in its spa and racing heyday, together form a unity compacted by Time. It is in the general impression created by the whole ensemble, rather than its individual components, that the attractiveness of Old Ewell lies. But therein lies a danger. If a plan is put forward to demolish any individual cottage or other property it is difficult to prove that it has architectural merit. However, if you pull down a Tudor cottage and erect a chromium-plated supermarket it is as conspicuous, and as damaging to the unity of the whole, as a silver tooth in a denture. Such a plan was proposed in 1958, and the applicants made great play of the fact that the tall lamp standards in the village—which rise 25 feet high, several feet above the adjacent roof tops, and were required because the High Street is a bus route and is therefore graded a Class 1 road—had already destroyed the village's rural character. Notice how insidious the process of despoliation is; one mistake is used by the unscrupulous as a rung for the next.

However the defendants quoted from Mr Gordon Cullen's article on Ewell in the *Architectural Review*, 27th June 1957:

Ewell Village . . . is on the brink of disintegration. As a personality it is faced with extinction. And that would be a pity. This is not a sentimental attitude, it is practical sense for, if the feeling of identity goes, then we become nomads living in a world to which we do not belong, for there is nothing to belong to.

The Tudor cottages were saved, and Old Ewell survived to fight another day.

Ewell has no village green or market place, which is rather curious since it was at one time the main market for the sheep of Banstead Downs. Before 1800, however, there was a market house, which was pulled down in that year to make way for road widening—an early example of 'progress'! But Old Ewell does have a village lock-up, an old church tower without a church, several old mills on the Hogsmill River that were used for gunpowder centuries ago, and in the grounds of Ewell Court a perfect example of an old pack-horse bridge which once carried the road to Kingston over the Hogsmill. In short it has all the character and interest that neighbouring places like West Ewell, Stoneleigh and Worcester Park lack. Surely we will not let the 'improvers' destroy what Mr Cullen called "a charming and ancient oasis in a sprawl of subtopia".

Epsom was first set on the road that was to make it the best-known town of its size in the world when Henry Wicker tried to enlarge a water-hole in the drought year of 1618, only to discover that his cattle would not drink from the bitter water that issued from it. Soon the "bitter purging salt" of Epsom became world famous for its medicinal qualities, and people suffering from gout and liver complaints flocked in their thousands to this little village to take the waters.

Luckily for Epsom the chemical composition of the salt was not diagnosed as magnesium sulphate for at least a century, and thus could not be manufactured artificially during that period. People therefore either had to go to Epsom in person, or pay for the water to be brought to them. Testimony to the high regard in which Epsom Salts were held is given by this epitaph discovered on a West Country tombstone:

Here lies I and my four daughters
Died thro. drinking Baryta Waters,
If us 'ad stuck to Epsom Salts,
We wouldn't be lying in these 'ere vaults.

People wealthy enough to go to Epsom, and with the kind of malaises (real or imaginary) that took them there, needed entertaining as well as curing. Epsom's hotels and inns were often crowded to overflowing (Samuel Pepys once had to go on to Ashtead to find accommodation), and many forms of entertainment sprang up: for the daytime there was cock-fighting, cudgel playing, foot running, wrestling, hawking and horse racing; and in the evening, dancing, music, cards and dice. The fashionable London set made for Epsom, and it became a fertile seedbed for scandal until the new resort of Brighton not only stole this unenviable title, but also most of Epsom's clientele for the newly fashionable pastime of sea-bathing. In its heyday Charles II was often at Epsom with Nell Gwynne discreetly lodged in an adjoining inn, whilst the Prince Regent was also often to be seen there with his secret spouse, Mrs Fitzherbert—and they once had to invent a ghost story to camouflage the demise of the dissolute Thomas, second Baron Lyttleton.

By the end of the seventeenth century the well was beginning to dry up. With as many as 2,000 people a day taking the waters this is hardly surprising. Celia Fiennes in 1702 caught them replenishing the well in the early hours of the morning with water from another well (which probably contained only a weak solution of salts), and when a German chemist came to Epsom in 1713 to study the salts he found only half an ounce of saline matter per 100 quarts of well water. At about this time a local apothecary, Dr Livingstone, built assembly rooms, gambling saloons and a bazaar, in Epsom—and a new well (which had no medicinal qualities). To ensure the latter's popularity he closed down the original well. Not unnaturally people began to desert Epsom, and historians generally blame his duplicity for the decline of the spa. In reality, however, the spa was already on the decline; other watering places like Tunbridge Wells and Cheltenham were becoming more popular, and in due course Brighton and sea-bathing gave Epsom its *coup de grâce*. By an irony of fate the sea also yielded the magnesium sulphate from which 'Epsom' salts eventually came to be manufactured artificially, some 20,000 tons per annum now being produced in this country. All that is now left of the spa at Epsom is the site of the old well, near Well Way, and a plaque which reads: "The medecinal waters that in the seventeenth century made Epsom a place of great resort, and its name known throughout Europe, were drawn from this well."

Epsom as a spa town died in the early eighteenth century; but Epsom as a town of popular resort was reborn at the end of that century when horse racing became established on Epsom Downs, and when the Derby and Oaks were instituted. The story of horse racing at Epsom belongs to the chalk downs and to a later chapter. Suffice it to say that Epsom of today looks more to the Downs and the race course than to the common and the well. Regrettably, few visitors walk along West Hill to the pond on Stamford Green, with its old inn and its air of having been there just as it is from time immemorial—one of those scenes that please most because it is least expected.

Leatherhead is the last of the spring-line villages that lay directly on a historic route from London to the south coast, and hence became, like Epsom, a true country town. The spring-line villages west of here were never on a direct route south and so remained insignificant little villages until the railway suddenly transformed them into outlying commuter suburbs of London. Leatherhead's setting at the northern embouchment of the Mole Gap is very impressive, the finest in fact of all the spring-line settlements. I like best of all the oddly named Gimcrack Hill, which carries the Leatherhead to Dorking road and which is for me one of the finest beginnings to one of the finest roads in Surrey. My mental image of this road was formed in the days when I was mostly walking and cycling, and I sometimes wonder if it is possible to gain such a sharply focused impression of a short stretch of countryside if one merely motors along it. One travels so fast in a car that the mind hardly has time to register the fact that the countryside is attractive before it has passed—the impression always is fleeting. Maybe only long continuous stretches of scenically beautiful road could have the same impact on a motorist travelling at 40 miles per hour as the Leatherhead to Dorking road had on me as a walker and cyclist. Leatherhead owes its existence in part to its position at the crossing of the River Mole, and down by the bridge, with its fourteen brick-built arches, lies one of the town's oldest buildings, lately the 'Running Horse', built about 1520, where Eleanor Rumming, the subject of Skelton's poem "The Tunning of Eleanor Rumming", was the proprietress. During the war years there was a youth hostel nearby, and when I stayed there as a lad in my 'teens I had never heard of Eleanor Rumming; but I knew every inch of the Mole from West Humble to Leatherhead, and I loved it as I loved no other part of Surrey. It has always been for me, as for Matthew Arnold, "the most enchanting country in England". I have a notion that everyone treasures in their memory some fragment of countryside that they associate indelibly with the first deep stirrings within them of an awareness of the beauty of Nature—vague "intimations of immortality"—and in my case that fragment is this part of the Mole Valley.

Leatherhead town for me is busy narrow streets and more traffic lights than any other town of its size possesses; blind people from the Royal School for the Blind tapping their way along Highlands Road; boys from St John's School hurrying along to the town to spend their weekly pocket money; buses heading out in all directions, and cars heading inwards for the shops and the theatre; genuine Tudor cottages and mock Tudor restaurants; and, above all, those decaying but still distinctive Victorian mansions along Gimcrack Hill, with their wonderful aspect across the Mole Valley.

Until the construction of the Leatherhead to Guildford railway in 1886 the string of villages from Fetcham to Merrow presented a picture of idyllic charm—provided, that is, one could overlook the grinding poverty of the agricultural workers, estate servants, gardeners and domestics, who inhabited these ancient villages. Wages in all these occupations were miserably poor, and the few surviving cottages in the district, such as Yew Tree Cottage in Fetcham (1617) with its ceilings only 6 feet high, give some idea of low material standard of living of the village people. Yet in another sense they were rich; for there was an ordered serenity about the life of those days that must have gone far to compensate for the lack of material possessions. And the housewives with their families shared their husbands' interests and lives, whereas today the husband rushes off to catch the 8.15 to London and she does

not see him again until seven o'clock. Then again, there were the
great houses in the neighbourhood—Fetcham Park, Eastwick
Park, Horsley Towers, Clandon Park and others—which brought
reflected colour and even glamour into the otherwise drab existence of the villagers, even though, like vagrants with their noses
pressed flat on the shop window, they could not themselves enjoy
the riches they observed. Then along came the railway, and in a
flash all this was changed. Populations doubled, doubled again,
and yet again; hamlets became commuter suburbs as dependent
upon the railway line as the original hamlets had been dependent
upon the spring line; the great houses mostly passed out of private
ownership, or at least occupation, and became, like Fetcham Park,
Effingham Hall and Horsley Towers, schools or training establish-
ments. High and low estate disappeared and were replaced by a
dreadful middle-class uniformity differentiated only by the particular train they caught each morning and by the make, but not
the size, of their motor car.

It is a curiosity that the main Leatherhead to Guildford road
passes very near, but not through, most of these spring-line
villages, so that the motorist is only aware of their presence by a
succession of name boards. The railway followed the low ground
a little to the north, and the villages therefore tended to grow in
lateral fashion—that is, at right angles to the Leatherhead
Guildford road. Since nearly all the new residents were commuters
and depended entirely upon the railway, the new houses were built
north and south of the stations, so elongating the villages still
further. Thus from East Horsley on the Leatherhead to Guildford
road almost to the outskirts of Ockham is about $2\frac{1}{2}$ miles of un-
broken residential development, and a similar pattern is repeated
at the other stations along the line. Seen from the air the district
has a fish-bone pattern of settlement, with the railway as the spine
and the roads as the ribs. South of the Leatherhead to Guildford road
there has so far been little residential development, and much of
this countryside still has something of the wide-open aspect it
enjoyed as the last of the great commonfields of Surrey. Here and
there, however, residential development has been creeping, like
Birnam Forest, on to the chalk downs under cover of woodlands,
particularly at Great Bookham and East Horsley, menacing
the hitherto unspoiled wedge of chalkland between Ranmore

Common and Newlands Corner—the last remaining extensive area of really natural chalkland left in Surrey.

It is an indication of the importance of London in the development of this part of the spring-line that, although East and West Clandon are only a mile or two from Guildford, they have not grown to anything like the same extent as the villages further east along the line—the few extra shillings a week on the season ticket put the brake on their development. Another contributory reason may have been that Clandon Park, the home of the Onslow family, occupied a large part of the parish of West Clandon. Here is situated Clandon House, standing in the park laid out by Capability Brown (who acquired this odd title from his habit of saying that such and such a piece of land was "capable of improvement"). The house, somewhat geometrical in appearance, but conveying a great sense of nobility, was built in 1729 to a design by the Venetian Leoni. It is administered by the National Trust and is open to the public during the summer months.

We end our journey along the spring line at Merrow, a village which, between the mid-seventeenth century and the time of William IV, was Guildford's Epsom, where the burghers and their families would come out to enjoy the horse-racing on Merrow Downs, followed by a glass of ale at the 'Horse and Groom'. Now there is a course of another sort, for golf has replaced horse-racing, whilst the players work mainly in London rather than Guildford. However, Merrow still has its homely flint church at the foot of the Downs, and something, too, of its old village atmosphere. Maybe Merrow is no longer, as it was in Kipling's day, an hour out of Guildford:

> There runs a road by Merrow Down
> A grassy track today it is
> An hour out of Guildford town
> Above the River Wey it is

but still, as in Kipling's day:

> On Merrow Down the cuckoos cry
> The silence and the sun remain.

# 7

# THE HEATHLANDS OF BAGSHOT AND CHOBHAM, AND THE SURREY BORDER COUNTRY

The huge segment of Surrey north of the Hog's Back as far as Windsor Great Park was for centuries part of the Royal Forest; but now it belongs to the Queen's army and all the Queen's men. The military shoot at Bisley, run their armoured fighting vehicles over Chobham Ridges, camp at Pirbright, educate their young at Sandhurst or at the General Gordon Memorial School, tend their sick in the hospital at Mitchet and bury their dead at Brookwood, the 'Camp of the Dead', the largest cemetery in all England. The army is your companion wherever you go; the more remote the heath the more likely it is that a Centurion tank will come crashing through the undergrowth; if the soil is too poor for a farmer to cultivate it will carry a prolific crop of army cantonments, wooden huts ridiculously equipped with verandahs as if this were Cawnpore not Camberley; if the road goes nowhere the military will be sure to be going there; if it is a fine clear day for rambling over the heath it is also a good day for shooting and the red flags are up; if you are immobile in a traffic jam like as not it is because the military are on the move. The army is in command—and so it has been ever since Queen Victoria reviewed her troops for the first time on Chobham Common in 1853. You have to love the army to enjoy living in West Surrey.

The busy, if unlovely, little town of Bagshot has given its name to the rural district that covers most of the northern part of army-dom; whilst, thanks to the army, the once-insignificant little villages of Frimley and Camberley have now acquired the status of an urban district. At the time when it figured in *The Beggar's Opera*, Bagshot Heath was far more extensive than it now is and stretched from Chobham Common in the north to Chobham Ridges in the south. Bagshot itself was equivalent to what we today would call a 'pedestrian refuge'—a place of safety in the middle of the road. Highwaymen infested the heath north and south of Bagshot (a pistol dropped by one of them has found its way into the local museum at Camberley), and many a tired and frightened traveller found refuge and a night's lodging at Bagshot before facing the rest of the road over the heath in the morning. Hanging was thought to be too kind a fate for the highwaymen. On Bagshot Heath there was a special erection where captured highwaymen were incarcerated in tarred canvas and chains and left to rot. However the 'gentlemen' were not the only hazard to be encountered on Bagshot Heath as Defoe found in 1724:

From Farnham . . . I took the coach road over Bagshot Heath, and that great forest, as 'tis call'd, of Windsor. Those that despise Scotland and the north part of England, for being full of waste and barren land, may take a view of this part of Surrey and look upon it as a foil to the beauty of the rest of England, or as a mark of the just resentment shew'd by Heaven upon the Englishman's pride . . . here is a vast tract of land, some of it within seventeen or eighteen miles of the capital city, which is not only poor but even quite sterile, given up to barrenness, horrid and frightful to look upon, not only good for little, but good for nothing; much of it is sandy desert, and one may frequently be put in mind of Arabia Deserta, where the winds raise the sands so as to overwhelm whole caravans of travellers, cattle and people together; for in passing this heath on a windy day, I was so in danger of smothering with the clouds of sand, which were raised by the storm, that I could neither keep it out of my mouth nose or eyes.

Bagshot Heath has given its name to one of Surrey's best-known geological formations—the Bagshot Sands—to which belong so many landmarks north of the Chalk, including St Anne's Hill, St George's Hill, Esher Common and Chobham Ridges. Sixty years after Defoe, the agricultural surveyor, Marshall, dismissed the Surrey heathlands as "the most unprofitable tract of country to the community of any district of equal extent in the Islands —the mountains on the north-west coast of Scotland perhaps excepted". In an age when nobody ever walked across Bagshot Heath for pleasure, if it yielded no crops it had no value. And so the army came and made the area a vast parade ground.

I first saw Chobham Common many years ago when following a 'beat-the-traffic' map to the South-west. I have never forgotten the deep impression created on me by this seemingly vast expanse of gorse and heather with here and there an isolated clump of pine trees—the whole aspect one of limitless space, although in reality it is of relatively small extent. Here, where travellers of a past age would spur their horses to a gallop as they sped across the heath with anxious glances behind them, we stopped and enjoyed the view. It was the first real piece of deep country we had enjoyed since leaving London. How far one has to travel through the Low Country before one leaves the Capital behind, compared for instance with the journey across the Chalk or the Weald. Chobham Common still has the same infinite capacity to delight. Only recently I was crossing the common early one morning when I saw the sun rising behind the obelisk on Ship Hill and wished, as I have so often wished on such occasions, that I had my camera with me. What a mercy it is that the military have on the whole left Chobham Common alone—perhaps a reluctance to foul their own nest, for, as the obelisk reminds us, their sojurn in Surrey began here. Part of Chobham Common is now a Nature Reserve.

Chobham Village has some very attractive corners—not least being the 'Cloche Hat' restaurant nearby. I was fortunate enough to see the 'Sun's' new inn-sign, a bikini-clad maiden, before the local residents decided that it was unseemly and mine host bowed to pressure and removed it—at least this little incident proves that it is the matrons and not the military who rule in this corner of army-dom. Chobham has no less a charming village atmosphere than its namesake without the 'h', and it possesses a lovely old church with a curiosity, a wooden font lined with lead, a reminder that just as Anglo-Saxon churches were usually made of wood so fonts were at one time also made of this same material.

The country along the Worplesdon to Lightwater road is one of Surrey's great disappointments. It is frankly a terrible mess, only rivalled by another road in this same unfortunate corner of Surrey, the Camberley to Ash road along the Blackwater Valley. Rather naïvely, perhaps, Eric Parker wrote of the Bisley-Knaphill-Donkeytown district: "It is a little difficult to understand why the cheaper forms of village building should spread in this part of the county which, so to speak, leads no-where." Surely he gives the reason himself. This area lay in a backwater between the main routes to the South-west from London, and it was ill-drained and infertile. What the army did not need the squatter and small-holder and 'shacker' took. In due course more permanent, if no less ugly, houses, followed. Recently some property of a better type has been introduced, but the damage has been done. This is ribbon development—not on a major radial route as is usually the case, but on a minor transverse road, and somehow this seems even worse.

Surrey has two disused canals, the Wey-Arun and the Basing-stoke Canal. Of these the latter was the first to be built (1793–6). It connected the Wey Navigation near Woking with the town of Basingstoke, 37 miles and twenty-nine locks away; the canal rose 195 feet, and the two principal staircases of locks were at St John's and Brookwood. Barges of up to 50 tons could navigate this canal. The Basingstoke Canal was the offspring of the canal 'mania' of 1792–7; it seems to have been conceived out of what Manning calls "flattering and fallacious representations" on the part of the proposers, and born of the public's insatiable optimism. How any intelligent person could imagine that a canal passing through what was then deep rural countryside to the small coun-try town of Basingstoke could ever make a profit is to me a mystery. The canal served a useful purpose during the Napoleonic Wars, particularly in supplying materials of war to the army en-campments *en route*, but in a fit of patriotic fervour (and presum-ably over-optimism regarding the canal's commercial prospects) the proprietors refused to charge tolls during the period 1803–5 and so the canal did not profit greatly as a result. The main weak-ness of the canal was that there was never really any prospect of a substantial downward traffic. That, however, was the direction in which the canal company's shares steadily moved. By 1818 they had slumped to one-tenth of their original value and it was clear that the Basingstoke was no Bridgewater Canal. Traffic continued to use the canal for many years, and indeed rose to a peak of 42,346 tons in 1838, but the arrival of the railways in the mid-nineteenth century destroyed any hope that it might redeem itself economically. Today the Basingstoke Canal is almost entirely

*The Wey Navigation at New Haw*
*Chertsey Bridge and lock*

disused, commercial traffic having come to an end about 1949. However, although down, it is not yet out. Arguments rage furiously in the district as to what the future of the canal should be. "Restoration would cost only £26,000 using volunteer labour," says the Surrey and Hampshire Canal Society and the Inland Waterways Association. "It is unlikely that revenue (that is from recreational traffic) will ever be sufficient to maintain the canal in working order," writes Paul Vine gloomily in his book *London's Lost Route to the Sea*—although in his latest book *London's Lost Route to Basingstoke* he writes: "Every effort must indeed be made to restore and preserve the beautiful but neglected waterway as far as Greywall." "Replace the locks with weirs and use the water for angling, nature reserves and small boating," says the New Basingstoke Canal Company, owners of the Canal. The Surrey County Council have settled the debate by acquiring the Canal with the aim of rehabilitating it and opening it for recreational use. They plan to do this by using voluntary labour. What a wonderful opportunity for the youth of Surrey to help the County and themselves. Meanwhile the old canal lies forgotten and weed-choked, the lock gates rotting, whilst here and there a derelict barge lies on the overgrown towpath where the local urchins relieve themselves uninhibitedly. It is a sad fate for such an enterprise. I have followed the course of the old canal for many miles with the deepening sadness that stagnant water and the demise of Man's endeavour alike engender. If another Horatio Bottomley came along with a specious plan to restore the Basingstoke's long-lost glories (as indeed happened in 1906), I believe I would fall a willing victim: almost anything is better than just to see it die in ignominy.

The Camberley, Yorktown, Frimley area is decidedly one to avoid if possible, especially around 5.30 in the evening when the many factories in the area disgorge their workers to swell the already considerable traffic on the Great South West and Portsmouth roads. Camberley and Yorktown occupy one side of the Great South West road, and on the other lie the Royal Military Academy and the Royal Staff College, where men learn the art of war, by a beautiful peaceful lake fringed with trees. Here is the very heart and soul of army-dom; on a wet wintry evening these mean looking terraces of bricky villas, the Inkermans, Sebastopols

6

*Outside the 'Kings Head', Shepperton*

and Balaclavas of Yorktown and Camberley, that were all the Victorians thought were appropriate for a garrison town, serve only to bring on an attack of the deepest melancholia. It is a relief to escape to Chobham Ridges, where the rain lures the scent from the pine trees and imparts a glistening sheen to the silver birches.

The Blackwater River is the formal boundary of Surrey, but, as suggested earlier, a river is usually more a unifying influence than a dividing one. Mountains, hills and other watersheds make natural boundaries—but rivers seldom do. Their only advantage is that they are often clearly visible from the ground. The country along the eastern side of the appropriately named Blackwater belongs in every meaningful sense to Farnborough and Aldershot in Hampshire—that is if it really belongs anywhere at all. The whole area is so hideously criss-crossed by railways, roads, canal and river that it seems as formless, and about as attractive, as a jellyfish. If it has a redeeming feature at all it lies in the distant prospect of the Hog's Back on the southern horizon.

In sharp contrast, the countryside immediately to the north of the Hog's Back is still marvellously unspoiled and rural. Here can be seen Tongham Church with its independent bell tower, and from which village a road leaps up the side of the Hog's Back at its steepest point in sheer exuberation at having escaped what has been described (with considerable restraint) as "the rather untidy mixture of town and country" that comprises the Blackwater Valley; here is Wanborough Church, one of the smallest in the county and measuring only 45 feet by 18—not much bigger in fact than a typical Surrey stockbroker's lounge, together with its huge neighbour, a barn big enough to swallow the church and still leave room for a vicarage; here also is Flexford, whose name is a reminder of the days when flax was grown in these parts; and here is Normandy Farm where William Cobbett, who had begun life as a crow-scarer and ploughboy, and who had more than once come back to this same farm as if to keep alive his close ties with the soil, returned at last to end his days. How fitting are these words on his memorial in Farnham Church:

> For Britons honour Cobbett's name
> Though rashly oft he spoke,
> And none will scorn and few will blame
> That low-laid Heart of Oak.

As you look northwards from the Hog's Back itself the ugliness of the Blackwater, and Aldershot and Farnborough beyond, is mercifully lost to view; instead the eye takes in only the ordered landscape that so delighted William Cobbett, who, of all men, was fitted to be a judge of these things, and who decided that this was the part of Surrey he liked the best.

PART TWO

SURREY ON THE CHALK

# 8

# THE SPIRIT OF THE CHALK COUNTRY

Imagine a spear-head sliced vertically down the centre—and you have the shape of the Chalk Country. The tip of the spear lies at Guildford, or, if it is a long, thin, pointed spear, at Farnham, and the thick edge represents the escarpment of the North Downs, with the rest of the half-spearhead representing the dip-slope, as it is called by geologists, which slopes gently northwards until it disappears beneath the London Clay. The long thin point, between Guildford and Farnham, represents, of course, the Hog's Back (see map on page 18).

For the whole of the county's recorded history the chalk country has dominated Surrey's development. Long before London even existed as a city, when the Thames Valley was a densely forested, swampy, almost uninhabited and unhealthy barrier, and when the Weald was almost equally forbidding and impenetrable, the open springy turf of the chalk country was an obvious route-way and a natural site for settlement. All over the chalk country one finds archaeological evidence of ancient settlement. Only recently I noticed in our local paper that a resident of Caterham had picked up a Mesolithic flint axe-head some 7,000 years old—in his own garden. The paper headed the story with the words: "With a piece of black flint some two and a half inches long, a member of the Bourne Society, has added some 5,000 years to the history of Caterham." Of course, it was nonsense—Caterham's history, as does that of almost any settlement on the chalk, has long been known to date far back beyond the year 31 B.C. I was amused when a week later, a letter appeared from another Caterham resident headed "No New Chapter in Local History" in which the writer entered a "wild protest" against the claim and added "I have before me as I write at least three specimens which I have picked up in my own garden" and adds: "surely it is well known that this was a populated district long before the Iron Age? . . . the Neolithic flint mines at Riddlesdown, plain for all to see in the quarry opposite Whyteleafe Station, but now in the final stages of destruction, indicate a substantial local population." One has only to compare a map of the archaeological discoveries in the Weald with those on the Chalk to realize that the former was to all intents and purposes terra incognita to Iron Age Man—he knew about as much about it as the Victorians knew about atomic energy, or we knew about the other side of the moon until the astronauts circumnavigated it. The world of the Iron Age Man in Surrey comprised the half spear-head of chalk and little else. Flints you pick up in the garden and toss away without realizing they are 7,000 years old—these are very much part of the spirit of the chalk country.

The chalk was attractive to primitive man because it was open country, unencumbered with great oak trees that could not easily be felled, or swamps and rivers that were impassable—but therein lay their greatest problem—water. Water was the basic essential of life in primitive times, and the location of settlement on the chalk was generally determined by the availability of water. Generally speaking the Downs were literally 'high and dry', but sometimes there was a capping of clay or gravel over the chalk, and in such places there would be shallow springs and brackish water just sufficient to support a small hamlet. Nearly all the villages and hamlets situated actually on the chalk owe their origin to this cause. Walton on the Hill, Burgh Heath, Chipstead and Sanderstead have their ponds still, although they are rather liable to be used as rubbish dumps these days; whilst other villages have lost theirs in recent times—a garage stands at the end of Banstead High Street where the pond once stood and where the sheep jostled for a place at the water's edge; and worshippers at St Mary's, Caterham on the Hill, park their cars where the pond once stood opposite old St Lawrence's Church. For drinking water, however, the shallow springs were inadequate, and deep wells were dug to the pure water at the base of the chalk hundreds of feet below. At Canons, near Banstead, is a well 360 feet deep, while the old well at Banstead itself, with its huge wheel and attractive canopy, and small fortune in children's pennies, is 300 feet deep. Even these, however, are still shallow beside the deep wells of the Weald, which sometimes go down over 1,000 feet. There are only two rivers that flow across the chalk country, the Wey and the Mole, and only the Mole actually flows over the chalk itself for part of its course. The result is the extraordinary 'swallows' which we will discuss later. As for the rivers that rise within the chalk country, they are usually flowing below the surface, the strange 'bournes' that appear on the surface only every few years after some particularly heavy fall of rain, as if to reassure themselves that they are still flowing in the right direction. Curious legends have attached themselves to these bournes, like the one about the 'Woe-water' that flows through Whyteleafe to Croydon. It is said that the appearance above ground of this bourne is a sure sign of impending disaster, as indeed happened in 1665 just before the Great Plague. I once heard a church-warden at St John's Church Caterham Valley make effective use of this old tradition when welcoming to the parish a new incumbent who arrived a few days after the bourne had overflowed causing considerable damage in the valley! In times past the water wagon touring the streets of the towns and villages in the chalk country was a common sight, and farmers would not infrequently have to borrow water from their neighbours during dry periods. An octogenarian of Sutton recalled some years ago that his mother, in 1876, was rationed to one pail of water a day for drinking and cooking. A consequence of the shortage of water for drinking was the large number of alehouses, additional to the licensed premises, which have long since faded from memory. Ale was then the universal beverage, the old people stirring a little ginger into it and sometimes inserting a red hot poker to provide a hot nightcap in the colder weather. The absence of surface water, and all that it entails, is as much part of the spirit of the chalk country as the abundance of it is part of the spirit of the Weald.

Colour of soil is seldom a distinguishing feature of the landscape, as the red soils are at Teignmouth, or the black soils in the Fen Country (although Redhill derives its name from the characteristic red soil in the neighbourhood), but in the chalk country, wherever the surface vegetation is denuded for whatever reason, the underlying chalk emerges in its striking whiteness, impelling attention and dominating the landscape. In places, as at Box Hill, the sheer passage of feet has eroded the grass and left gashes of white down the steep hillside; elsewhere great mechanical excavators, aided by explosives, have quarried huge quantities of chalk and stone from the escarpment, leaving often a sheer cliff of dazzling white, sometimes so near the old Pilgrims Way that the latter has collapsed into the quarry below, taking the modern metalled road with it. This indeed happened a few years ago above Oxted, and a new road has been built a few yards back from the new cliff edge, the remains of the old road providing a magnificent scenic viewpoint. For centuries past chalk from the North Downs has travelled northwards and southwards. Northwards in the form of mortar for the building of London Bridge, St Paul's Cathedral, the London Docks and a host of lesser buildings. And southwards to 1,000 limekilns scattered among the farms of the Weald, a few of which can still be discovered here and there, although now usually heavily overgrown. It is altogether appropriate that one of the most interesting memorials in Cranleigh church is to the memory of Richard Mower (1630) who discovered the use of lime in agriculture. The great chalk and lime quarries of Betchworth and Oxted seem to repel some people and to attract others, but either way they cannot be ignored. Here is Nature's own way of signposting the Great White Way. The chalk gleams white in the sides of railway cuttings, where road works are in progress or where a new trunk sewer is being laid across-country. They remind us of the fact that the whole of Southern England is, in the words of G. K. Chesterton, "not only a grand peninsula and a tradition and a civilization—it is something even more admirable. It is a piece of chalk." Every gardener in the chalk country knows that if he digs too deep he will bring to the surface the pure white chalk, and there it will lie, its whiteness refurbished with every shower of rain until in desperation he gets down on hands and knees and removes each offending piece one by one. Poor Man! He is trying to remove part of the very spirit of the chalk country —its whiteness.

The chalk soils support a fine springy turf that is to cricket what the sand dunes of St Andrews are to golf. In 1711 John Toland wrote enthusiastically of Banstead Downs "being covered with grass finer that Persian carpets and perfumed with wild thyme and juniper". Cricket is not, of course, confined to the chalk country, but it seems to belong to that part of Surrey in a special way. It is a fact that the earliest known reference to the game in Britain dates from a lawsuit of 1598 concerning land on the chalk downs above Guildford; one of the litigants recalled that forty years earlier, when a pupil at the 'Free School' (now the Royal Grammar School), he "did run and play there at cricket". In those far-off days the runs were notched onto a piece of wood—hence the word 'score'.

What would Old Coulsdon be without its cricket green—or Banstead, Tadworth or Headley—or a hundred other clubs whose pitches were largely the gift of Nature? The same springy turf is ideal also for horse-riding, and long before the first willow was cut for a cricket bat men were riding on the downs for pleasure. James I was fond of horse-racing on Banstead Downs, long before the Derby was established. In 1700 or thereabouts, Celia Fiennes, that intrepid traveller, was writing of Epsom Downs: "On the hill where are the race posts they have made a ring as in Hyde Park, and they come in coaches and drive round. Epsom shall be cluttered with company from Saturday to Tuesday, and then they many times goe, being so neare London, so come again on more Saturdays." The famous chalk downs, Epsom, Farthing, Merrow, and so many others, were already becoming 'cluttered' two and a half centuries ago! All over the chalk country you will see horses being ridden: racehorses at Epsom ("a string of delicate tremulous creatures"), hacks at Headley, hunters at the Horsleys—and even perhaps a farmhorse or two where a farmer cannot bear to pension off his old friends before their time.

This same downland turf has down the centuries provided wonderful pasture for some of our most famous breeds of sheep—the Downland sheep. In 1454, when the price of wool was fixed by Parliament and forty-four different grades of quality were established, the wool from Banstead Downs (at that time covering a huge area between Banstead and Croydon) were graded eighth in the list and higher than any other wool from Surrey. None of the Surrey breeds have the magnificent horns of the true Dorset Horn, but they are fine-looking animals and formed the foundation stock for the great flocks in South Island, New Zealand. They were particularly renowned for the sweetness of their mutton, although regarded as rather small-bodied sheep.

Today the downland pastures seldom carry sheep flocks. With no sheep to graze the grass, many of the uncultivated areas of the Downland, especially the open commons, have reverted to gorse and bramble and have assumed a wilder character than they once had. On the other hand, the cultivated areas have been mostly ploughed up since the 1939–45 war and now carry heavy crops of barley which yield a higher profit to the farmer than sheep as a rule. Ironically, it was partly the absence of hedges and the very large open fields of the chalk country that made them so suitable for highly mechanized corn growing. The 'open fields' or 'commonfields' of medieval England lingered longer on the chalk downs of Surrey than in most other parts of Britain. Those of Epsom, for instance, were not enclosed until 1869. Even when they had been enclosed, the fields remained very large and well adapted for cereal growing. Although the Surrey downs have few of the 'barley barons' one associates with the much larger chalk area of Hampshire (although they now call themselves the 'cereal serfs'!), there are nevertheless some prosperous corn-growing farms in the chalk country, and their large combines can be seen busily at work during the summer months. However, even the power-driven combines cannot negotiate the steeper slopes, and these are still the preserve of the Downland sheep that centuries ago were the main source of the prosperity of the whole region, particularly the 'wool towns' of Guildford, Godalming and Farnham. A woolpack is the centrepiece of the crest of the Banstead Urban District Council, and it figures also in the crests of Guildford and Godalming. Thus we are reminded that Martin Tupper's "tinkling bells of the bleating ewes" were for centuries a vital part of the spirit of the chalk country.

The chalk soils are valued not only for their surface cover but also for the flints they contain. In a country otherwise lacking in building stone these flints were very useful for that purpose, and the flint-clad churches of St Lawrence, Caterham, All Saint's, Banstead and, in fact, the majority of old village churches in the district, are eloquent testimony of the value of this material. Perhaps the 'flint' style of architecture reached its zenith at the village of Whyteleafe where it has been called the 'Whyteleafe Style', although I find the combination of the age-old flint material with typical Victorian style architecture, complete with gothic arches and battlemented bays, particularly distasteful. Rather than the zenith, I would call it the nadir, and perhaps it is no sad thing that a major road improvement will soon sweep away the centre of Whyteleafe and with it most of this unhappy episode in architectural history. In times past, of course, the flints were even more valuable as weapons and tools, and in places, such as at Riddlesdown, mines have been discovered where the people of pre-Roman times excavated their valuable flints. By chance these Neolithic flint mines at Riddlesdown have been partially excavated by a chalk and lime company, and as you sit in the train at Whyteleafe Station you can see a cross-section of their workings neatly exposed in the side of the quarry. This same quarry is unique in that a railway line crosses the middle of it on a steel viaduct—it seems a simple enough solution, but it must have caused some heart-searchings when the railway engineers were planning their route in 1884. Looking for Neolithic arrow-heads, or flint axes, is as much part of the spirit of the chalk country as looking for fossils on Charmouth beach.

The open chalkland, in addition to being a natural site for settlement, was also one of the historic routeways of Britain. Many centuries before the murder of Thomas à Beckett is supposed to have brought the pilgrims along the road to Canterbury (I prefer to believe that the 'Pilgrims' Way' is not wholly invention despite the fact that many authorities now doubt the veracity of much of the tradition that has grown up around it), the herdsmen and tradesmen of Pre-Roman times followed the 'Old Road' from the ancient heartland of England, the chalk country of Salisbury Plain, to the Straits of Dover whence a ship could be found for Gaul. We are prone to imagine the Ancient Britons as primitive woad-smeared savages, ignorant of all the finer arts, the aborigines of their times, but this is an entirely false picture. The people of this land, and especially the people of the chalk country, its most densely settled parts, had evolved a high level of cultural and commercial life, and had acquired such a high reputation on the Continent for the quality and abundance of their corn and wool (Britain was exporting both commodities to Europe before the Roman period) that Julius Caesar could not resist the tempta tion to add this conquest to his already long list of military triumphs. Were it otherwise, he might have left this misty sea-girt island alone (the Romans hated the sea) and saved himself one of the most anxious moments of his life as he watched his ships being pounded to destruction on Deal beach in a storm. Nor was he disappointed; he noted with admiration the prosperity of the farming he saw being practised. Yet I noticed the other day that my son was using a history book with the absurd title *History before Britain*, and on inspection I found, as I had suspected, that it ended at the Roman conquest of Britain! The great trackways of England, the Old Road, the Icknield Way, the Fosse Way, they all linked together the chalk and limestone areas of Britain. The Surrey chalk lands take their place in this ancient network of communications and settlement. The Hog's Back, for instance, is the arch-type of a communications corridor, it is barely wide enough for a drove-way and little else. This network was not the creation of Man but the legacy of Nature. The companies of young people hiking along the Pilgrims' Way in the mid-summer of 1970 to join the celebrations of the 800th anniversary of the murder of Thomas à Beckett at Canterbury, were demonstrating that the Pilgrims' Way, Massingham's "green way sidling under the crest", has become an integral part of the spirit of the chalk country, as the Roman Wall is to Northumberland, or Offa's Dyke is to the Welsh Border country.

We have left to the last that feature of the chalk country which is perhaps its most important—at least to many people, both those who live on the Chalk and those who do not. This is the magnificent succession of views to be obtained from the crest of the escarpment. Martin Tupper captured this attribute of the chalk country, together with others in these lines, from which a fragment was quoted earlier:

> The breezy Downs and a spirited horse
> And the honeyed breath of the golden gorse,
> And the tinkling bells of the bleating ewes
> And a bright panorama of changing views
> And all that is peaceful and cheerful beside.

Every resident of the chalk country has his own favourite view, and one or two viewpoints that he keeps carefully to himself if he can. The famous vantage points are the property of all, Newlands Corner, Ranmore Common, Box Hill, Colley Hill and the rest. He leaves these to the crowds who throng them in the summer, and only goes there when the sun unexpectedly shines on a winter's day and the townsman dare not go for he knows that the sun will have gone before he arrives. But in the summer he makes for his local viewpoint, known only to him and his fellow-residents of the Chalk. It may be Hanging Wood near Godstone, Viewpoint near Caterham, Shepherds Hill near Merstham, Gatton Park, or a hundred other spots on the escarpment where he can enjoy the view in comparative peace. To him this view is his birthright as one who lives on the Chalk—the view belongs to him as much as the escarpment belongs to the dip-slope on which he lives. The pity is that a few people have tried to filch the birthright of the many by building their homes right on the edge of the escarpment and clearly visible from the valley below. There is a vital need for fewer houses and more public viewpoints along the crest of the escarpment, and I believe the local authorities should tackle this problem as a matter of urgency. They should provide many more open spaces where trees do not obscure the view (but are so arranged as to shield the cars and ancillary buildings that may be required) and also scenic routes following the crest of the hills, miniature versions of the Skyline Drive, or the Blue Ridge Parkway, along the Appalachian Mountains in Eastern United States. It is true that the Countryside Commission have now received Ministerial approval to the creation of a 141-mile pathway along the crest of the North Downs, the eleventh such route to be approved in Britain; but, admirable though this is, it does not meet the even greater need for motorized access to selected places along the crest. The view from the escarpment is the most valuable gift the chalk country has to offer. Yet this gift lies virtually unexploited, or reserved for a favoured few. It must be made available to the many in such a tasteful way that its beauty is not destroyed but preserved for all time. When land right on the crest is put up for sale the local authority should buy it and make it available for the public. Only if they do this are they being true to the spirit of the chalk country.

# 9

## PIERCING THE CHALK WALL

Nature built a great wall across Surrey, and provided only three
gateways, the valleys of the Blackwater, the Wey and the Mole.
However, these have never been adequate to meet the need for
north-south communication and transport, and a vital part of the
history of Surrey has therefore been the problem of piercing the
chalk wall.

Even Nature's own gaps were never so convenient as they may
appear on the map. I always remember the late Professor Wooldridge, of Kings College, London, when he was leading a group of
geography students (of whom I was one) on a study walk along
the North Downs, pointing to the Wey Gap at Guildford and
saying: "You must be on your guard against assuming that because this looks an obvious gap it was an obvious choice for a
routeway." He went on to emphasize that the Wey Valley was a
marshy area and densely wooded in early times, so that it was
avoided by travellers as much as possible. I remembered this later
when I discovered that the old road from Betchworth to Leatherhead went slap up the side of Box Hill rather than through the
Mole Valley, and that the old Brighton Road took the route over
Reigate Hill rather than the much easier gradient via Merstham.
It is indeed very probable that the Wey 'Gap' was more a hindrance than a help to early settlers in the region, who kept to
the high chalk trackways whenever they could. The Romans,
it is true, made some use of the Mole Gap, for they took
their Stane Street through it, but it is noteworthy that they
branched off it at Mickleham and headed straight for Ewell bypassing the present site of Leatherhead. It could even be that
their choice of the Mole Gap was dictated more by the problem

of crossing the higher Greensand Ridge on which Leith Hill stands.

Having said all this, however, there can be no doubt that as the size of vehicles using the roads increased, and as the bulk and weight of goods being transported grew, so the need for better roads with easier gradients became more pressing. London's requirements for timber were rising every decade, and as shipbuilding activity on the Thames increased so the problem of transporting the timber and the heavy cannon from the iron foundries in the Weald became worse. It is some indication of the difficulty of transporting goods in Elizabethan times that an Act was passed which referred to the damage done "by the carriage of coals, mine and iron" and which compelled those engaged in the traffic to repair the roads. Later another Act was passed forbidding any wagon, cart or carriage, drawn by more than seven horses or eight oxen, or carrying more than 30 hundredweight, to use the roads between 1st May and 1st October. These had little effect, and in the mid-seventeenth century the Guildford to London stage coach took a whole day to travel 30 miles. Just what road travel meant in the days before Telford and McAdam is shown by this quotation from a letter written by a courtier who accompanied the Prince of Denmark on a coach journey to Petworth House in 1703:

> His Highness gave direction for his coach to be ready at 6 o'clock in the morning on Monday to go to Petworth. Accordingly we set out at that time by torchlight, and did not get out of our coaches again, save only when we were overturned or stuck fast in the mud, 'til we arrived at our journey's end. 'Twas hard service for the Prince to sit 14 hours in the coach that day without eating anything, and passing through the worst ways that ever I saw in my life.

If the reader needs further convincing perhaps this quotation from Salmon (1736) will suffice, although I fear it is almost as tortuous a piece of writing as the Wealden ways he is describing:

> At this place (i.e. Leigh) begins one of the dirtiest counties in England. The dirt, almost without bottom, goes on upon the borders of Sussex for many miles, but whoever it was that, describing Surrey dry and pleasant elsewhere, which Speed mentions, compares it to a garment fringed at the bottom, meaning its fertile heavy earth hereabout, might have added that this fringe is intolerably draggled. The

7

*Conversation piece, Carshalton Ponds*
**The old packhorse bridge, Ewell**

men, and the horses who draw their corn to market, of which seven, eight or nine are in a team, with a weight for which four are sufficient in other places, look as if they had wallowed in the mud.

The deep ruts in the clay tracks dried to iron hardness during the summer and were cruel to both man and beast. Arthur Young in 1813, with considerable restraint of language, noted that "in dry weather the hardness of the clay is very prejudicial to the feet of the cattle."

In such circumstances any form of transport that did not depend upon the roads was at a premium. The river gaps now sprang into prominence, not so much for the easily graded passage they afforded as for the possibility of water transportation. The River Mole, it is true, had never been of much use for navigation because of its swallows. But the River Wey was another matter. The Wey presented a potentially valuable water route from Guildford to the Thames, but its course was beset with many impediments to navigation, such as the many watermills and weirs utilizing the flow of the river. It would need a man of drive and vision, endless patience—and a considerable private fortune—to cut through the Gordian Knot. Such a man was Sir Richard Weston of Sutton Place. He had travelled in Holland and Flanders and had returned to his home at Sutton Place by the River Wey (or 'Wye' as it was called at this time), fired with enthusiasm to harness the potential of the river. At first his main object was to improve the agriculture of his own estate and prevent the regular flooding that occurred, but soon he saw the possibilities of making the Wey commercially navigable from Guildford to the Thames. Two rivers had already been successfully canalized, the Lea and the Thames to Oxford—he would now do the same thing for the lower Wey. In 1651 he began his great enterprise. Hitherto navigation over the numerous weirs had only been possible by using the extraordinary system of 'flashes', whereby a miller would (by opening a sluice gate set into a dam across the river) release a volume of water over his weirs sufficient to carry a barge over the shallows to the next stretch of deep water. But Sir Richard decided to straighten out many of the awkward meanders in the river and to instal pound locks of the type familiar to us today to overcome the problem of changes in levels—thus the 'Wey Navigation' is partly a river and partly a canal. Some 200 men were employed on the works, and within

nine months ten of the 14 miles to Weybridge had been completed.
With its four weirs and twelve bridges, it had cost some £15,000,
but the annual income was soon £1,500 and financial success was
assured. For nearly a century the canalized river was the principal
outlet for the timber, wool, grain and other products of the part of
the Weald centred on Guildford, whilst in turn it enabled this
region to be supplied with flour, meal, manures, coal and stone for
improving the Wealden roads.

Some idea of the commercial importance of the Wey Navigation may be gained from the information quoted by P. A. L. Vine
in his book *London's Lost Route to the Sea* (1965); he says that in '
1664, only eleven years after it was finished, 4,000 barge loads of
timber alone passed along it. Defoe commented in 1724:

This Navigation is a mighty support to the great corn market at
Farnham . . . for the mealmen and other dealers buy the corn at that
market, much of it is brought to the mills on this river [i.e., at
Guildford] . . . and being first ground and dressed is then sent down
in the meal by barges to London.

In 1754 the Wey Navigation was extended to Godalming. At
the same time an Act was passed by which the Canal Commis-
sioners were obliged to raise the banks of the river to prevent
flooding. This may have been easier than dredging, but it was a
great mistake since in the course of time the river came to be flowing between raised banks several feet above the level of the surrounding land, and the danger of flooding was greatly increased.
At Send the Wey Navigation flows 8 to 10 feet above the adjacent
Broadmead.

The Wey Navigation had come a century early. The real canal
fever did not begin until towards the end of the eighteenth century, and although the bulk of the projects carried out at this time
were in the great mining districts of Britain, Surrey had her share
of outlandish proposals—and even a few sensible ones that had a
lasting effect upon the county's development. The war with
Revolutionary France was making coastwise movement round the
English Channel extremely hazardous because of the harassing
activities of French privateers; it has been estimated that they captured £3 million worth of shipping during the Napoleonic Wars
between the Isle of Wight and the North Foreland alone. The sea

journey from London to Portsmouth Dockyard had become very dangerous, as also was even the short journey down the Thames estuary to the Medway ports. In these circumstances attention naturally turned to the possibility of an inland water link between London and Portsmouth, whilst a canal linking Gravesend with the Medway at Strood was actually built early in the nineteenth century.

In 1801 the Grand Surrey Canal Company was formed to build a canal from the Thames at Rotherhithe via Camberwell to Mitcham and eventually, it was hoped, to Portsmouth. Another proposal, by Rennie in 1803, was for a canal from New Cross to Portsmouth via Croydon, Redhill (through a tunnel $4\frac{1}{2}$ miles long between Coulsdon and Merstham) and Horsham. This would have cost nearly $£\frac{3}{4}$ million and was rejected, partly on the grounds of cost, and partly because of the opposition of the industrial interests along the River Wandle. Although these grandiose schemes were never realized, the canal to Camberwell was completed and in 1809 was extended to Croydon, terminating in a large basin where West Croydon Station stands today. The barges, pulled by horses, had to negotiate twenty-five locks, and it is hardly surprising that the canal was never much of a financial success. In 1834 it was sold to the London and Croydon Railway Company, which drained it and used the bed of the canal as the track for their new line from London Bridge. I wonder how many commuters crammed on to the 8.30 a.m. realize they are travelling along an old canal bed! So the attempt to pierce the chalk wall south of London by canal ended in failure.

Other abortive projects at about this time included proposals for canals linking Kingston to Ewell (1778), Deptford to Kingston (with branches to Epsom and Croydon) in 1798, and from Thames Ditton to Holmwood via Leatherhead and Dorking (1811).

Despite the relative lack of success of the canals elsewhere in Surrey and Kent, the pressures for a direct canal link to Portsmouth were still strong and now came to be focused upon the route of the old Portsmouth Road. Why not link the waters of the River Wey with the upper reaches of the River Arun? Had not a Bill been tabled in the House of Lords as far back as 1641 for a canal linking the Wey at Cranleigh with the Arun at Dunsfold? And as recently as 1798 had not Marshall, in his great Survey of the

County of Surrey, suggested a Wey-Arun Canal? He had, it is true, been mainly concerned to find a way of improving upon the roads of this part of the Weald, which he called "the worst in the Kingdom", with "roughnesses as high as the horses' knees and ruts to the axles". But if a canal was justified for this limited purpose how much more so if it could become the principal route for heavy traffic between London and Guildford! So it came about that in May 1811 at a meeting in the 'White Hart', Guildford, it was decided to build such a canal, and two years later an Act was passed for the Wey Arun Canal to be built. It was to be 17 miles long and would run from Shalford to Wisborough Green. Thanks largely to the generous financial backing of the Earl of Egremont it was successfully built within the next few years, and was opened by the earl on 29th September 1816. In his book, mentioned earlier, Vine quotes an eye-witness account of the occasion: "The sunshine which now broke out, combined with the unrivalled scenery of the favourite spot (St Catherines Hill, Guildford) the music, the numerous assembly of spectators and the merry peal of the bells . . . gave an effect to the senses which could not be contemplated but with the most lively and pleasing emotions." But the canal did not prosper as had been expected. In the first seven years only 10,000 tons per annum were carried, a mere fraction of the 130,000 tons hoped for. The main snag was the need for transhipment at Arundel, whilst the ending of the Napoleonic Wars removed the element of risk. Coal and building materials were carried inwards from London and Littlehampton, and agricultural produce and timber in the reverse direction. In addition a wide variety of miscellaneous goods were carried ranging from bullocks' horns and faggots to bullion and carrots, not to mention homely items like soldiers' baggage and groceries, and dangerous items like explosives that could not be carried by road. The peak year of traffic on the canal was 1839-40, when 23,000 tons were carried; but, compared with the 300,000 tons per annum being carried on the Kennett-Avon Canal at the same period, this was nothing. Thence onwards traffic steadily declined, and the construction of the railways in the district, particularly the Guildford to Horsham line in 1865, sounded the canal's death knell. By 1868 the local inhabitants were appealing to the Railway Company to buy up the canal as it had by then become disused, and in that same year an Act of Parliament was passed by which the canal was officially closed. Within three or four years the canal was no longer navigable above Bramley, so quickly does Nature reclaim her own. Fortunately, for lovers of rural Surrey at least, the Wey-Arun Canal came 200 years too late. One wonders what the whole district, and particularly the town of Godalming, would look like today if the canal had been there in 1600 to facilitate the import of coal for the iron and glass industries and the export of the finished products. Today the line of the old canal can still easily be followed on the ground, and in places it still holds water, as well as rusting bed springs and old paint canisters. Most of the old bridges that crossed the canal with a deferential bow are still there, but the modern roads cross at the level so that the traveller is unconscious of the existence of the old canal. There is a poignancy about this, Surrey's most intriguing industrial antiquity, which exceeds even that of the now-disused railway that caused the canal's demise. Happily the end of the Wey-Arun story has not yet been told. A new Trust has been set up to restore the canal and it is hard at work, on both sides of the border. They have our admiration—they also need our support.

There were a few later schemes for canals across the Surrey Chalk, the major one being the proposed Grand Imperial Ship Canal, to be built from London to Portsmouth via either Guildford or Dorking. This scheme was conceived on a scale that takes one's breath away. The proposal was for a ship canal with 25-foot depth of water, capable of taking first-class ships, between Deptford and Littlehampton, and the cost was estimated at about £4 million. Two alternative routes were suggested, one via the Mole Gap and Dorking, which would have involved a four-mile cutting 130 feet deep at Holmwood, and the other via Cuildford and following the line of the Wey-Arun Canal. However, Rennie was appointed to advise on which was the best route, and when he reported that the cheapest estimate would be £7 million the scheme was as good as dead. This indeed was the swansong of the canal era in Surrey. By this time George Stephenson had appeared on the scene, and everyone knew that railways were just around the corner. Interest in canals faded, the Railway Age was about to dawn, and, with it, great new opportunities and terrible new dangers for the county of Surrey.

Before the railways came, however, the chalk wall was being breached, albeit in a minor fashion, by the new turnpikes that were springing up all over Surrey at this time. The story of the Brighton Road—or rather roads, for there were several—will be told in the next chapter, but a comparison of the map of turnpike roads in Surrey in 1768 (when they were mostly so bad that Arthur Young said of them: "It is a prostitution of language to call them turnpikes.") with that for 1825 shows clearly that during these fifty-seven years an elaborate network of reasonably passable roads had been established on both sides of the chalk wall, and that metalled roads were beginning to be built across the wall itself, especially through the major gaps. In addition to the new roads to Brighton, other major roads that were improved at this time were the Leatherhead-Dorking road through the Mole Gap (replacing the old road up the side of Box Hill), the London to Portsmouth road through the Wey Gap (no doubt Professor Wooldridge would accept the phrase in this context), and the London to Southampton road via Farnham. There is no doubt that these roads made a great difference to road traffic, and the Prince of Denmark could have travelled to Petworth without any great difficulty by 1825. However, for heavy goods the horse-drawn carts were still slow and expensive, and the real breakthrough in cheap and fast travel awaited the arrival of the railways.

It was no accident that the first railway in Surrey, indeed in the world, the old Surrey Iron Railway, should have been designed not for the carriage of passengers but for the transport of heavy goods—in this case limestone and building stone from the quarries of Merstham. Merstham limestone vied with that from Dorking for the distinction of yielding the finest mortar in Britain. The railway was built from Wandsworth to Croydon in 1799-1803 and then extended to Merstham two years later. Judging by old prints of this railway that I have seen, it must have looked very much like a mineral railway—perhaps in an ironstone quarry— would look today—a long line of hoppers piled high with stone— except that it was drawn not by a locomotive but by a horse travelling at about $2\frac{1}{2}$ miles an hour. A distinguishing feature of this railway, however, was that the rails themselves were flanged rather than the wheels; this had the great advantage that the trucks could simply be wheeled off the rails and continue their

journey along the road as required. It was a great moment in 1967
when Mr W. G. Tharby, the well-known local historian in the
Croydon-Caterham area, unearthed several yards of this ancient
track with its stone sleepers, the earliest in the world, still lying *in
situ* at the Merstham end of the line (a specimen section of the
original sleepers and plates can be seen in the grounds of Wallington Town Hall). Another peculiarity of this line was that the
proprietors did not provide any wagons but merely the track, for
the use of which customers paid a toll and provided their own
rolling stock. Mr Tharby, in reporting his find in the local press,
quoted how the railway engineers had laid a wager with local
members of the Merstham Hunt Club who had turned out to see
the trial run of this strange contraption, that one horse could pull
over 36 tons of stone. To their amazement the horse did this without difficulty, and to drive home the point the engineers added
another four wagons and fifty workmen for good measure. That
'train' of crude wagons, trundling along the rails to Croydon,
covering the six miles in one hour and forty-five minutes, was
heralding a new age, although probably few people at the time
realized it. Before long other railways came to pierce the chalk
wall, and it would largely cease to be the great barrier to communication it had hitherto been.

In 1823 William James, an early railway pioneer, proposed extending the Surrey Iron Railway to Brighton, and Sir John Rennie
was actually appointed to survey the line. However, the project
came to nothing, and it was another decade before the railway
mania really gripped the nation. Then new proposals for steam
railways came as thick and fast as rumours on a jittery stock
market. South of London three new lines from London to the
South Coast were being discussed, via Merstham, via Dorking and
via Oxted, the latter to be entirely laid in a tunnel, the piston-like
carriages being sucked through by vacuum. Eventually Sir John
Rennie's proposal for a line via Merstham won the day, and in
1841 this line was built—the first public railway through the chalk
wall and a vitally important landmark in Surrey's history. This
line spawned many new towns, such as Purley, Coulsdon Valley,
Redhill and Earlswood, and gave a new importance to old settlements like Merstham and Horley. On 21st April 1842 Reigate
Parish requested financial help from the railway company to build

a new church at Redhill, and asked if the prospective brides could be brought from New Cross at less than the usual rates. The railway was moved by this unusual request, which came very appropriately from a Mr Hart, and allowed the brides to travel at cost price. So it was that Redhill was colonized by immigrants on assisted passages!

However, the new railways were not universally popular—many people still preferred the old coaches which now began to acquire an aura of romance.

A young man who entered the coach at eight o'clock in the morning at Brighton [reminisced Shergold, a contemporary writer] took his seat perhaps opposite a young lady whom he thought pretty and interesting. When he arrived at Cuckfield he began to be in love; at Crawley he was desperately smitten; at Reigate his passion became irretrievable, and when he gave her an arm to ascend the steep ridges of Reigate Hill—a just emblem by the way of human life—he declared his passion and they were married soon after.

Travelling by rail, on the other hand: "You learn nothing except the number of persons killed or injured in the last accident."

The next rail piercing of Surrey's chalk wall was not, as one might expect, through the Mole Valley, the next gap nearest London, but at Guildford. The landowners of the Mole Valley were still successfully resisting the intrusion of a railway through their lovely valley, as they had been since the first proposals were made in the 1830s, and for the time being there was a stalemate. Meanwhile in 1845 the first line through the Wey Gap was built from Woking to Guildford; four years later the line was extended to Godalming, and in 1858 to Haslemere and Portsmouth. Further west the first line to utilize the Farnham gap was in 1870, when the line from Woking to Farnham was built. With all this railway construction going on around them, the landowners of the Mole Valley finally realized that they could not hold out indefinitely. However, they did what they could to ensure that the railway when it came would do the least possible damage to the landscape. Although John Stuart Mill was unsuccessful in his attempt to prevent the railway running through Norbury Park, he and the other landowners in the district were at least able to minimize its adverse effects. They made it a condition of the sale of their land that the buildings erected should be of a high standard, and that there should be the minimum of disturbance to the amenities —even to the extent of insisting that the tunnel through Norbury Park should be built without sinking a shaft down from the surface! They seem to have been remarkably successful since the railway does very little visual harm to the Mole Valley and indeed adds interest in places.

By now all the natural gaps through the chalk had been utilized, but still there was an urgent need for another line to relieve the overcrowded London to Brighton line. One of the discarded ideas of the 1830s was now revived—to drive a tunnel through the chalk wall at its narrowest point, the head of the Marden Valley above Oxted. This line was built in 1878, and remains the only Surrey line which passes through, rather than over, the chalk wall. Because it defied geography in this way it has had in many respects a greater impact on the development of Surrey south of the Chalk than any other line. The Oxted tunnel, like the Riddlesdown tunnel on the same line,* is curving and is regarded in engineering circles as quite a feat.

By the end of the nineteenth century the piercing of the chalk wall by railways was complete. It remained only to improve the rail and road routes already established—no further new lines were needed and none were built. Among these improvements were several new bypass roads. The Caterham bypass was completed before the war, and in the last few years a major improvement of Godstone Hill has been made. This involved using heavy grading machinery over the top of the Godstone Caves, some of the most extensive in Surrey, and whenever I watched some of these monster machines at work in the vicinity I fully expected to see one of them disappear into the bowels of the earth; I understand that lighter machinery only was used on the most dangerous section immediately above the caves lying nearest the surface, but there must have been some anxious moments for the engineers. These caves represent the worked-out galleries of the old hearthstone mines that first attracted the railway to Caterham. The Brighton Road through Coulsdon and Merstham has been little changed so far this century, but a new motorway is now being built which will transform this road out of recognition. It will cross the South Orbital Motorway in a giant fly-over near Merstham, which will make the old coaching days seem positively antediluvian. Two other bypasses were built during the 1930s in the river gaps, the Mickleham Bypass in the Mole Valley and the Guildford Bypass in the Wey Gap. The latter links to the Godalming Bypass and takes the Portsmouth traffic round both towns. It overcomes the problem of the constricted Wey Gap by simply going straight over the top of the Hog's Back and down the other side. In an age before the Planning Acts it would have had as great an effect on the landscape south of the Hog's Back as the Oxted line had futher east, but in fact it passes today through lonely unspoiled countryside and does the minimum damage to the environment.

So the chalk wall has been breached. But it has not been flattened. It still acts as the best of all breakwaters against which the urban tide of London suburbia continually spends itself and withdraws to renew its strength for another assault. Every proposal for large scale urban development south of the chalk wall receives twice the attention that a similar development north of the wall would receive. Would the decision to develop old Croydon Airport for residential uses have been accepted so readily if the airfield in question had been at Lingfield, Ockley or Cranleigh? The white wall symbolizes a determination to keep seeping suburbia at bay; and the eagerness with which the fringe authorities like Caterham and Warlingham and Banstead have opted to stay out of the Greater London Council area shows that Surrey 'South of the Chalk' has some powerful allies on the top of the plateau. Let canals, railways and motorways pierce the chalk wall by all means, but if once seeping suburbia pierces the wall, Surrey is on the way to extinction. To the Surrey man the white wall is as meaningful in its way as that other white wall—the White Cliffs of Dover—is to every Englishman.

# 10

# THE NEW CROYDON, CATERHAM
## AND THE BRIGHTON ROAD

Croydon stands at the apex of a large segment of the chalk country spreading southwards to the escarpment between Tatsfield on the east and Merstham on the west. It may no longer lie in Surrey (it is now the London Borough of Croydon and incorporates the old Urban District of Coulsdon and Purley), but still it is the natural focus for a substantial part of Surrey on the Chalk, and historically it belongs firmly to Surrey. It is in London—but not of it.

No other borough of its size in the south of England, save possibly Plymouth, has changed so much since the war as Croydon. A few years ago the local Dorking newspaper arranged for an old lady, who had at one time been a resident of the town but had moved north and had not revisited it for fifty years, to come back and to describe her impressions. She was astonished by what she saw; the few new blocks of flats here and there, the new shops and a new road or two. But what would a resident of Croydon who had not been back for fifty years—or even twenty-five years—make of Croydon today? Croydon is the first heart-transplant city in Britain. In twenty years the town centre has shifted from its original position at the junction of George Street and North End to its new position at the junction of Wellesley Road and George Street. Here are located the great new blocks of offices, clustered round the twenty-eight storey tower block of St George's House, soaring 260 feet high (and now another twenty-two storey block where the old Whitgift Trinity School used to be), the new shops and restaurants, the technical school with a reputation many of the younger universities would be proud to have, the Fairfield Halls (where no less than 200 local men and women act as voluntary stewards, proving that this is a truly community venture), the new Courts of Justice, new multi-storey car parks, and the under-pass to take care of through traffic. It is true that the three big department stores, Debenhams, Grants and Allders, are still in the old town centre, and the ancient open market is still in Surrey Street, but increasingly the centre of commercial gravity is shifting to where the centre of civic gravity is now firmly anchored. Of course, mistakes have been made. The new parade of shops on the north-east side of Wellesley Road and George Street is alto-gether too mean for such a dominant site, whilst the underpass is probably a mistake—it would have been better to keep through traffic out of the centre altogether. But these are minor criticisms. No one can deny that the overall effect of what has been done is magnificent, and as the grand design gradually unfolds—with the wholesale redevelopment of the old Trinity School site, for in-stance, and the new fly-overs south of the city centre—one has an increasing sense of a new city being created almost from scratch under the direction of a master mind. I have watched the New Croydon come into being over the last twenty years, and no-where else in Britain, except perhaps in the new towns themselves, have I had such a strong sense of an overall strategy being followed stage by stage as each new phase becomes due. It has been rather like watching a conjuror perform an intricate trick—at first he seems to be in such a muddle that you doubt if he will get out of it successfully—but then as he goes on you realize that he knows exactly what he is doing, until in the end a feeling of inevitability seizes you so that you are hardly surprised when eventually he performs the impossible. That stage of inevitability has been reached at Croydon—everyone knows that out of this present creative turmoil will come a fine and finished product—the conjuror will not fail and everything will come out right in the end. To see how much has already been achieved, go to some high spot or other and look down on the new Croydon. The best is from the Purley Way looking across the extensive playing fields. The new town centre soars skywards from the two-storey mediocrity of its Victorian setting and dominates the whole land-scape around as a city centre should. I passed this way not long ago after touring the United States for five months and I found myself looking at Rayleigh (North Carolina) or Battle Creek (Michigan) or

Lexington (Kentucky)—or indeed almost any of the middle-sized cities of the mid-west states. Croydon, like all those American cities, belongs firmly in the twenty-first century.

Yet Croydon has one inestimable advantage over its American counterparts which to my mind sets it apart in a special sense—as indeed it sets apart any town or city in England from its counterpart in the New World. I refer to its rich heritage of history. What citizen of Rayleigh could direct you to a sixteenth-century almshouse right in the centre of the city, or a parish church whose tower is over 500 years old, or an archbishop's palace with an undercroft dating from the time of Magna Carta? Croydon people are proud of their past, and the casual visitor underestimates them if he looks at the ugly welter of Victorian villadom that still remains and concludes that this is all there is to Croydon outside the new city centre. As the author of the Croydon millenary booklet, *Croydon 1000*, remarked a few years ago,

> If the stranger, trusting the evidence of his eyes alone, insists that we are really only an offshoot of London, he is as mistaken in this as in believing that we are merely a mushroom growth of the nineteenth and twentieth centuries. For a thousand years and more, Croydon has been a separate entity, a community, a town of character and importance living its own life and making its own history, as distinct and personal as if the Metropolis were a thousand miles away.

It is a bold claim, but the statistics prove that it is becoming increasingly true as more and more Croydon people are finding work locally rather than in London. Already the town centre provides office jobs for 30,000 people, and 15,000 cars converge on the central area every morning. Incredible as it may seem, this will put Croydon on a par with such cities as Manchester, Birmingham and Liverpool so far as office employment is concerned. A smaller proportion of Croydon people commute to London for work than for instance in Coulsdon and Purley and places even further out, and the Croydon proportion is steadily falling. Croydon sat like Canute whilst the tide of London's vast urban expansion during the nineteenth and early twentieth centuries flowed about its heels; rather than try to stem the tide it waited patiently until it had spent itself and had begun to recede—or at least to lose its menacing aspect. Meanwhile it nurtured its own independence and character; and so it survived and achieved that remarkable miracle of new birth from within itself. Croydon today is a product of Croydon energy, Croydon enterprise and Croydon individuality—it is almost as though Croydon people are fiercely determined to show that those 12 miles that separate it from Westminster are as sure a guarantee of independence as the 22 miles of the Straits of Dover are to England.

The ancient heart of Croydon lay down by the headwaters of the River Wandle—Surrey's third largest river. Like its lesser neighbour, the Hogsmill, the Wandle rises at the foot of the dip slope of the Chalk, where springs rise and give birth to streams that make their way across the London Clay to the River Thames. Thus Croydon lies at the margin between the Chalk and the Low Country and it belongs, geologically at least, to the line of towns and villages, from Sutton through Epsom and Leatherhead to the Clandons, that marks the northern edge of the Chalk. In our scheme of things therefore, Croydon belongs properly to Chapter 6. However, Croydon has grown so large, and occupies so dominant a position at the apex of valleys through the Chalk, that we are justified in regarding it as belonging to the chalk country. So we return to the low marshy site where the 'Old Town' was born. These springs from below the Chalk fostered the young settlement that was to become the Croydon of today, just as that settlement and its history spanning so many centuries still fosters a sense of the past in the citizens who daily see a new city rising about them. In the Old Town was built the first church, a century before Domesday. Here, in the fourteenth century, was established the market that still flourishes today. Here, a century later, the Archbishops of Canterbury established their country residence before Croydon had become so urbanized that they took another stride further out to Addington in the late eighteenth century (their old palace is now used as a girl's school, but at certain times the staff will proudly show visitors round the older parts of the building). Here, in 1867, occurred the great fire that destroyed the nave of the parish church during a snowstorm and blackened not only the tower, but also the tombs of six archbishops buried there —including Archbishop Sheldon, whose corpse must have stirred uneasily in its grave, for it was he who had instituted the rebuilding of St Paul's Cathedral after the Great Fire of London. Here then lies Croydon past, but many visitors know nothing of its existence; all they know perhaps is the Surrey Street Market—but that is five centuries away.

It was the Whitgift Hospital almshouses that began Croydon's slow climb up the hill. They were located here because the new road to London had forsaken the former route through the 'Old Town', which was very wet at times, and had adopted the line of what is now High Street and North End. It is almost miraculous that they could have survived intact on such a site. Yet there they are for everyone to see—a beautifully proportioned haven of peace (before 7 a.m. and after midnight) right in the centre of a borough of 330,000 people. Forty aged and infirm persons live here, barely a yard or two from the swirling traffic, the hooters and exhaust gases, the hustle and bustle of one of the busiest cities in the kingdom, pre-empting a site that all the town planners who ever tried to solve Croydon's traffic problem would give a month's salary to eliminate. Yet still it is there, and Croydon has now moved a little further up the hill, and George Street carries one-way traffic only. Perhaps the Whitgift Hospital, said to be the finest example of Elizabethan domestic architecture in the south of England, will yet survive intact (though I hear rumours that it may become a museum) to prove to all the world that the people of Croydon value their past as much as they look forward to their future. Probably in any other city this would be asking for a miracle—but in Croydon they perform miracles.

Apart from the Whitgift Hospital, Croydon has few other buildings of architectural merit outside the Old Town. There are a few sixteenth and seventeenth-century houses in the High Street, but they are so overshadowed by later development that they are scarcely noticed. However, one outstanding legacy of the past is Wrencote, an imposing eighteenth-century building in the High Street that might well have been designed by its namesake, although it was in fact given this name only at the end of the nineteenth century; it is a beautifully proportioned building and an excellent example of the architectural style of its period. The latter comment, or rather the latter half of it, might apply equally well to the town hall, which is as uncompromisingly Victorian in character as the stern-looking statue of that monarch that stands guard over it. All one can say of this miniature version of Westminster's Roman Catholic Cathedral is that the alternative design,

*The chalk escarpment at Viewpoint near Caterham*

a kind of cross between the Mormon Temple at Salt Lake City and the Opera House in the Amazon city of Manaos, would have been even worse. Such is the fantastic progress of Croydon's redevelopment that soon the Victorian town hall will stand in lonely isolation as a memorial of a past age; it might even begin to acquire a curiosity value in this age of stark simplicity and functionalism.

If Croydon is the principal oasis in a desert of Victorian, Edwardian and Inter-war suburbanity, there are at least a number of other oases of different kinds which relieve and refresh the traveller as he passes through these unrewarding regions. Some of these are tiny, like the glimpse of the beautifully restored windmill at Shirley, more a single spring than an oasis but important nevertheless. But others, like Addington Hills, Selsdon Woods and Croham Hurst, are green oases that sustain not only those who live in or near them but people who live several miles away. New Addington is both a desert and an oasis. What an extraordinary decision it was to build what is virtually a new town on this exposed and windswept plateau that had been ignored by everyone who visited the region except the Romans (who built a road across it). The first houses built there before the war had virtually no social facilities or local employment and were all one-class dwellings. Even today New Addington must be the largest one-class community in the country—it has virtually no dwellings of the four-bedroomed detached type. The only public means of transport provided was the bus service to Croydon. Today the town has grown a great deal in size and has acquired industry and excellent social facilities including a fine swimming pool that attracts people from as far away as Caterham. But still it has almost no communications eastwards—certainly no public communications, and the roads eastwards out of the town degenerate almost immediately into the narrow country lanes that existed before the town was built, and which wander in the vague direction of Tatsfield or Biggin Hill—or just lose themselves in the maze of steep sided valleys that the Romans so skilfully avoided. The heart of the town is a green swathe of common, as wide as a droveway, that leads the eye to the church strategically placed at the southern end. This is the oasis. New Addington is just an oddity, the like of which probably does not exist anywhere else in Britain.
8

*The Burford Bridge Hotel and Box Hill*
**Stepping stones over the Mole**

Nearby lies Old Addington, with its attractive old church, its authentic village atmosphere, that still survives despite the ever increasing volume of traffic that now takes this convenient and recently widened cross-route between Surrey and Kent, and its cricket field well placed to catch the evening sun. Above the village lies Addington Palace, once the country residence of the Archbishops of Canterbury, but now the home of the Royal School of Church Music. And above the palace lie the Addington Hills, with a viewing platform thoughtfully provided by the Croydon authorities so that the visitors may as it were climb a palm tree and view the rest of this charming oasis.

Coombe Woods, another oasis, is justly renowned for its magnificent rhododendrons which people travel miles to see; Selsdon Woods has its bird sanctuary; but my favourite oasis is Farleigh, with its tiny Norman church of St Mary's, damaged badly by fire in 1964 but still standing, as it has stood for 850 years, the smallest and one of the oldest churches in Surrey. Yes, in Surrey! For Farleigh resisted its incorporation into the Greater London Council area so fiercely that eventually the mandarins of Whitehall relented, and this little community was handed back to Surrey. The essence of Farleigh's claim was simply that it was not an oasis at all, since it did not lie within the desert but belonged to the green country outside it. Farleigh, they said, was rural in character, had been rural for all its recorded history, and wanted to stay that way—and they won their case. The whole story of this remarkable episode is written up in Vol. VIII of the Bourne Society's series, Local History Records.

The green country beyond Farleigh brings one to the edge of the escarpment, to the Pilgrim's Way, and to two villages which lie a little back from the edge, Tatsfield and Woldingham. Tatsfield is a hamlet curiously detached from its church, hiding itself away in a fold of the hills as if it never properly recovered from the shock it received when the Romans left Britain, after which their road, (which passed by the front door of Tatsfield) fell into disuse. Woldingham is an affluent hill-top village of expensive residences, that possessed its own golf course before it built a village hall only a year ago.

Sanderstead and Warlingham are frontier posts on the edge of the Croydon desert. Sanderstead has a pond, but no longer has the

large flocks of sheep that used to use it, and it has an old village
church which is curiously symbolic of these new suburbs on the
outer fringe of Greater London; seen from the road it looks like
an old church much modernized, with a battlemented extension
tacked rather incongruously onto the northern side, but seen from
the south or 'country' side it still looks like the old village church
it once was. Thus Sanderstead Church neatly symbolizes the
ambivalence of the community it serves. Across the road is a quiet
cemetery where the panoramic view of London from this spot is
lost on those who lie there. We buried a close relative there last
year, and this thought I found hard to bear. Nearby, the new
Sanderstead Village has captured something of the spirit of the old,
sufficient of the half-timbered houses remaining to give the whole
an authentic air. As much can also be said of Warlingham, a
village with two greens, and a church surprisingly far from either
of them. The old Atwood Almshouses (1663) at Warlingham
Green are a miniature version of the Whitgift Hospital, and they
perform a similar vital function of tying the old in with the new.
But the building I like best in Warlingham is the old vicarage on
the opposite side of the green from the Almshouses. I recently
watched seventy young people set out from here to walk all night
to Guildford, 30 miles away, to help 'Shelter', and to help remind
us at the same time that today's youth is not all pop and pot.
Whilst waiting for them to move off, I noticed the curious
Grecian-style columns built into the brick facade of the Vicarage
—a feature I do not remember ever having seen before. Beyond
Warlingham lies its unhappy neighbour Chelsham, a kind of poor
relation at the end of the road, fit only for an ugly bus depot—
although, unbeknown to most people, it has a lovely church
buried deep in the countryside over a mile away with only a
farmworker's cottage or two within half an hour's walk. Why
these three churches, Farleigh, Chelsham and Warlingham, all
now linked under one vicar, were located so far from their respec-
tive villages is another of those mysteries I would like to resolve—
provided I could find another to replace it!

South of Chelsham and Warlingham lies the beautiful Haliloo
Valley. It is as if you had passed from the Libyan Desert to the
green lushness of the Nile. The road through the Halliloo Valley,
which my family call the 'Secret Valley' whenever we drive along

it, is one of the most attractive in Surrey, and although a huge gas main was driven through it recently the evidences were mercifully covered over and obliterated and the countryside restored to its former unspoiled beauty. Happily the area was nominated a Site of Special Scientific Importance by the Nature Conservancy some time ago and therefore may be preserved from urban encroachment with a little luck and a lot of public vigilance. The house of Slines Oaks beside the hill leading up to Chelsham pond is one of the prettiest stone houses in Surrey with an incomparable setting and a great air of tranquillity.

Second only to the Halliloo Valley in its quiet beauty is Marden Park in a tributary valley. Unfortunately the casual visitor cannot easily see the house, now the Convent of the Sacred Heart, a Roman Catholic school for girls, for it lies at the end of a long private drive branching off the Woldingham Road at the Mumbles railway viaduct. However, if the reader could accompany me to one of the ecumenical conferences held there each year he would not only enjoy a moving experience of being present as an Anglican bishop and a Roman Catholic monseignor conduct a joint service together, but he would also be able to appreciate for himself what an excellent choice Sir Robert Clayton made when he selected this spot, untouched since the village of Marden had been wiped out by the Black Death in 1348-9, as the site for his new mansion in the mid-seventeenth century. It was a site worthy of a mansion worthy of a man whom his friend Macauley described as "The wealthiest merchant of London". When John Evelyn visited Marden Park in 1677 he said of the mansion: "'Tis seated in such a solitude among hills, as being not above 16 miles from London, seems almost incredible, the ways up to it are so winding and intricate." In its setting in a steep-sided valley, and in its approach along a narrow winding lane, Marden Park reminds one of Fountains Abbey in Yorkshire—except that there are no lakes by the roadside. Indeed, as Evelyn himself noted (obviously mindful of his beloved Wotton) the site "wants running water"; the Bourne rises in this same valley a mile or so further down, but here it is dry. As to the house itself, it is an impressive Victorian gothic pile (the old mansion was destroyed by fire in 1879), now rather unbalanced by the new buildings erected in connection with the school, although these have been well designed to blend with the rest as far as possible. However, it is not the house that is the glory of Marden Park but the setting. Driving along the valley on a September evening, the cows contentedly munching the grass on one side and the evening sun gilding the autumn leaves on the other, one has to agree with the opinion expressed by William Wilberforce, a one-time tenant: "a fine place, one of the prettiest spots that I ever saw". They say that the school is one of the most expensive in the country, but to go to school in such a place! No parent able to afford it should grudge a penny of the cost.

The principal centre of the part of the Surrey Chalk we have been exploring is Caterham. It is really two towns in one, for Caterham Valley and Caterham on the Hill are distinctive communities that keep very much to themselves; they share the same station, and the same Urban District Council, but otherwise they have little else in common. All the old settlements on the chalk seem to have been located on the hilltops rather than down in the valleys, which were often thickly wooded and which often ended abruptly at the escarpment itself. This is true of Old Coulsdon, Chipstead, Sanderstead and Woldingham—and it is supremely true of Caterham. Strange as it may seem to the casual visitor today, Caterham Valley was virtually uninhabited, save for a few scattered farmsteads, up to the middle of the nineteenth century, whilst Caterham on the Hill was an ancient village with a church (St Lawrence's) dating back to the twelfth century and with several cottages of Tudor age. Caterham Valley was born when the branch line was constructed from what is now Purley Station to the terminus at Caterham.

The story of the Caterham railway, as indeed of the other lines in the area also, makes fascinating reading. The first proposals for a railway came as far back as 1836 when the South Eastern Railway surveyed the Caterham Valley with the object of building the new London to Dover line through a proposed mile-long tunnel under the 'Godstone Gap' and so on to Edenbridge and Dover. It was thought that this would be a better proposition than the alternative route via Woldingham and Oxted, which would have necessitated building five miles of tunnel (this line, as we have seen, was eventually built in 1878), but even this less ambitious project was found to be too costly, and it was decided to use the existing line to Redhill and to build the Dover line from there. So it came about that Caterham only had a branch line which was built by a private company in 1856. Later on there were many proposals for extending the line but they came to nothing. There is no space here to tell of the bitter squabbles that broke out between the private company that built the Caterham line and the London and Brighton Railway who owned the station at Purley—then called Godstone Road Station, which led to the lines remaining derelict for nearly a year after they had been laid, and eventually to the bankruptcy of the private company—or of the frustrations caused to the local inhabitants through the train from Godstone Road Station to London being timed to leave precisely one minute before the train from Caterham drew in! Like the quaint little stations at Kenley and Whyteleafe, these incidents belong to a now remote and picturesque chapter in Surrey's railway history.

The proprietors of the Caterham Valley branch line undoubtedly hoped to attract residential development along the valley, but their immediate objective was to provide a more convenient means of transporting the valuable building stone from the Godstone quarries to London, where it was so much in demand during the mid-Victorian building boom. At this time, of course, Kenley and Whyteleafe did not exist—even in name. However it was not many years before the original objective was virtually lost sight of as Caterham began to develop rapidly, both hill and valley, under the stimulus of this railway link with the Capital. Many wealthy Victorian city men built themselves huge Victorian mock-Gothic mansions in the valley, and many of these still remain as reminders of a world long since passed away—a world of armies of domestics, rambling stable blocks, walled gardens, glass conservatories and a sublime conviction that Britain ruled the waves and all was well with the world. A contemporary writer summarized the process of development, currently being repeated in a hundred suburban railheads at this time, in these words:

The main army is preceded by an advance of villas, seizing a few picked positions . . . then come the more solid ranks of the semi-detached, along the high roads and in the neighbourhood of railway stations. They are followed by rows of shops. The houses have that cramped and mean appearance which speaks of pressure on the dingy crowds of London. They bear the stamp of their origin.

It was not only the wealthy who came to live in Caterham. In 1877 the Caterham Guards Barracks were constructed on Caterham on the Hill alongside the new lunatic asylum, and very soon rows of mean little houses began to spring up between these two huge and gaunt blocks of buildings and the attractive old village of Caterham on the Hill. By the turn of the century the old church of St Lawrence had been superseded by a new and larger church on the opposite side of the road, symbolizing the final incorporation of this ancient village into the modern Victorian suburb. Caterham on the Hill is today a place altogether unworthy of its magnificent location a mile or two back from the escarpment of the North Downs. Barely a quarter of an hour's walk away lies one of the most sublime views in Surrey, yet there is no point between White Hill and Merstham where the motorist can gain real access to it. He might as well be in the middle of Manchester or the Black Country. For 99 per cent of their waking time the people of Caterham on the Hill are as oblivious of their view as the passengers of a tube train are of what lies above them. Such a view, like access to light, is an inalienable right: there should be a law like 'Ancient Lights' guaranteeing the motorist access to magnificent views. A tastefully laid-out viewpoint, accessible by road, would open a window in the shuttered room that is Caterham on the Hill.

Caterham Valley, and indeed parts of Caterham Hill away from the barracks, are still beautiful places in which to live. Few towns only 18 miles from London contain within them such wonderful viewpoints as Church Hill, Tillingdown Lane, Newstead Rise and Burntwood Lane. The sides of the valley are so steep that in places handrails are required for pedestrians, and paths become steps, so that the whole area is reminiscent of some Welsh mining valley— although happily without the pit-head gear. High up the side of the valley ran the Roman Road from Portslade to London; a friend of mine in Caterham recently conducted me round his garden and pointed out where this old road crosses his lawn—that is quite an *object d'intérêt* to have in one's garden! The great expert on Roman roads, I. D. Margary, conducted an excavation at this very spot some years ago and found the road to be about 25 feet wide and 12 inches thick. The Bourne Society excavated a section in a neighbouring garden recently but must have been disappointed

to find no Roman remains other than the road surface itself
—just one coin would have been very satisfying after the
labours of digging a trench some 30 feet long and up to 10 feet
deep, but I suppose the Romans did not go around dropping
coins for the sake of amateur archaeologists 2,000 years later. They
did find a medieval knife blade and some thirteenth century pottery, which suggested that the road may have remained in use as a
track, although the Roman surface had by then disappeared. The
Romans bypassed the valley, presumably because it was wooded
and because, in any event, they could not avoid the climb to the
top of Godstone Hill. In the 1930s Caterham was again bypassed.
The Caterham Bypass was one of the earliest built in Surrey and
must surely be one of the most successful. I regard it as the classic
example of what a bypass should do. The road threads its way
through hilly country to the east of Caterham, which has never
been settled residentially, and emerges near the top of Godstone
Hill, thus diverting all through traffic from Caterham Valley
whilst being itself invisible from the town and causing the very
minimum of disturbance to the landscape. It was a triumph of
planning skill, and without it Caterham Valley by now would
surely have been throttled to death.

We come now to the principal north-south valley through this
part of the Surrey chalk country—and the ancient trackway and
line of communication through it—the historic Brighton Road.
The railway from Merstham passes through such places as
Coulsdon North, Reedham, Purley, Purley Oaks, South Croydon
and East Croydon—the names come automatically off the tongue
of any commuter on what is one of the busiest lines on the Southern
Region. Gazing out of the window as the train glides along the
wide valley towards Croydon is apt to be a depressing experience
(apart from the fine view of the skyline of the New Croydon in
the distance) unless one can see beyond the endless rows of suburban dwellings to the time barely a century ago when this valley
was virtually uninhabited and undeveloped.

It seems almost unbelievable now that when the Caterham
branch line was built to what is now Purley there was no settlement of any kind there, and the station (which had been closed
down for some years for lack of traffic) had been called, as mentioned earlier, 'Godstone Road Station'. It then became Caterham

Junction Station, and only in 1888, after the Purley residents had complained that their mail was repeatedly sent to Caterham by mistake, was it changed to Purley Station.

The story of how Purley Oaks Station got its name is even more extraordinary. It seems that the Superintendent of the Railway was walking down the track soon after the lines had been laid and asked one of the gangers what the name was of an isolated farmhouse by the railway. "It's called Purley Oaks," he replied. "That's what we'll call the station," said the superintendent. And so Purley Oaks came into being. Of course, these places began to grow rapidly once the railway arrived. By 1878 Purley had a population of 500 people and was obviously going to expand very much more. Already its first church, Christchurch, had been opened (as there were no villages in the valley there were no churches, of course), and villas were springing up on both sides of the valley. Measures were taken to deal with the occasional flooding at the Purley crossroads (after heavy storms the road is still often flooded at this point), and with the arrival of the motor car Purley never looked back. The hamlet became a village, the village a town, and the town a vast sprawling suburb of 74,000 people which is now part of the London Borough of Croydon.

Why had the valley been left for so long undeveloped? The basic reason is that the villages had long ago been established on the neighbouring hilltops at such places as Sanderstead, Coulsdon, Farleigh, Woodmansterne and Chelsham, whilst much of the valley was owned by great landowners like Lord Howard of Effingham, who lived at Haling House, now the site of Whitgift School. Another reason was that the old Roman Road from Portslade did not run through the valley for the whole of its route through the Chalk but went up over Riddlesdown and came down near South Croydon, thus bypassing what is now Purley. There must have been little of interest in the valley to divert the traveller at this time. Cobbett came this way in 1832, and all he could find to comment on were some cabbages!: "Came from the Wen through Croydon. From London to Croydon is as ugly a bit of country as any in England—poor spewy gravel with some clay. Croydon is a good market town but swelled out into a Wen. At Mearston (i.e. Merstham) there is a field of cabbages."

The route over the North Downs via Coulsdon and Merstham

is so much easier than the Godstone Road that it is surprising the Romans did not bring their road by this route. It is suggested later that the reason is probably that they wanted their road to serve the iron-fields in the Weald, which were located east of the Merstham-Portslade line. Nevertheless some Roman remains have been found along the Coulsdon Valley (Roman coins and pottery at Farthing Downs, Coulsdon Woods, Marlpit Lane Quarry and Starrock Wood), and there is little doubt that they used this convenient route across the escarpment even if it petered out in the Vale of Holmesdale. The huge stone quarries of Merstham have been worked for many centuries and were certainly being exploited as early as 1176 when the first stone bridge across the lower River Thames, London Bridge, was built with Merstham stone. This same material was also used in the building of Westminster Palace, Windsor Castle and Old St Paul's. As indicated earlier, it was the prospect of a more economical method of transporting this stone to London that led to the construction of the Surrey Iron Railway in 1805. Apart from this rather mundane traffic the Coulsdon Valley was not at this time a major route and was certainly not the road to Brighton.

There were two alternative routes to Brighton in this period, the older route followed the Roman road over Riddlesdown and through Godstone and Lewes to Brighton. A 'Flying Machine' left Brighton at 5.30 a.m. every morning by this road and arrived at Southwark in the evening. But since the construction of the new turnpike in 1755 the route via Mitcham, Sutton and Reigate had become the more popular. This was by no means an easy route since it involved the steep ascent of Reigate Hill, and just what this could mean in the days of horse-drawn coaches is brought home vividly in this account by Shergold dated about 1790:

When the coach arrived at Reigate Hill, all passengers inside and outside, were requested to descend. The Hill was the most formidable tug on the road. The best and easiest way of arriving at the summit of the hill was to follow humbly the movement of the coach; but some ladies and gentlemen ventured up a steep which led almost perpendicularly up the hill, adjoined the road by a transverse path. Here was the trial of sound lungs and easy and comfortable lacing. Ladies who looked more to dapper shapes than easy respiration were sure to be brought to a non-plus about the middle of the path, and it was sometimes necessary to despatch a deputation of the gentlemen, who were walking near the coach, to aid in dragging the impeded ladies up the path . . . when we arrived at the top of Reigate Hill we considered the journey to London almost as completed.

Why they underwent all this inconvenience when there lay an easily graded route only a mile or two the other side of Gatton Park is a mystery—until one learns that the main instigators of the Reigate route were the gentlemen of Sutton who naturally wanted a road to Brighton that passed their front doors! However eventually geography was bound to prevail, and in 1816 a turnpike road was opened along the Coulsdon Valley through Merstham to Reigate (later going direct through Redhill to link with the Reigate to Brighton road near Horley) and so the Brighton Road came into being. As it happened the new road only had a short period of popularity before the railway was built in 1841, which brought road traffic to Brighton almost to a halt. However, in that short time it acquired a great reputation for the number and brilliance of the coaches and their ebullient drivers and passengers who followed the Prince Regent pleasure-bound to London-by-the-Sea. Already Brighton had become the largest town in Sussex, and some fifty coaches a day passed along this road. They had to change horses frequently, and there was much coming and going at 'The Greyhound' and the 'Green Dragon' in Croydon and the 'Red Lion' at Coulsdon. There seems to be an idyllic quality about this colourful and gay chapter in our nation's history which may help to explain how the Brighton Road came to acquire such a secure place in the affections of Surrey people despite its relatively short life. But, even making allowances for a degree of poetic licence, one finds it difficult to accept that all was as idyllic as this contemporary description would paint it:

From Brighton to London it is merely a street of twenty leagues, bordered with parks, gardens, smiling farms, pretty country houses, charming pavilions covered from top to bottom with hangings of roses, and preceded by courts or terraces shaded with cool bowers under which dance young girls, whom Raphael might regret not to have seen.

Many were the contests fought out on the Brighton Road and old prints adorn the walls of a hundred public houses along the route to Brighton, showing coaches at full pelt, their axles almost touching, and the drivers (obviously adherents of the 'hit 'em and hold 'em' school) flourishing their whips to coax yet another effort from the horses whose legs are already almost horizontal. These contests continued long after the railway had taken away most of the commercial traffic along the road, and on 13th July 1888, James Selby drove the 'Old Times' coach from London to Brighton and back in seven hours and fifty minutes—so winning a £1,000 wager with only ten minutes to spare. Unfortunately, however, his success was dearly bought, for he had defied his doctor in making the run and died three months later. As a boy I spent long hours devouring my father's old copies of *The Strand Magazine*, and I think it was through the pages, and particularly the illustrations, of 'Rodney Stone' that I absorbed into my system the magical lure of the coaching era. The Brighton Road is still the place for contests of all kinds: the annual walk, the penny-farthing race, the annual Old Crocks run—they are all in the true tradition of this great road. As Vidal de la Blache said: "The road is branded on the soil; it sows the seeds of life, houses, villages and towns." The Brighton Road is surely branded on the soil of Surrey.

# II

# THE CHALK DOWNS OF BANSTEAD, EPSOM AND MICKLEHAM

The best-known natural feature of the chalk country, second only
to the magnificent escarpment itself, are the rolling Downs that
comprise so large a part of the dip slope. Farthing, Banstead,
Epsom, Merrow—the names of the Surrey Downs have become
household words, and so have those other Downs that are not so
called—Box Hill, Ranmore Common, the Hog's Back and so
many others. They all share the same distinguishing features; the
high open rolling country—likened by more than one poet to the
waves of a vast green sea—with springy turf and few trees, and
here and there substantial areas of bramble, gorse and heath.

At one time virtually the whole of the chalk dip slope was open
downland. Aubrey in the late seventeenth century described
Croydon as "lying at the foot of Banstead Downs", indicating
that these must then have been very much more extensive than
they are today. But a century of urbanization has covered large
areas of the chalk country with houses, so that only here and there
—in places like Riddlesdown, Croham Hurst, Coulsdon Common
or Banstead Downs—can one catch a glimpse of what the country
was like before the builders came. One can hardly blame people
for wanting to live on such an attractive terrain compared with
the damp sticky clays of the Wandle and Hogsmill basins, but
because of the very scarcity of trees on the Chalk the effect of
urbanization on the landscape is often more painfully obvious
there than elsewhere. Fingers of residential development grope
up the valleys off the Coulsdon Valley, and the lower slopes are
clothed with long rows of houses which stop dead as the ground
becomes too steep for building. There are no trees to mask the

margins, as there are at Hindhead or Chobham Ridges, for instance, and the effect is aesthetically disastrous. As you climb Farthing Downs you are accompanied by a long fence and the backs of houses, and the same story is repeated all along the northern edge of the Downs as far as the Mole Valley. Surrey's ever-present dilemma of trying to meet the needs of people for residence and recreation without in the process destroying the very assets the people come to enjoy is highlighted in the chalk country as no-where else in the county.

The Surrey Downs fall into two main sections. The first lies east of the Mole Valley and, being nearest to London, is subject to heavy urban pressures, the chalk country south of Croydon being, as we have seen, almost entirely urbanized save for the watersheds between some of the valleys. The second section, which is very much smaller in extent as the tip of the half spear-head is ap-proached, lies on the west side of the Mole and so far this section has escaped any significant urban development except near Guild-ford. This is indeed a very remote piece of country, with no village worthy of the name and only one or two tiny hamlets. "In all my wanderings," wrote Louis Jennings in 1877, "never have I seen in a civilized land such a deserted tract as this." Because it is so different from the eastern section, this part is dealt with separately in the next chapter.

The fact that all the ancient villages of the Downs were located on the tops of the hills, whilst most of the modern development has been in the valleys (where access to roads and railways was easiest), has brought about some remarkable contrasts. All over the chalk country can be found old and seemingly very remote villages and village churches that are in fact only a mile or two from densely populated suburbanized valleys. Take Woodman-sterne, for instance, a little hilltop village with an ancient church, which until recently had no public transport of any kind, although it is now served by a private shuttle service of buses to and from Banstead—and yet it lies within a mile or two of the densely popu-lated areas of Chipstead Valley and Banstead. Another example is Chaldon, a little, hunched-up-looking country church set in a remote country location near the chalk escarpment, with its curious medieval wall paintings (said to be among the oldest in England) of devils and ladders and people being boiled in cauldrons—all savouring very much of an age of superstition and witchcraft and endlessly embroidered travellers' tales as they passed this way. Yet only half a mile away is the rapidly growing residential part of Chaldon and Caterham on the Hill. Across the Coulsdon Valley lies the 800-year-old Chipstead Church, a full mile from the old hill-top village and two from the new suburb by the railway station. Perhaps it was partly due to its distance from the village that, in the eighteenth century, Chipstead Church was greatly neglected; the local cricketers used it as a pavilion, marking their scores, or rather scoring their marks, on the wooden furniture of the church and drinking beer or eating their bread and cheese inside. Then there is Headley, not very far from Epsom and Ashtead but still retaining its village air, especially if you approach it as it should be approached—from across the fields or over the downs from Epsom. Its hilltop companion is Walton on the Hill. Here the urban tide laps the very doorstep but has still not quite robbed the village of its rural charm, to which the Mere pond, the green, and the nearby stump of an old windmill, contribute not a little. Both these villages have long had a reputation for being exposed to the high winds which sweep unopposed down the dip slope of the Chalk from the nearby scarp edge. John Toland, in 1711, commented: "Sutton and Cheam are too dirty (i.e. for riding) as Walton and Headley are too windy in winter, and too woody, and therefore too close, in summer."

These few villages have survived more or less unchanged over the centuries, but many others only a mile or two away, which happened to lie in the main path of urban development, have changed almost out of recognition. Old Coulsdon is one of these. It calls itself 'Old Coulsdon' to distinguish it from the new suburb in the valley, but few old buildings survive other than the church, Bradmore Farm, Cherrytree Cottage and the cottages at Coulsdon Street. Another of these newly developed villages is Banstead, the largest village on the top of the chalk downs and the one which has given its name to a large and scattered urban district of over 40,000 people, comprising no less than nine distinct villages. Despite the great changes that have taken place these have mostly managed to retain a village atmosphere. This is particularly true of Banstead itself with its ancient flint church dating, together with the orchard in front (surely the oldest in Surrey), from 1170; the old well and the Well Farm opposite dating back to Tudor times; and a modern High Street that has been designed (save for the most recent additions) so successfully in mock-Tudor that the appelation 'Banstead Village', to which the residents so bravely cling, does not seem too hopelessly out of place. But the old church is the real treasure of Banstead, and therein lies a cruel dilemma. For decades now the Parish Church Council have intermittently been debating the agonizing problem of how to make a twelfth-century church suitable for the demands of a twentieth-century population without in the process destroying the rich heritage from the past. Should they build a new church, enlarge the old, or just squeeze the people in as best they can and leave well alone? I took part in some of these debates, and I realize only too well what a difficult decision this is to make. On balance I prefer the solution adopted at Caterham on the Hill, i.e. to leave the old church alone and build a large modern one nearby. The next best solution would be to enlarge the old church as tastefully as possible (as at Sanderstead); and far and away the worst solution is to simply do nothing in the belief that preserving a beautiful building from the past is more important than serving the spiritual needs of the people of today. Beyond Banstead Church is the cricket green, a tranquil haven of peace with as rural a backcloth as any green in Surrey. To watch the cricket here on a summer's evening, whilst listening to the ringing of the bells of All Saints as the bell-ringers practice for the Sunday services, this is indeed the *Ultimun Refugium*, the term used by London physicians centuries ago when recommending the sweet and wholesome air of Banstead Downs to their patients. The ringers of All Saints, like those of cruciform churches such as the 'Cathedral of the Downs' at Alfriston in Sussex, stand in full view of the congregation whilst they are ringing, shirtsleeves and all—it would cost a bell-ringer the traditional fine of 6d. if he kept his jacket on whilst he was ringing. It is not always realized how deeply embedded in our nation's life bell-ringing still is; there are no less than 40,000 bell-ringers in Britain. No wonder they call ours the 'Ringing Isle'.

Because Banstead has no natural feature inviting urban development, such as a valley or a river or a major intersection of roads, it was not developed residentially to any extent until the twentieth century. The Old Brighton Road, it is true, passed through the

*The Old Town Hall, Reigate*

present urban district when it was built as a turnpike in 1755, but it headed straight from Sutton to Reigate across Banstead Downs, and thus completely bypassed Banstead Village. Today it is probably true to say that for every hundred Londoners who have passed through Banstead Urban District there is only one who has ever passed along Banstead High Street, which is orientated in an east-west direction and has no direct access from the Brighton Road. You have to turn off the Brighton Road to see Banstead, and this is the last thing the thousands of motorists heading for the coast on a typical summer weekend want to do. Because of its late development there is hardly a building in the village older than 1900. I have in my possession a copy of a tithe map of Banstead dated 1841, and it shows only a few cottages clustered, very characteristically, round the old well, with the church some distance away along the ridge, and here and there a few gentlemen's houses, the rest being all fields, Downs and parks. That is what Banstead was like until the turn of the century. The first major intrusion on this rural scene was the building of the railway to Epsom Downs across the middle of Banstead Downs in 1865, and this was followed in 1877 (as at Warlingham, Caterham, Netherne and Reedham at about the same time) by a huge mental asylum. This sad little city of 2,500 people occupied a beautiful location high up on the Downs where a windmill had once stood, commanding a panoramic view of London that none of the inmates could see from the ground because of the twelve-foot-high wall surrounding their 'prison'. Eric Parker has a poignant passage written shortly after these huge mental asylums had been built in Surrey:

> County Councils have decreed that in this part of Surrey must be massed together the thousands of poor souls who have lost the reason which county councillors must be supposed to possess; but why insist on their unhappy presence? A building to hold such sadness should be a quiet thing, hidden among trees, silent, alone. But that would suit neither councillors nor architects. For them asylums must stare, scar, insist that they will be seen and known, and here, in what should be tranquil and lovely country, they violate the hills.

As late as 1901 half the people of Banstead, statistically speaking, were out of their mind, for the population was 5,624, of whom 2,677 were in the asylum. At Epsom today there are 7,000 patients

9

*Castle draughts, Guildford*

in the local mental hospitals, compared with a population of about 70,000, and the authorities are very worried lest public tolerance and understanding may suffer in the face of what they term "over-saturation".

Considering the high reputation that Banstead Downs had enjoyed for so long, it is surprising that the healthy were so slow to follow the sick. In 1760 Bowen had described Banstead as "famous for its wholesome air", and a contemporary poet of the period wrote of:

> spacious airy downs
> With grass and thyme o'erspread and clover wild,
> Where smiling Phoebus tempers every breeze,
> The fairest flocks rejoice—
> Such are the downs of Banstead, edged with woods
> And tow'ry villas.

As the last line of this verse indicates, there was some urban encroachment even as far back as the Napoleonic Wars, especially on the various commons of Epsom, Ashtead, Sutton and Banstead, and, while the men were away fighting and the price of food rose very high, more of the commons were ploughed up. This led to bitter complaints, and one contemporary poet expressed the feeling of the time in the following couplet:

> The law forbids the man or woman to steal the goose from off the common
> Yet it lets the villain loose who steals the common from the goose.

However it was not until the first decade or two of the present century that Banstead began the transformation that was to take it from a village to a large and growing outer suburb of London. The few large houses were mostly pulled down and gave their names to new roads or semi-detached houses which filled the northern slopes of the ridge and thus spoiled the view of All Saints Church which must have delighted the eyes of travellers in times past as they toiled up the long climb from Sutton and across the Downs. Unlike those of most Wealden towns and villages, the High Street of Banstead, or 'Hye Street' as it was called in 1433, really is high—some 500 feet. One wonders indeed if the location of these ancient chalk villages high on the top of the chalk plateaux gave rise to the term 'High Street' centuries ago.

The Old Brighton Road across Banstead Downs and through Burgh Heath, was once a dangerous one, and the various pits and shallow depressions on the Downs (some of them now put to good use as bunkers on the golf course) were at one time known as the 'Highwaymen's Stables'. Today, however, highwaymen of a different kind travel the Brighton Road. They are the motorists in their hundreds of thousands, bound for the coast or a trip in the country, who say at every wayside parking place: "Stand and deliver—petrol, cups of tea, antiques, toilets, accommodation, amusements. . . ." Their demands are endless. Reversing the old order, they give their money, but in so doing suck the life blood from the villages through which they pass. To meet their demands there have sprung up in recent years a welter of roadside facilities, and nowhere is the effect more disastrous than at Lower Kingswood, which has come to look like a Mid-West prairie town in Goldrush days. It came as a shock to me, some years ago, to discover that this village possesses an ancient church and is indeed a settlement of great antiquity, for it seems today to be merely a waste product of the motorcar age. I suppose it all began when the Prince Regent used to drop in at the Tangier Inn, Burgh Heath, for a glass of Miss Jeal's famous elderberry wine to help him on his way to Brighton; but, multiplied a million times over, the modern highwaymen, among whom, ashamedly, I must include myself, have robbed the age-old villages of the Downs, that happen to lie in their path, of their peace and beauty. And in exchange for this birthright they have given only a mess of pottage.

Banstead Downs have been for many centuries a great playground and were the scene of horse-racing in the sixteenth century long long before Epsom Downs became associated with this sport. The parish register of Banstead for 1625 contains a reference to a William Stanley who "on running the race fell from his horse and broke his neck". During the Civil War the Royalists planned a rising on Banstead Downs under cover of a race-meeting to be arranged there. The peak of horse-racing on Banstead Downs was probably on 20th November 1683, when it is recorded that both King Charles II and the Duke of York watched the racing. After this Banstead Downs seems to have declined in popularity as a venue for this sport, whilst Epsom Downs increased, and eventually they ceased altogether to play any part in horse racing.

Horses still enjoy the Downland turf, however, and little equestrian columns can be seen any day wending their way along the
track of the long-since disused race course on the Downs. What
was perhaps the spiritual home of modern horse-racing, the mansion called 'The Oaks' between Banstead and Woodmansterne,
has recently been demolished. When Edward, the 11th Earl of
Derby, acquired the lease of this property in 1759, he did not know
it at the time but he was adding two names to the racing calendar
that were to become famous the world over. He constructed on
the site an extraordinary building, half mansion and half summer
house, a Regency folly of mock turrets, arrow slits and battlements, designed primarily for the entertainment of guests during
the racing season. I visited the site when the building was being
demolished in 1957, and the foreman told me that it was the
worst-constructed building he had ever had to demolish in his
twenty-three years experience; the bricks were so soft that they
were useless for anything else, and the turrets had not been properly keyed into the rest of the structure. In this building had been
enacted scenes of opulent splendour that caused even Horace
Walpole to complain of extravagance. He wrote to a friend:

> This month Lord Stanley [Derby's grandson] marries Lady Betty
> Hamilton. He gives a most splendid entertainment at his villa in
> Surrey and calls it a 'Fête Champetre'. It will cost £5000. Every
> body is to go in masquerade, but not in mask. He has bought all the
> orange trees around London, and the haycocks, I suppose, are to be
> of straw coloured satin!

Robert Adam was commissioned to build a magnificent Corinthian pavilion in the grounds, which included a state room 120
feet long. Here was a display of opulence to match even that of
the Royal Pavilion at Brighton, another structure that seems
hardly to have been designed to last for ever. It was after this
curious house, 'The Oaks', that the famous race for fillies at
Epsom (sometimes referred to as the 'Garter of the Turf') was
named in 1779. The Derby itself being established in the following
year. Because of its historic associations, rather than for any
architectural interest, a portion of the old building was kept intact
when the demolition took place and is now used as a restaurant,
the surrounding park being open to the public.

At Preston Hawe, near Burgh Heath, is one of the oldest, and at the same time one of the newest, villages in Surrey. For centuries Preston Hawe was just a meadow on which sheep contentedly grazed, the existence of the village being altogether unsuspected. Then in August 1952 along came the bulldozers and giant excavators to lay the foundations for the huge new estate to be built there—a unique venture whereby three neighbouring local authorities, Merton and Morden, Sutton and Cheam and Mitcham, combined together to build an estate for 3,000 people in another local authority's area! Soon a wonderful hoard of medieval remains began to be unearthed: skeletons, pottery, remains of timber buildings, and many other items which together comprised, in the words of an expert at the time: "the most complete picture of life in the Middle Ages so far discovered in this country". So Preston Hawe joins the ranks of lost villages in the chalk country such as Cuddington (near Banstead), Watendone (near Kenley), Marden (near Caterham) and Goldwhurd (near Tatsfield). No one knows exactly why these villages died (except Cuddington), but the Black Death and its aftermath is often thought to have been one reason, whilst a contributory factor may have been the incidence of sheep disease in Britain in the latter part of the thirteenth century.

Near Banstead Village is the ancient inn known as 'the Mint'. It is a reminder of an industry that has long flourished in this area —the growing of peppermint. The district around Tattenham Corner and Banstead is said to be the best in the world for the growing of this crop, and a few years ago there was one farm growing nearly thirty acres of peppermint, although by now the farmer may well have decided that houses are an even more lucrative crop. The oil is sent to Mitcham where it it used in the sweet factories there. The plants have to be cut by hand, and an unusual feature of the crop is that after four consecutive harvests have been taken the soil has to be rested for twenty years.

Two curious railways work their way up the dip slope of the Chalk and terminate within a mile of each other high up on Epsom Downs, like two rivers rising on opposite sides of a watershed and flowing off in different directions. The first, as we have seen, was built in 1865 and, as if in shame at its intrusion, it hides itself in a deep cutting as it crosses Banstead Downs on its way to Epsom

Downs. In 1897 the second line began its sinuous course along the Chipstead Valley with apparently as little idea of where it was going as the valley itself; when the valley petered out the builders seem also to have run out of ideas. They took the line to Kingswood, and there it stopped. But then Sir Cosmo Bonsor of Kingswood Warren (now the B.B.C. Research Centre) formed a syndicate to take the line on to Tattenham Corner in 1901—surely a remarkable tribute to the secure place horse-racing had in English social life at that time. The first train ran, very appropriately, on Derby Day 1901. These two railways are the only ones in Surrey that venture onto the high chalk plateau—all the others keep to the valleys through the Chalk.

The Chipstead Valley line brought a residential boom to places like Chipstead, Kingswood, Tadworth and Tattenham Corner. At Chipstead it gave birth to new settlements both near the railway station in the valley and high on the hilltop where the old village was—although happily it had little impact on old Chipstead Church, safely out of reach of any railway line on its hill by the green, the least spoiled of any village green in Surrey.

Kingswood is almost wholly a creation of the railway, including its Victorian church by the Reigate Road with a soaring steeple that has provided a useful homing beacon to many a walker who has lost his bearings on Banstead Heath. On one occasion before the war, when I was a young army cadet scarcely in my teens, I remember spending the best part of a day dead and alive—and very lost! It was the annual manoeuvres and mock battle, and in an early encounter with the 'enemy' I had the misfortune to be pronounced 'dead' by the umpire and so became detached from my platoon. The 'battle' drifted further away and after a while I became tired of being dead and decided to set out in search of someone, friend or foe. But the heath seemed huge and empty, and I was lucky to fall in with a party on their way back to the coaches or I might well have spent an uncomfortable night on Banstead Heath. At Tadworth and Tattenham modern housing areas sprang into being sustained by the same umbilical cord to the Mother City.

And so we come, as millions of Londoners have come before us, to the finest of Surrey Downs—Epsom Downs. They are high, bracing and invigorating, as made for sport and pleasure as any lake, beach or mountain side. Epsom is the hub of the racing world—or rather, on Derby Day, its hubbub. Just when horse-racing started on Epsom Downs is not known for sure, but as we saw in Chapter 8 the Downs had been laid out for the sport as early as 1700, and it is only natural that horse-racing should flourish here rather than at Banstead because Epsom had by this time become a favourite spa town, and anything that would help entertain the visitors from London was welcome. However it was not until Lord Derby and his friends, over their glasses of port at 'The Oaks', decided to hold their race on Epsom Downs that this became the leading racecourse in the country, if not in the world. The Derby is said to be the most testing 1½ miles of any course in the world, thanks to its being laid out over the rolling downland country. The Derby and the Oaks soon became household words, and when Thackeray named a character in *Pendennis* 'Sir Derby Oaks' he had no doubt that the readers would gather he was a sporting gentleman! In 1829 the first stand was built, and this was the one Charles Dickens described in his famous account of Derby Day 1851. In 1926 the present grandstand, now capable of accommodating 25,000 to 30,000 people, was built.

Although I cannot claim to be a 'sporting gentleman' myself, I do enjoy the atmosphere of Epsom on Derby Day. Perhaps this is how it came about one year that I was deputed to place bets on a number of horses for office colleagues. The crush was so great that I was unable to see the horses pass and had to listen to the radio commentary instead. According to this none of my horses had come in the first three, and so I went home in disgust. It was only later that I discovered that the commentator had made a mistake and that one of the horses I had backed on behalf of a colleague had come second. That experience cost me quite a bit when I met my colleague next day! During a visit to the United States in 1964 I visited the famous Spendthrift Stud Farm in the Bluegrass Country of Lexington, Kentucky, and saw there several well-known Derby winners including 'My Babu' and 'Tudor Minstrel'; for all I know, I may have seen the horse that had cost me dear a year or two before. Horses are in the blood of Epsom and of Epsom people. It is fitting that two horses' heads should adorn the borough's coat of arms superimposed on a background of green and white representing the turf and the chalk of the Downs.

But Epsom Downs stand not only for racing—they are for walking on also; were it not so the two stations terminating on the shore of this green sea would certainly have made a loss. Before the war, and still to a lesser extent today, every train arriving at these two stations on a summer weekend disgorged its crowd of haversacked walkers, lighthearted and lightfooted as they faced a ten, fifteen or twenty-mile walk across the Downs. Here the real country begins: mile after mile of open downland, heath or common, with few farms or fences to impede the walker, and at the far horizon a rich prize for the effort entailed in getting there—the view from the escarpment at Colley Hill, Pebble-coombe or Box Hill. There is no finer walking country on the Surrey chalk than this triangle with its apex at Epsom and its base along the edge of the Downs from Reigate Hill to Box Hill; it must be the most walked-over piece of countryside in the whole of Britain. There is wonderful variety of scenery here, ranging from the open north-facing Downs of Epsom, the rolling hills and valleys of Headley, the heaths of Walton and Tadworth, the woods of Burntwood, and the crowning exhilaration of the escarpment itself. And, because of the great variety of scenery, there is also a great variety of entomological life. On Mickleham Downs there are said to be seventy varieties of butterflies and 300 varieties of moths. Whether one is on foot or travelling by car, the valley from Tot Hill to Mickleham, with the steeple of Ranmore Church beckoning one onward on the far horizon, is one of the loveliest in the chalk country.

As is so often the case, the very beauty of the countryside is its own worst enemy in this age of mass travel, and Box Hill is the most threatened of Surrey's famous beauty spots. Some years ago we took a young French visitor to Box Hill one sunny Sunday afternoon in summer, but we were horrified at the huge crowd there, the serried ranks of motor bikes with leather-jacketed youngsters lounging round them apparently oblivious of the view to be enjoyed a short distance away, the queues at the ice-cream parlour, tea-rooms and toilets, the traffic jams, the noise, and indeed the total absence of any sense of rural tranquillity. It certainly seemed true at that moment that, as Katherine Kenyon has put it: "The second half of the twentieth century has a craving to get away from crowded towns into the diminishing countryside in order to mix with other crowds." We vowed to give Box Hill a miss in future and indeed have not been back there since; I suspect other people have had a similar experience. One wonders if this degradation of Nature's finest gifts is inevitable. It seems to me that the problem is not insoluble, provided the cars can be tucked away in parking places in the woods, excessive noise forbidden and any development out of keeping with the environment prohibited. The damage is not beyond repair, and the Surrey County Council has wisely chosen to nominate Box Hill as a Country Park under the new Countryside Act, thus enabling more money to be spent on providing adequate facilities to accommodate the people who want to come here than has been possible in the past. Despite these problems, Box Hill is still a sublime viewpoint; it is still the only place that you approach by anything resembling a mountain road in the South of England, complete with hairpin bends; the eastward facing slopes are still the only place in Surrey that I know where skiing is regularly enjoyed; and it is still the only place in Surrey where the box trees grow in such profusion, clinging to the precipitous slopes which were too steep to be ploughed. If it were not for these slopes, indeed, the box tree might by now have become extinct, and, as William Gilpin observed as far back as 1808, "it might perhaps be doubted whether Box were a native of England".

# 12

# THE MOLE GAP,
## AND THE DOWNS TO NEWLANDS CORNER

Box Hill could almost have been so named because it is like a box
at the theatre—and what finer scenery could any theatre have than
the surpassingly beautiful Mole Valley.

The Mole Valley is the offspring of the river, geologically
speaking, but, exhausted perhaps by the immensity of its achievement in breaching the chalk wall, the river sinks gratefully into
the womb of the earth every dry summer. The 'swallows' of the
Mole have excited the curiosity of travellers down the ages. The
poet Spenser wrote of:

> Mole that like a Mousling mole doth make
> His way still underground, till Thames he overtake.

Celia Fiennes, about 1700, notes that the Mole

runns twining itself about and is called the Swallow, and just about
Dorken and Leatherhead it sinkes away in many places which they
call swallow holes; this must be some quick sand, but the report of it
is it sinkes here and runnes underground a mile or two and rises
about Molesey and runnes again. Camden does credit this and
repeates a tryal one made of forcing a duck into one of these falls
which came out at the other side by Molesey with its feathers all-
most all rubbed off.

When Mr C. C. Fagg was appointed Warden of the Centre for
Field Studies at Juniper Hall soon after the war, he decided to conduct a scientific investigation into the nature of the swallows of the
Mole. As a result of his painstaking work we now know exactly
what happens. Mr Fagg discovered that the swallow holes were

fissures in the chalk, and that most of them were located either to one side of the bed of the main stream or in the bank at the side of the river. These fissures in themselves could not bring the flow of the river to a halt. However, he also found about eight 'swallows' that actually lay in the main bed of the river, and he estimated that these were capable of absorbing 30 million gallons of water a day. Once the flow of the river drops below this level the stream bed begins to dry up. To quote Mr Fagg:

> In what may be called a normal year the river ceases to flow above ground, often intermittently, for $3\frac{1}{2}$ miles of its meandering course, during the summer and autumn months. During dry periods the whole of the flow entering the gap sinks into the chalk at certain points and pursues an underground course in fissures until it re-appears as copious springs on Thorncroft Island near Leatherhead or perhaps in the similar springs in the Fetcham Road. There are some 30 active swallows concentrated mainly in four areas.

I once spent a weekend at Juniper Hall Field Centre studying the local geography. The highlight came when Mr Fagg showed us where the swallows were, and, although the river was not dry at the time, it was intriguing to watch the swirls and eddies in the stream denoting where the chalk was gulping down its daily ration of 30 million gallons of water. In the evening we would compare notes under the chandeliers and embossed ceilings of Juniper Hall with the moonlight filtering through the magnificent cedars with which the mansion is surrounded and which as far back as 1823 were described as "of the finest growth in England".

On 6th February 1940 occurred the most extraordinary of the many incidents associated with the swallows of the Mole. This account from the local paper captures the scene well:

> It was cold and snowy in the early days of 1940 and Mr Middleton's (the local policeman's) wife had for some time before the incident heard rumbling in the earth. On the night of February 4–5th, when the snow was melting and there was plenty of water about, further heavy rumbling (clearly of earth settling) was heard, and again at breakfast time on February 6th. It was shortly afterwards that Mr Middleton witnessed what must surely be one of the most unusual sights ever seen in Mickleham, or anywhere else come to that.
> Mr Middleton was amazed to see a large oak sway slightly and subside straight down into the earth leaving a large crater about

20 feet across and full of water. When at last the tree came to rest its top branches were about 15 feet below the surface.

Local explanation of the phenomenon was that underneath the tree was a huge subterranean hollow, caused by the carrying away of the soil by the Mole, and that the weight of the tree finally broke down the shallow crust causing the whole thing to sink.

There is a quality about the Mole Valley that sets it apart from anywhere else in Surrey. It seems to be compounded of the best of Nature's creative activity and the best of Man's also. For the Mole Valley contains in Mickleham a picture-postcard village and a genial church that Leigh Hunt once remarked was "as plump as an abbot"; in Burford Bridge Hotel an historic building little changed since Lord Nelson stayed there just before Trafalgar and Keats put the finishing touches to his "Endymion"; in Juniper Hall a fine house in a finer setting just oozing the spirit of its times; in Norbury Park, with its 'Druid's Grove' of yew trees specifically mentioned in Domesday Book, as fine an achievement of Man as can be found in the realm of Nature; and in the arterial road bypassing Mickleham one of Man's happiest achievements in the realm of transport engineering. In short, Man and Nature have worked in league in the Mole Valley and have together created a thing of beauty. Even the small things are right. The petrol station at the junction of the Leatherhead-Dorking road and the bypass is designed to merge as well into the landscape as a petrol station can. The railway station at Box Hill, with its sculptured porch, fancy-tiled roofs and iron-crowned tower— once christened by someone "a lodge to a French chateau"—and the three railway viaducts over the Mole with their coloured brickwork and stone corries and other enrichments, may not be altogether to our taste today, but they represent an honest attempt to create something worthy of its setting. The landowners of the valley insisted upon these embellishments, and in so doing they were demonstrating that they too had caught something of the spirit of this valley. But above all the valley has been preserved in large measure from sporadic urban development. This was due in large measure to the far sightedness of the Surrey County Council who, in 1931, promoted a Parliamentary Bill (The Surrey County Council Act 1931) to obtain authority to purchase land in the Valley. Apart from the residential estate at West

Humble, the valley has remained inviolate. Even at West Humble they have restored and maintained a curious old barn-church which was used for services over a century ago when the railway was being built. It is a shame to end this eulogy on a slightly sour note, but what a pity it is'that the Leatherhead Bypass is not given a better bridge over the Mole than the rickety Bailey Bridge it has had for too long. Before this was built there was an even more ramshackle temporary bridge which so offended the Mole that she undermined the foundations and brought the bridge down in 1951—she tried to do likewise with its successor during the great floods of 1968. The Mole Valley deserves a creation of beauty here.

A place of great beauty, be it the Lake District, the Scottish Highlands, the Cornish Coast or, coming nearer home, the Devil's Punch Bowl at Hindhead, usually attracts people of unusual sensitivity and culture. The Mole Valley is no exception; it has enjoyed a rich cultural life centred on its great houses of Polesden Lacey, Norbury Park, Juniper Hall and Denbies. Much has changed, but still the tradition lingers on in different ways, in the open-air theatre at Camilla Lacey, for instance, founded in 1949. This cultural life was not confined only to the great houses; there were many London gentlefolk who were attracted by the beauties of the Mole Valley and bought cottages to convert into county pieds-à-terre. As far back as 1787 The Gentlemen's Magazine commented: "Mickleham is a place deservedly a favourit in which several cottages have been fitted up in a very neat manner and have been inhabited by persons of fashion." Fanny Burney's name is indelibly associated with the Mole Valley and of course with Camilla Lacey in particular; it was named after her successful novel Camilla and indeed built out of the proceeds. In her earlier days, however, she was mainly connected with the brilliant group of French emigrées who found shelter from the revolutionary storm in Juniper Hall. One of them, General D'Arblay, found more than shelter there—he found a wife. He taught Fanny Burney to speak French, but she must have decided that the subject required a lifetime's devotion for she gave him her hand and they were married in 1793 in Mickleham Church. They were desperately poor, but then Fanny wrote Camilla and their financial worries were at an end. Another famous literary figure associated with the Mole Valley is Richard Brinsley Sheridan, author of The Rivals and The

*School for Scandal*, who lived in a house on the site of Polesden Lacey before the present mansion was built. In more recent times the literary tradition of the valley was continued by George Meredith, who lived in Flint Cottage a little way along the zig-zag road at the foot of Box Hill. He chose to live in humble circumstances, but the literary world of London came to his hearthside to give and to take, and it seems to have been a very satisfactory arrangement. At any rate, Meredith produced some of his finest work whilst living beneath what he called "the long green roller of the down". Every morning he would climb Box Hill, often at 5.30 in the morning, to enjoy "the fresh loveliness of the downs, the fields, the velvet shadows, sharp and thin, and the exquisite sky".

These men and women lived in the valley, and so belong to it in a special way, but many other great literary and political figures visited it and its talented circle from time to time: men like Wordsworth, Scott, Coleridge, Macaulay, Huskisson, Lord John Russell, and Robert Louis Stevenson, who stayed at Burford Bridge in 1876 and later wrote of "the inn at Burford Bridge with its arbours and green gardens and silent eddying river". It must surely have been of men and women such as these of whom George Meredith was thinking when he wrote of his beloved valley:

> How barren would this Valley be
> Without the human lives now beating
> In it, or the throbbing hearts
> Far distant, who their flower of childhood
> Cherish here, and water it with tears.

These "human lives" helped to give the Mole Valley that indefinable quality that springs from the fusion of Nature's beauty and Man's genius.

There now remains a lovely and unspoiled stretch of Downland comprising the tip of the half spear-head of chalk referred to in Chapter 8. The Downs are here rather more wooded than on the eastern side of the Mole and very much more remote. There is only one church, that on Ranmore Common (the ancient chapel of West Humble, founded in the twelfth century, is now a ruin and is in the hands of the National Trust), and there are no villages to speak of and few roads. Apart from Ranmore Common and Newlands Corner, it has few viewpoints accessible to the public, and there is no road that keeps close to the edge of the escarpment such as the road from Box Hill to Pebblecoombe. This is one of the least explored and exploited sections of downland country, and as such has an appeal to the lover of natural countryside that is different from that of many other better known parts.

Ranmore Common (sometimes called Ranmer Common) can be reached by a frontal assault up the steep hill from Dorking, and you reap your reward during the ascent more than from the summit; for there are magnificent views of the Vale of Holmesdale and the Tillingbourne Valley to the south as the road climbs the steep face of the escarpment, and then, when the summit is reached, you plunge into a wood and the view is lost. Or you may take it by surprise from the rear, following the road that climbs gradually upwards from the valley at West Humble. One Sunday morning in spring, many years ago now, I took this route to Ranmore Common accompanied all the way by the peal of bells, presumably from the church on the common; it was one of those rare moments of ecstasy that C. S. Lewis described so well in his book *Surprised by Joy*. Ranmore Common delights because it is free of disfigurement of any kind, thanks largely to the vigilance of the National Trust, who own much of the land there. However the Trust have made only one mistake. They have provided a simple car park of gravel, with the minimum of associated 'furniture' so that it merges well into the landscape; but they seem to have overlooked the fact that the cars themselves do not! How much better it would have been to site the car park in the nearby trees, so keeping stationary vehicles away from the common itself. The 'common' comprises a wide drove-way reminiscent of the Hog's Back, surrounded by thick brambles and woodland, and a tiny village of a few houses, a shop and, of course, the church.

Ranking probably second only to Box Hill as the most popular viewpoint in Surrey is Newlands Corner. The road through the Tillingbourne Valley meets the sharp right-angled bend at Albury, hesitates for a moment as to whether to follow the valley to Guildford via Chilworth, and then suddenly decides to make straight for Guildford over the top of the Downs. Above where it crosses the Pilgrims Way lies Newlands Corner. The view from here is superb, in my estimation the finest in Surrey if not in the South of England and the Surrey County Council have located a picnic site here under the new Countryside Act. In the foreground lies the green Tillingbourne Valley and St Martha's Chapel on its sandy ridge, beyond lie the tree-clad hills which rise higher in the receding distance so forming a magnificent backcloth to the whole scene. Sidney Allnutt, in a poem published in the *Spectator* in 1907, captured the essence of the view from Newlands Corner:

> Far southward from St Martha's Hill
> And to the east and west,
> The downs heave up green shoulders, till
> The distance with its magic blue
> Envelopes every other hue,
> And crest is lost in crest.

Many times I have returned with my family from a holiday in the south-west or Wales, and we have remarked as we passed by Newlands Corner that nowhere have we seen a finer view. Writing to a friend in February 1876, Matthew Arnold expressed a similar opinion: "As I looked at the landscape from the hills above Horsley, the backbone of England, I felt how pleasant a country it was, and how well satisfied I could be to remain all my days in it."

# 13

# GUILDFORD, GODALMING AND THE HOG'S BACK

If you climb the eastward slopes of the Hog's Back and look back across the River Wey and straight up the steep High Street of Guildford, you will realize both how narrow the Wey is at this point, and how inevitable it was that a town should grow up to control the gateway and to serve those who used it. Guildford owes its origin, at least in part, to the existence at this spot of a ford across the River Wey at the foot of what is now the High Street in the centuries before the river was deepened in the interests of navigation. From our vantage point on Guildown we can see on the opposite hill what remains of the 'gate-keepers lodge'—the old Norman castle. And there, at the foot of the hill by the river, lies old St Mary's Church in Quarry Street, its Saxon tower making it the oldest building in Guildford, where travellers in the pre-coaching era found a ready welcome and a resting place before continuing along the chalkway or plunging into the still-dangerous forests of the Weald. Its situation at the nexus of routes has always made Guildford a place of passage. Even the prisoners incarcerated in the castle scratched figures of St Christopher, patron saint of travellers, on the walls of their cells. When vehicular traffic came the High Street was so steep that it had to be paved with granite setts like those of Rye in Kent or in many Belgian roads today. The old road over Guildown, which was so steep that they had to poke poles between the spokes of the rear wheels of coaches descending the hill, was eventually abandoned in favour of the lesser climb along what is now Farnham Road.

Here on Guildown we are standing among the graves of 200 travellers whose need of St Christopher's help came to a sudden and savage end. They were Normans who were on their way to

Winchester when they were met by Earl Godwin, welcomed and feasted, and then treacherously murdered, their bodies being buried by the roadside. In 1928 the skeletons were discovered, showing every sign of violent death, a grisly confirmation of historical record. Guildown's associations with violent death did not end there, for Defoe noted, on one of his journeys through Guildford, that the gallows had been set up on Guildown so that the people in the High Street could the more conveniently watch the felons suffer their last agonies.

However Guildford does not usually massacre her visitors. As befits a place of passage it has provided food and lodging to travellers over the centuries and at one time the High Street was a major posting station on the coach routes to Portsmouth and the South Coast. When 'The Angel' was built, one of Guildford's old coaching inns that still survives, Guildford was a day's journey by coach from London. In his diary, Samuel Pepys tells of the many occasions on which he stopped overnight at Guildford during his journeys to and from the naval dockyard at Portsmouth and he was particularly appreciative of the hospitality of the 'Red Lion'. On one occasion, on 6th August 1688, he hired a guide at Guildford for the journey to London but even so they were lost for several hours around Cobham. Even at the time of Jane Austen travelling conditions had not much improved as she writes in her diary of breakfasting at Guildford, after the ride across the Hog's Back in the early morning, and then not arriving at Sloane Square until 6.30 in the evening. Apart from the Angel the old coaching inns have now mostly disappeared, but it takes only a little imagination to stand at Tunsgate and see them jangling off down the cobbles towards the bridge, the passengers alert with that air of anticipation that every new morning, and the fresh phase of a journey, bring.

At Guildford the old chalk trackway crosses the north-south river route along the Wey; and because the Wey has always been a more important river than the Mole, it was Guildford, and not Dorking (which is nearer the geographical centre of Surrey), that became the historic county town. It is wholly appropriate that the Guildhall is the most prominent building in the High Street, for if Farnham, seat of the Bishops of Winchester has historically been the ecclesiastical centre of West Surrey, then Guildford has been its administrative centre. The town now houses no less than three local authority headquarters, Guildford Borough, Guildford Rural District Council and Hambledon Rural District Council. If the current proposals to move the County Hall from Kingston to Stoke Park are realised (there is considerable opposition from Guildford residents) Guildford's importance as an administrative centre will be greatly increased and its ancient status as the County Town of Surrey finally confirmed. Guildford has recently acquired a cathedral and a university, but these came largely because it seemed appropriate that a county town should have these facilities—unlike Canterbury, Cambridge and Chichester, for instance, Guildford was an administrative centre long before it became significant as an ecclesiastical or university town.

Guildford is as typical a country town as one could find within such a relatively short distance of London. It is the matured product of Time. I never cease to admire the wonderful variety of design, age and mood, that the High Street possesses—that hotch-potch of buildings that grew up so slowly and evolved so naturally that it looks 'right' although no one could possibly have planned it so 'in cold blood'. Guildford people know full well that their High Street is the glory of their town. How otherwise could it have come about that, by mutual consent, the shopkeepers of the High Street have agreed not to erect exterior neon signs, or to undertake any development that might destroy the character of what Charles Dickens called "the most beautiful High Street in England". In recent years the High Street has been pedestrianised on an experimental basis and the results have been so satisfactory that there is every prospect of its being made permanent—even if there is quite a high price to be paid in the provision of large multi-storey car-parks on the periphery. The first words of the official guide to Guildford are: "The great problem of town planning is to encourage new growth without impairing the dignity and character which are the heritage of centuries." Guildford has gone further than many other towns in finding an answer.

In times past Guildford, together with its neighbours Godalming and Farnham, was a centre of the woollen cloth industry that spread along the chalk Downs and was most extensive in Hampshire, where the chalkland widened out to become Salisbury

Plain. It was for this reason that the cloth made in West Surrey was often called 'Hampshire Kerseys'. However, the Guildford district made a particular type of blue cloth, and the old brothers and sisters of Abbott's Hospital in the High Street, founded in 1619 to alleviate some of the poverty caused by the decay of the woollen industry, have worn clothes of this material ever since. Just when the industry started in West Surrey is not known for sure, but an Assize Act of 1391 contains words suggesting that it was by then well established: "of old times divers cloths were made in the town of Guildford, called 'Cloths of Guildford', which were of good making and of good value, and did bear a good name." In a recent lecture on 'The woollen industry of Guildford', Mr George Underwood, the local historian, said that the industry in Guildford dates back at least to 1251, when Henry III sent a request to the Sheriff for space to be set aside for a fulling mill in the royal park. In 1574 every alehouse keeper in Guildford was obliged to have a signboard outside his hostelry on which was painted a representation of a wool sack. Guildford Borough shares with Godalming and Banstead the distinction of having a woolsack in its coat of arms—only Guildford goes one better than the others and has two! It is an indication of the importance of Guildford during the late fifteenth and early sixteenth centuries, thanks to its wool trade, that it received a royal charter from King Henry VII in 1488, and in 1534 came within an ace of having a Suffragan bishop; an Act was passed in that year providing for the appointment of a Suffragan bishop, but in fact it was never implemented and Guildford had to wait until 1874 before this came about. The woollen industry seems to have gone into decline at Guildford during the latter half of the sixteenth century. In 1557 an Act was passed which had the effect of prohibiting the manufacture of woollen cloth other than in the market towns of Farnham, Godalming and Guildford. However this did little to arrest the decline to the industry in Guildford, and when the Ship Money assessment was made in 1636 the town was assessed for only £53 compared with £90 for Farnham and Godalming. It may be, as Aubrey has suggested, that the Guildford clothiers were themselves mainly responsible for the decay of their industry because they were too fond of stretching the cloth to make it appear longer than it really was—an activity that was conducted at Racks Close, off Quarry Street (whose name has nothing to do with the supposed tortures inflicted upon prisoners in the castle keep). However, others have suggested that it succumbed to the pressures being exercised by competitors in London, particularly the London Drapers' Company. Some clothiers turned to framework knitting, but this industry was never of great importance in Guildford, and until the advent of Dennis, the vehicle manufacturers, in the late nineteenth century, Guildford seems to have survived mainly as a market town and service centre of various kinds. This 200 years of relative seclusion might have been a period of stagnation had it not been for Sir Richard Weston and the construction of the Wey Navigation in 1651. This made Guildford into a true river port and gave it a valuable commercial link with Weybridge and London in one direction, and later with Godalming and the south coast. Guildford became an important corn-milling and timber town, and a heavy traffic passed along the Wey. In 1838, the year when the railway from Woking to Weybridge was built, the traffic reached 86,003 tons. However this was the peak, and the railways gradually robbed the Wey Navigation of some of its traffic. Even so, however, a substantial traffic continued to use it and in 1953 the total was about 18,000 tons. Whereas in the earlier years most of the traffic was down-stream—taking Wealden products out—the main traffic in later years was in the reverse direction, especially corn and timber being imported through London. During its pre-railway days Guildford must have been a very delightful place in which to live. Like all erstwhile wool towns it had inherited an air of graceful elegance and prosperity, and its incomparable setting had not been disfigured by any unsightly development. William Cobbett, who, as he said himself, "have seen so many many towns", thought it "the prettiest, and taken altogether, the most agreeable and most happy-looking that I ever saw in my life". Guildford has changed since then and has grown far far bigger, but it is not a bad description still.

In 1845 the railway came to Guildford, and its era of rural seclusion was over. Other lines were built, and by the end of the century Guildford was a major railway junction with lines fanning out in several directions north and south of the town. The rest of the Guildford story is one of continued growth. Merrow, for instance, doubled its population between 1881 and 1891, and other new suburbs sprang up at Shalford, Stoke and Woodbridge. This was the period when people seemed, almost for the first time, to become aware of landscape in a positive sense (Witley became popular with artists at about this time), and the new railways enabled them to enjoy the landscape of the Downs whilst working in London. So the town grew, congestion in the High Street became intolerable, and in the 1930s they built the bypass that isn't a bypass because it slices right through the busy suburb of Woodbridge and is as crowded with traffic trying to cross it on a summer weekend as if it were the High Street. There is now a proposal to by-pass the by-pass by building a new road from Woodbridge to Burpham, but it has aroused a great deal of opposition and its future is uncertain.

Somewhere among the hundreds of thousands of rose-coloured bricks that comprise the Cathedral of the Holy Spirit on Stag Hill, and which were made from the very clay on which the building stands, are two or three that bear my name—my tiny stake, along with that of so many other tens of thousands of people, in the building of this beautiful cathedral. This modest gift enables me to feel possessive and at home whenever I enter the cathedral—as the monks of old must have felt when they had built their cathedrals with their own hands. The exterior is pleasing without being exciting (it is the site that really makes it what it is)—but the interior is the real joy of Guildford Cathedral. After all the monument-cluttered interiors of some of our older cathedrals, Guildford's is breathtakingly light and modern (save for the tattered regimental flags in the military side chapels that I think are an abomination)—it is Waterloo Bridge beside Tower Bridge, the Post Office Tower beside the Albert Memorial. The tall windows suffuse the interior with light; the building is about as far from the murky gloom of Liverpool's Anglican Cathedral, the first cathedral built on a new site in England since 1250 (Guildford is the second), as one can imagine. The only other cathedral that equals, indeed surpasses, Guildford for sheer intensity of light and uplifting interior, is the third newest cathedral—the Roman Catholic 'Wigwam' at Liverpool. Only fifty years in time, and a mile away in space, from the Anglican Cathedral, the wigwam is light years away in architectural conception.

Guildford is Surrey's only university town (although Croydon's technical college is surely not far behind), and fittingly the new university shares Stag Hill with the cathedral. Wisely, they have put the residential buildings at the top of the hill, near the cathedral and overlooking the town, and the lecture blocks and administrative buildings further down. Town, gown and cassock will soon be linked even more closely when the new road is driven across the railway and the river to link Stag Hill to the town centre.

Godalming, Guildford's twin town just four miles away up the Wey Valley along what Cobbett thought was the prettiest road in England, is certainly no identical twin although it shares with Guildford the same umbilical cord—the River Wey. Apart from this, and the fact that it has in common with Guildford a long association with the cloth industry, Godalming could hardly be more different. The town occupies the flat river valley bottom, whilst Guildford is situated on the chalk slopes that rise steeply at right angles to the river. Godalming lies on the main Portsmouth Road, or it did until recently, but its communications in any other direction are poor, all roads going against the grain of the river having to climb up the steep sides of the valley and negotiate the hilly country on either side. Only one railway serves Godalming. The Wey, it is true, was made navigable to Godalming in 1754, but when the Wey-Arun Canal was built Godalming was left isolated. A similar thing happened when the Godalming bypass was built in the 1930s diverting all through traffic so far from the town that few motorists bother to make the necessary detour to visit Godalming. Godalming is a borough, but it has no cathedral, no university and no space; hemmed in by steep hills it cannot expand as Guildford has expanded. Its attractive little town hall, known locally as 'The Pepper Pot', is more truly representative of God- alming in mind and spirit than the Guildhall is of Guildford. Godalming is a wool town that clung to its looms and frames longer than any other in the district, and when this ancient indus- try finally died the town never found a substitute; unlike Guild- ford, it never really experienced rebirth. It lives on its past, is proud of its past, and attracts people who like it more for what it is than for what it might become. The close mentality of the valley, rather than the expansive mentality of the Downs, belongs to the people of Godalming—friendly within, and indifferent, as the Scots say, 'outwith'. In this narrow valley lives a people as devoted to its glen as any Scottish clan.

But Godalming cannot escape the pressures of modern life. The bypass saved Godalming, as another built at the same time saved Caterham, from traffic asphyxia, but in the thirty-five years since then local traffic has increased to such an extent that the ancient High Street, and its narrow offshoots, can no longer cope at peak periods. An inner relief road is an urgent necessity. But where can it go? In such a restricted valley there is no obvious answer. Engineering-wise, the cheapest route is along the valley floor, and this indeed is the plan now being proposed by the Surrey County Council and accepted in principle by the Godalming Borough Council. But this involves tearing the heart out of Old Godalming and driving a three-lane road, 40 feet wide, right through the centre of the town, crossing historic Church Street a mere fifteen yards from the twelfth century parish church, and destroying many medieval buildings *en route*. The Mayor, Mrs Veronica Allen, has said: "I love Godalming as it is, but we have to look to the future." And the future, it seems, has no place for an historic old town like Godalming. However the clan are not accepting the proposed desecration of their glen without a fight. And they have strange allies. In November 1968, the Governor of the State of Georgia, U.S.A., the state founded by the famous Godalming resident General James Oglethorpe in 1733 declared Sunday 17th November 1968 'Godalming Day' in his State, and the Godalming Trust has received a strong message of support from their American clansmen. So the battle continues. Is this steep-sided valley, that has made Godalming what it is, to become the cause of its own destruction? Surely a generation that can take the Guildford Bypass slap over the top of the Hog's Back can find a solution to Godalming's traffic problems that will keep the old town inviolate for future generations to enjoy, even if it means tunnels or cuttings such as the Americans have made at Williamsburg to preserve the centre of the restored colonial capital from destruction by the motor car.

Godalming's history can be summed up in a word—wool. The industry seems to stem from about the twelfth century when it was introduced by Flemish weavers and dyers who settled in this

part of England during Edward III's reign. By 1620 the industry
had obviously been established a very long time for a contemporary record describes Godalming as "an ancient clothing town,
and the inhabitants thereof of long time and before the memory of
any man to the contrary, have been principally employed in the
making, dyeing, fulling and dressing of woollen cloth". At that time
the cloth industry of Farnham, Guildford and Wonersh was decaying; but Godalming alone continued, and concentrated upon mixed
kerseys and blue kerseys for sale to the Canary Islands, and which,
according to Aubrey at the end of the seventeenth century "for
their colour are not equalled by any in England". A framework
knitting industry was established in the town during the eighteenth
century and remained one of its staple industries to the present
day, so that the woolsack in the Borough coat of arms represents
800 years of continuous association with the wool trade.

Although not a major crossing-place of routes, as Guildford is,
Godalming's location on the main Portsmouth turnpike made it a
popular stopping place for coaches, and the town had its colourful
coaching days during the seventeenth and eighteenth centuries.
Some of the old coaching inns, like the 'King's Arms', the 'Great
George', and 'The Angel' (like its namesake at Guildford once the
largest in the town) still exist in the picturesque High Street.

Godalming has one other claim to distinction. A few years after
Cranleigh School had been founded a few miles away, Charter-
house School moved in 1872 from its cramped London quarters to
its present site on a hill above Godalming. Built in the Gothic
style, the school dominates its surroundings in the way that the
Royal Holloway College does further along the Portsmouth Road
towards London and also built at about the same period. In the
grounds of the school is a statue of William Haig-Brown the
school's famous headmaster—he is sitting in a chair as if resting
from the exertions of bringing the school to this majestic setting,
which he surveys every minute of every day with sightless eyes.
One wonders, sometimes, if it means any more to the boys who
jostle past him every day; or does their vision extend only to the
edge of the nearest touchline? I believe not. I know a professor
whose keenest memory of his public-school days is the before-
breakfast run to the top of the chalk escarpment to see the sun rise.
I believe a child seldom articulates its joy in such things, but they

give him deep wells of spiritual refreshment on which to draw in later life.

The Hog's Back is so familiar a title that it comes as a surprise to learn that the first recorded reference to its use comes in Greenwood's *Surrey Described*, written in 1823. It is a curious name, and as a child it always puzzled me a great deal. I could not imagine why such a razor-edged ridge should have been named after an animal that has as rounded a back as any in the animal kingdom. In fact, of course, the name has nothing to do with pigs. It is derived from the Old Celtic word *og* meaning a giant, as in 'ogre' or 'Gog and Magog'. In North Wales there is a similar ridge called the Hog's Back which is a mistranslation of *Cefn Og* or 'Giant's Back'.

The Hog's Back is the only example in Surrey where a Neolithic ridgeway along the crest of the Downs has become a busy modern road. In most other places along the escarpment the edge was so sinuous, and the surface so often rendered difficult by woodlands and thickets where patches of clay or sand overlay the chalk, that few stretches of the old ridgeway were metalled. Travellers often found alternative routes, usually half way down the escarpment face, that avoided the difficulties along the crest. As a result subsequent generations have been denied the thrill of travelling for long distances along the edge of the Chalk, except on foot in places—and along the Hog's Back.

There is nothing quite like the Hog's Back anywhere in Surrey, or indeed in Britain, except perhaps the road along the top of the Malvern Hills. For seven miles the Great White Way follows the ridge, its summit little wider than the road itself, from Guildford to Whitewaysend, where it slopes gradually down to the Farnham Gap. Often when I have been travelling along the Hog's Back I have wished that I were on the top of a double-decker bus. The view on either side is magnificent, but it is obscured from the motorist along most of the ridge by what Eric Parker calls "deep and exuberant hedges". Only at the occasional gateways and gaps in the hedge can the motorist enjoy the view he knows lies tantalizingly close. A new road has been built during the last two years along the north side to provide a second carriage-way, and this affords unimpeded views to the north, but because it lies a little below the ridge the views to the south are lost. I wonder if anyone has thought of the possibility of running open-topped double-decker buses along the Hog's Back; I am sure they would prove as great an attraction as the Bluebell Railway or the trip round the Great Orme. After all, where else in Britain can one motor seven miles with a view extending simultaneously many miles in all directions?

# PART THREE

# SURREY SOUTH OF THE CHALK

# 14

## THE SPIRIT OF THE WEALDEN COUNTRY

If ever there was a 'No Man's Land' it was the Weald. It was a great barrier of wet clay lands covered with thick forests that spread in places from the North Downs to the South Downs almost without a break. In early times the Weald was well nigh impassable, and, apart from a few isolated iron-working settlements (few of them in Surrey until the Middle Ages), it was virtually uninhabited. Even as late as 1798 a traveller commented: "In travelling over the Vale lands nothing strikes a person more than the extreme fewness of the inhabitants." Compared with the open chalk downlands to the north and south, and the well populated vales on either side of them, the Weald was a veritable Slough of Despond. John Bunyan, indeed, is reputed to have had in mind, when chosing this title in *Pilgrim's Progress*, the low country around Shalford near Godalming: significantly this was one of the few places on the Pilgrim's Way where the travellers were forced to come down off the Chalk onto the heavy Wealden clays.

The Weald was so much a no man's land that no one really owned much of it, and when the time came to draw a boundary between the people of the Mid-Saxon Kingdom (the southern part of which was Surrey), and the South-Saxon Kingdom (Sussex), they had to fix an arbitrary line that might follow an odd stream or two here and there but otherwise just cuts clean across country through the dense forests and across the heaths of what is aptly called the 'deep' Weald. There was no observable difference between the country one side of the boundary and the country the other. And so it is today. The Surrey Weald is virtually indistinguishable from the Sussex Weald, and both merge imperceptibly into the Kent Weald. As Gertrude Jekyll, who lived in West

Surrey, once commented: "One steps without knowing it from Surrey into Hampshire on the dry Heathland, and out of Surrey into Sussex from one clay puddle into the next, without being aware in either case that the land is called by another name." It is noteworthy that the names of Wealden villages often originate in landscape features like 'hurst' (wood) or 'fold' (pasture) rather than the names of people or tribes who first settled the land like the 'ings' and 'hams' of Dorking, Effingham, Fetcham, Caterham and Wallington—all places situated on or near the Chalk. As the well-known place-names authority, F. M. Stenton, has said: "they demonstrate human occupancy but not in the first instance permanent settlement".

The Romans tamed the Weald sufficiently to drive four roads across it, the most important being Stane Street from Chichester to London, probably the first to be built (in the first century A.D.) and designed primarily for military purposes. The others, from Brighton, Lewes and Hastings, were built later and were probably designed as much to serve the iron works in the Weald as for communications. Hilaire Belloc called them "bridges" and that is exactly what they were—narrow lanes of civilization in a wooded wilderness. After the Romans had gone, the 'bridges' fell into disrepair. Stane Street virtually disappeared from the map. By 1750 the people of Horsham were petitioning Parliament to complain that if they wanted to travel to London they had to go by the Dover Road! Communications across the Weald remained very bad right up to the time of the first railways in the mid-nineteenth century. The sticky clays made bad roads, and the farmers had the utmost difficulty in carting the chalk for their fields from the quarries on the Downs to their farms, each of which had a kiln of its own. As late as 1730 the road from Godalming to Portsmouth was so bad that Prince George, Queen Anne's husband, had to be conveyed in a litter from Godalming to Petersfield across the Weald. Bad roads were part of the spirit of the Weald—and twisting, turning ones (Stane Street excepted) still are!

God gave the Weald two major natural resources—iron and timber. The Romans built roads of iron (they were built largely of iron slag or 'cinder' as it was called locally, since stone was scarce in the Weald) to get the iron out. And they cut the timber to make charcoal to fire the furnaces. The ore of the Weald is of a low

*The 'Pepper Pot', Godalming*

grade, and a lot of timber was needed—it took twenty-four cart-loads of charcoal to produce 8 tons of pig iron. It has been esti-mated that an iron foundry consumed 3,000 loads of timber per annum. Not that the Romans were the first to make iron in the Weald. The Iron Age people almost certainly made iron there (so adding the 'Wealden Culture' to archaeology), and the Romans merely gave a stimulus to an industry that already existed. Iron is still an integral part of the spirit of the Weald. It lives on in the many beautiful hammer ponds, artificial lakes created by damming a stream to give the head of water required to drive the bellows and hammers; in the numerous half-timbered houses betokening an affluence not usually associated with Wealden agriculture; in the several 'iron' villages like Friday Street and Thursley; in the many trackways through the woods along which the felled trees were dragged centuries ago (and which make a compass more a necessity than a luxury on a walk across Leith Hill); and in the many distinctive churches in the 'iron country'. It is strange that we now remember an ugly industry by beautiful things.

Iron is the father and the child of war. The tribal wars of medieval times gave rise to little demand for iron. Yews may have been planted in the churchyards to provide the bows, but no one prospected for iron ore. But by Tudor times, with great warships mounting over a hundred guns being launched on the Thames, and artillery becoming increasingly important, iron became essen-tial. The Weald, being so near the great shipyards of the Thames, was an obvious centre for the iron industry which became very important at this time. It now spread across the Surrey Weald from the early locations near the Kent and Sussex border towards West Surrey. It appeared at Newdigate and Abinger in the mid-sixteenth century, and by the 1570s it had reached as far as Chid-dingfold, Haslemere, Cranleigh and Dunsfold. In 1610 the Thursley ironworks was established. However, by now the carnage in trees had become alarming. This was crude exploitation of Nature's bounty, with no provision for replenishment; if it continued un-checked the industry was doomed. Restrictions had to be imposed. Before the end of the sixteenth century a limitation was placed on the number of ironworkings, whilst taxes were imposed on the carriage of charcoal and iron. Charcoal was so widely used at this time that it was simply called 'coal', and charcoal-burners were

11

*Boxing Day meet of the Surrey Union Hunt, Forest Green*

called 'colliers'; when coal as we know it came into use in London it came to be called 'sea-coal' because it was generally brought down from the north-east coast by sea. Partly because of these restrictions—and the growth of other iron-working districts like the Forest of Dean—and partly as a result of Darby's invention of iron-smelting using coal, the Weald gradually declined in importance, and iron-working there had virtually died out by the end of the eighteenth century. In the churchyard at Thursley stands a gravestone with this epitaph:

> My sledge and hammer lie reclin'd
> My bellows too have lost their wind,
> My fire is out and forge decayed
> And in the dust my vice is laid.

It commemorates the death of Richard Court, blacksmith, in 1791, but it will serve also as an epitaph for the passing of the Wealden Iron Industry. The hammer ponds became 'naturalized', the one-time noisy iron villages became quiet backwaters, the roads deteriorated into cart tracks, and the deep Weald sank into the deep sleep of no man's land. And so it remained until the twentieth-century motorists discovered an unexplored and unknown corner of Surrey a mere afternoon's drive from the Metropolis. The long sleep was over.

Trees, as well as iron, are part of the spirit of the Weald. Even today Surrey is still, as it was at the time of Domesday, the most wooded county in relation to its size in all England. Today we think of trees primarily as part of the landscape, and we value them positively for their contribution to the beauty of so much of Surrey. But to the people of the Weald in times gone by they were regarded largely in a purely negative sense, as something to be cut down and exploited as a source of fuel, either for making into charcoal to fire the iron furnaces or for the hearths of a million homes in Surrey and the nearby Metropolis. Timber from Ewhurst parish was carried overland to the headwaters of the Arun and shipped down the river and so round the coasts of Kent to London. So important was firewood that the townspeople complained bitterly when the increasing demands of the iron-works caused timber prices to rise; there was such a case in 1562 when the people of Kingston protested that the establishment of ironworks south of Dorking had caused the price of their firewood to be doubled. But trees were not only valued for firewood, they were also in demand as divinely fashioned ships' timbers. Great Wealden oaks were carefully selected for the shape of their boughs in relation to the trunk, each one being destined to become part of a ship's vertebrae; they were chosen as carefully as a model-builder in an anatomical laboratory would select pieces of bone with which to construct his models of human skeletons. For the Weald, by Tudor times, had become the most important source of timber for the rapidly expanding ship-building industry. Oaks, and the 'Hearts of Oak' made from them, are part of the spirit of the Weald.

Ship's timbers often had a second reincarnation. Many a church or mansion house in Surrey has a roof constructed of ships' timbers, each still bearing the carpenter's signs signifying its place in the ship's hull, and they are as sound today as when they were felled centuries ago. I was talking recently to the vicar of Banstead Church and he told me that when they took down part of the roof a year or two ago to look for death-watch beetle infestation they found many of these signs indicating that the timbers had come from a ship. It was partly to preserve the supply of oaks for ship-building that quotas were issued to Wealden ironmasters during the sixteenth and seventeenth centuries, and at Cranleigh there is a record of an ironmaster who had his felling licence confiscated for exceeding his quota of oaks.

The lesser trees and bushes of the Weald have also been put to good use in the past. Alongside Wealden streams and ponds grew willows and osiers, and many a Wealden housewife made a little extra money for the household making baskets. In places the industry was conducted on a larger scale, as at Cranleigh, where the stone figure adorning the fountain in the High Street represents not only a crane but also an osier basket the two being equally symbolic of important aspects of the village's past. Osiers and baskets; beeches and walking sticks or broom handles; willows and cricket bats; these are as much part of the spirit of the Weald as the solid rough-hewn pews of Dunsfold Church or the massive lattice-work of oak beams supporting the bell towers of Newdigate and Tandridge churches.

Iron and trees are God's own contribution to the spirit of the

Weald. Man's particular contribution lies in the many scattered hamlets that are so characteristic of the region. Villages there are in the Weald, but they are relatively few. Instead there are many tiny groups of cottages, little Friday Streets with or without the hammer pond, some of them with a church or a pub, none really worthy of the name village. This pattern of scattered hamlets, still persisting throughout the Weald despite the changes of the twentieth century, owes its origins to the way in which the Weald was originally settled. In this wet and often water-logged country (it is a wonderful sight to fly over the Weald and see the sunlight glistening on the many ponds, and lakes), one of the main needs of the inhabitants, ironically enough, was water. Surface water there was in plenty,[1] but good drinking water was scarce. So it was that where a deep well had been sunk through the clay to the water-bearing pervious strata below, a small settlement grew up. Often these wells had to be very deep; there is a well at Blacknest Farm, Dunsfold, reputed to be over 1,000 feet deep. The old well on the village green—as at Leigh, for instance, with its tile-hung timbered canopy—is part of the spirit of the Weald. Once a settlement had become established the trees were felled in the immediate neighbourhood and the land was cultivated. Usually each such settlement was merely a clearing in the forest, and the woods remained untouched between one clearing and another. Even today you can seldom go from one Wealden village to another without passing through woodlands—the last remnants of the great Forest of Andredsweald.

For many centuries such settlements as there were in the Weald were outposts of parishes located on the more populated districts to the north. Thus Chiddingfold was for a long time merely an outlying appendage of the parish of Godalming. Sometimes parishes in the Weald have taken their names from hamlets that have almost disappeared, such as Peper Harow and Wanborough,

---

[1] That Wealden residents are well accustomed to surface water was brought home to me recently. I was being driven round the Cranleigh district by a friend who lives in that area when we suddenly realized that the engine was badly overheating. Without a moment's hesitation he grabbed the windscreen-washer bottle, filled it from the fast-flowing stream by the road, and poured it into the steaming radiator. I think if it had been a hot summer's day he would just as readily have slaked his thirst at the roadside stream.

whilst in the parish of Artington, the only settlement worthy of the name village is Littleton, the parish itself taking its name from a tiny cluster of cottages on the main Portsmouth Road.

The Weald was never farmed on the open-field system such as prevailed over the chalk country to the north, and which naturally gave rise to villages of substantial size. The Wealden farmers were individualists. They farmed their own compact rectangular holdings centuries before the huge hedgeless and communally run open fields were enclosed. They had relatively little contact with their neighbours, and lived in small hamlets near their holdings carved laboriously out of the forest. It was a Jutish type of settlement pattern, although there is no evidence that the Jutes of Kent penetrated this far. At the time of Domesday King William's enumerators found little to record in the Weald of Surrey (Ockley and Charlwood were virtually the only churches)—there was very little wealth, or land-ownership of any significance. It was a backward and remote area, just ideal for the Cistercian monks who wanted above all a place away from 'civilization'—which is why they established their abbey at Waverley in the upper Wey valley in 1128.

Trees and grass have traditionally been the crops of the Weald— the products respectively of the 'hursts' and the 'folds'. But wheat also grows well on the heavy Wealden clays, just as it does on the heavy clays of North Essex. The Wealden clays are difficult soils to work—"like cement in summer and soup in winter", as one farmer described them. Teams of four or six oxen were once a common sight on Wealden farms, and when oxen were replaced by horses some farms in the Weald had as many as thirty of these fine creatures to do the farm work. Often three or four horses at a time would be hitched to the plough and the land was often called 'three-horse' land in consequence. When Cobbett came riding through this region he reported that he had found "a country where strictly speaking only three things will grow well, grass, wheat and oak trees". The price of wheat had risen so much by the end of the eighteenth century that most of the clearings in the Weald, which had hitherto been used for pasture, had by then become almost entirely arable. In 1798 Marshall reported that "the present production may be said to be wool and arable crops. Excepting the commons and some numerous strips of brook land there is scarcely an acre of natural herbage or old grassland, and this notwithstanding almost every acre of the District is fitter for permanent herbage than for any other species of produce." The Napoleonic Wars brought about a quiet revolution in the agriculture of the Weald. However, within a generation the wheel of fortune had changed again, the flood of cheap wheat from the New World had brought the price in Britain crashing down, and the Weald largely reverted to pasture, or just tumbled down to bracken and thicket. This was a low point in the history of Wealden agriculture. The Second World War brought a recovery and today the farms of the Weald are as prosperous as any in the south of England. Yet agriculture is not really part of the spirit of the Weald—it seems almost to exist in spite of the natural environment rather than because of it. The trees are biding their time at the edge of every clearing—waiting for the farmer to relax his vigilance so that they can creep back and reclaim their rightful territory.

Of course not all the Weald was no man's land. At the northern and southern edges was well-populated territory. The Valley of the Tillingbourne and the Vale of Holmesdale along the foot of the North Downs gave rise to many villages and several important gap-towns such as Guildford, Dorking, Reigate and Redhill. These strictly belong to the Weald, but they are really an intermediate stage between the Chalk and the Weald proper. This zone has a character and spirit of its own, which is different from that of the Weald. To the Weald alone belong the moated houses, the wide village greens, the raised causeways, the timbered cottages and wooden towers, and the roads wandering inconsequentially across the countryside as if the trees were so dense that the original travellers had all lost their way and just followed whatever tracks they came across—even in a motor car the interminable twisting and turning of the Wealden lanes can make a short journey seem a long one. All these are part of the spirit of the vast tract of marsh and scrub that was called in Tudor times simply the 'Wyld' or 'Wilde', but which we today know by its former Saxon title 'The Weald'.

# 15

# THE VILLAGES OF
# THE TILLINGBOURNE, AND DORKING

The little Tillingbourne rises near Leith Hill and, after being joined
by a tributary flowing northwards from Friday Street, flows
westwards along the foot of the North Downs to join the River
Wey at Shalford. In this short ten miles it once drove no less than
eight water mills, and provided power for five industries, corn-
milling, gunpowder manufacture, iron furnaces, weaving and
tanning; not a bad record for an overgrown rivulet! Even more
important, the Tillingbourne has spawned a succession of beautiful
villages, including Albury, Shere, Gomshall and Abinger Hammer, villages which belong not just to Surrey but to countless
thousands of Londoners who have found there a healing antidote
to the Great Wen. Any illustrated book on Surrey must include
a picture or two of one of the Tillingbourne villages, and like as
not a book on the beauties of the English Countryside will include
one as well. Yet this rich heritage is under threat. The valley in
which these villages stand has become the most important east-
west route south of London and carries such a weight of traffic that
the villages are being pummelled, pounded and poisoned to death.
Thus our journey through this most highly favoured valley is
overlain by a deep anxiety for its survival.

Travelling eastwards from the confluence of the Tillingbourne
with the Wey, the first village we encounter is Chilworth, nestling
below St Martha's Chapel as a faithful dog waits at its master's feet.
So close are they, in fact, that the parish is called 'St Martha with
Chilworth'. To bring them even closer still, there is said to be a
tunnel between the chapel and Chilworth Manor in the green
hollow immediately below. Surrey, like any other county with a

high proportion of chalk or sandstone strata, has its prolific crop of 'tunnel' stories, but this one may have more substance than most because Lady Heald of Chilworth Manor, in an interview with a reporter from the *Surrey County Journal* in 1955, spoke of having met an old lady in the village who had actually walked along the tunnel in her youth.

Industry seems so far removed from the Tillingbourne Valley of today that one can easily overlook that its past prosperity was largely based on its industries rather than upon agriculture which could not alone have supported so many villages so close together. Thanks to a slight change in land level as the Hythe Beds give place to the Atherfield Clay, and the consequent extra fall of the Tillingbourne at this point, Chilworth was a good site for a water wheel and quickly became the leading industrial centre of the valley. From the mid-seventeenth century right up to the end of the First World War the village was an important centre of the gunpowder industry. The full story of gunpowder in Surrey is told by Mr Montague Giuseppi in an article in the *Victoria History of the County*. In this he tells how the industry began with the building of powder mills on the little Hogsmill River by George and John Evelyn at the end of the sixteenth century. These were soon transferred to Godstone because supplies of charcoal were more plentiful there. However, the Evelyns ran into trouble with the Crown, and when the powder mills were opened at Chilworth by Sir Edward Randyll in the mid-seventeenth century those at Godstone closed down. By the end of the century there were sixteen powder mills at Chilworth, and the industry continued to exist, although with varying fortunes (some of the mills turned to paper manufacture later), for another 200 years. After one last great heave during the First World War, when several thousand workers were employed here, the industry finally expired. The tall chimneys were demolished, the land was sold, and Chilworth reverted at last to the rural peacefulness that Cobbett thought was more fitting for this "narrow, exquisitely beautiful vale of Chilworth" than "two of the most damnable inventions that ever sprang from minds of man under the influence of the devil! namely the making of gunpowder and of bank notes!"

It is not only the road that twists and turns at Albury, the next village along the valley, but the chimneys as well. Albury's fan-

tastic chimneys are one of the sights of the Tillingbourne Valley.
In respect of their chimneys at least, commoner and lord are on
the same footing, for the cottages of Albury have chimneys as
twisted as those of Albury House, which has sixty-three of them
and never two alike. Curiously enough, the lords of Albury Park
down the ages were themselves responsible for both the twisting
road and the twisting chimneys; originally Albury village lay
about where Albury House now stands, but it was removed, the
road being diverted round the perimeter of Albury Park, while
'New' Albury was erected in its place—complete with chimneys.
Albury House has just recently been acquired by the Mutual
Households Association Ltd, and will be converted into thirty-six
private apartments for retired and semi-retired people. The passing
motorist never sees Albury House, which lies secluded in its park,
but he cannot avoid seeing the impressive church on a hillock near
the 'Silent Pool'. This was built by Henry Drummond, the famous
banker, in the nineteenth century and is dedicated to the faith to
which he subscribed, the Catholic Apostolic Church. It sits there
on the little eminence seemingly specially prepared by the Creator
for it, tempting the motorists as they rush along the new dual
carriageway to Newlands Corner and Guildford to continue instead along the Valley of the Tillingbourne. I will confess that, in
common with probably 95 per cent of motorists using this stretch
of road, I never succumbed to its allurements until the imperative
of writing this chapter drew me for the first time to Albury—and
its fantastic chimneys. Often I had wondered what lay along this
attractive-looking valley—it is good sometimes to keep a pleasure
like this in store.

Almost in the centre of the Tillingbourne Valley lies its centrepiece—the village of Shere. If the Tillingbourne belongs to Shere,
it is equally true that Shere belongs to the Tillingbourne. It was
the Tillingbourne that drove the hammer mills of the local iron
industry centuries ago, as well as the old corn mill incorrectly
called 'Shere Mill' (correctly 'Netley Mill'). The mill still stands,
but its interior has been gutted and filled with modern machinery,
for the building is now a pump-house of the local water company.
Humans, like the watercress beds of the neighbourhood, prefer
pure water from below-ground rather than the water of the
adjacent river, utterly pure though it seems to be as it flows under

Shere bridge. The mill pond, which formed the subject of Seymour Haden's fine etching incorrectly titled 'Shere Mill Pond', has now been filled in and is an allotment, but there is too much of beauty left in Shere for us to grieve overmuch about this. In its industrial days the Tillingbourne served the needs of the local weavers of Shere who made the 'Guildford Cloth'.

The Tillingbourne's working days may seem to be over, but still it serves an increasingly important industry—recreation. Shere may now have been bypassed by the cars, but certainly not by the visitors who come in ever-increasing numbers to enjoy its peace and beauty, magnified now by the virtual cessation of through traffic. They saunter through the narrow streets gazing at the old half-timbered houses; they walk round the old Norman church which was built on the site of a church that had stood there for several centuries; they cross and recross the bridge over the Tillingbourne; and when they have enjoyed the village they rest by the sparkling waters of the river that brought it into being. To walk over the heaths and woodlands from Holmbury St Mary to Shere, and to sit by the Tillingbourne on a summer's evening enjoying the serenity of it all—this is something we must preserve for our grandchildren.

And the Shere bypass is a fine example of how timely action can avoid the destruction of what we hold most dear. Shere could not have withstood much longer the pressure of through traffic, but now the old traffic delays through Shere Village are a thing of the past, whilst the motorist with time to spare, or who happens to need to go into the village, can make his journey there in peace. The only difficulty is that what was Shere's problem yesterday is still Gomshall's today, and Abinger Hammer's, and perhaps Albury's tomorrow. The only satisfactory long-term solution would seem to be to route all through traffic along a parallel road running at the foot of the Downs on the other side of the valley. The railway paved the way as far back as 1849. It runs south of Albury, skirts Shere in a wide arc (it is a rather odd experience to climb the steep hill out of Shere and then to find oneself crossing the railway at Brook, the line lost to view in a deep cutting), crosses the Tillingbourne at Gomshall where the main road is forced to take a vicious 'S' bend which is a menace to motorists and potentially lethal to pedestrians, and then hugs the base of the

Downs all the way to Dorking. You can motor right through the Tillingbourne Valley and be quite unaware of the existence of the railway, save for a fleeting moment at Gomshall. By the same token, one can take a railway journey from Dorking to Guildford and be quite unaware of the existence of the Tillingbourne villages. This indeed is one of the loveliest and most rural railway journeys one can take so near London. Gomshall is the only railway station in the nine miles between Dorking and Chilworth. The Tillingbourne villages grew up along the south side of the valley because the river was there and because springs emerge there to give a plentiful supply of water. Thanks to this geological chance, the planners have a clear run, so far as human development is concerned, along the northern side of the valley, although of course the value of agricultural land has to be taken into account and the soils at the foot of the chalk escarpment tend to be of a high fertility. This is only one of the agonizing decisions planners have to take. On one side of the scales—high-quality farm land. On the other side—the Tillingbourne villages in danger of death by asphyxiation. We need a latter-day Solomon, but for my part I believe farm land, or rather the produce of farm land, is less irreplaceable than the villages of the Tillingbourne.

Gomshall is more than the axis of the road and rail 'scissors', it is also an attractive village in its own right. Compared with Shere it has a more work-a-day air, with its petrol-stations, restaurants, antique shops, pottery, and large tannery. The latter befits a village that has an ancient industrial tradition. It has been claimed that Gomshall is the most ancient site of a leatherworks in Britain—dating back certainly to Domesday times. Several tanneries existed here at one time, but eventually these were concentrated into one large factory called the Shere Tannery, which by the latter part of the nineteenth century had become one of the best equipped in the kingdom. At that time one-third of all the leather produced in Britain was manufactured and dressed in Surrey. Today the Gomshall factory makes light leather goods, including suede clothing, handbag leather and leather for shoes and jackets. Probably few people are conscious of the existence of this industry in Gomshall, for the factory is decently tucked away and does not intrude upon the village. For myself, I like the idea of a self-supporting community rather than a glass-case showplace, and if the industry is one that has existed there for nine centuries so much the better.

Probably most people who pass through Abinger Hammer imagine the name is derived from the famous hammer clock in the village, but of course it comes from the forge that once stood by the River Tillingbourne; the suffix 'Hammer' was added to distinguish the settlement that grew up round the forge from the village of Abinger itself. The Old Forge is believed to date from about 1530—the Tillingbourne is here constricted to a width of only 4 feet by strong stone walls. Between these walls stood the water mill, that drove the furnace, that made the iron, that was made into the two cannon balls unearthed a few years ago when a trench was being dug for a sewer (cannons for Elizabethan warships were also reputed to have been made here, but you would have to look on the bottom of the ocean for these). It is also said that the iron from which the gates of Old Temple Bar were made was forged at Abinger Hammer. Abinger Hammer was of course only one of many iron villages in Surrey, but the hammer clock is unique. It is representative of the iron industry and was erected in the memory of the first Lord Farrer by his second wife, Euphemir of the Wedgwood family. The clock projects over the road, and it is a wonder that some tall vehicle has not carried it away long ere this. 'Jack the Smith' strikes the bell every hour, but I have never seen him in action although I have passed through the village hundreds of times. The motorists passing underneath pay little heed to the inscription "By me you know how fast to go", except that if one of them is in a hurry the sight of the clock spurs him on—until the Gomshall bend curbs his enthusiasm. The villagers have a private joke that if you are there at midnight you will see Jack the Smith change his grip on the hammer as he strikes.

Near Abinger Hammer, down by the Tillingbourne, lies one of the most perfect farmhouses in Surrey—Crossways Farm. Built in 1610, as an addition to a building that had existed on the site for another century before that, it is probably the earliest gentleman's residence in Surrey built specifically as a farm and used as such ever since. But Crossways Farm is probably better known to devotees of the writings of George Meredith (if any still exist), as the setting of his novel *Diana of the Crossways*. During his forty-two years at Flint Cottage at the foot of Box Hill he must often have walked across the valley to Abinger Hammer, about the span of a brisk morning's walk. The house itself shows unmistakable Dutch influence, especially in the windows with their flat-topped relieving arches. The building's ornamented brick work is characteristic of other buildings in the locality—one sees it again in the old Mill House beside the spot where Abinger Mill (sometimes called 'Crane's Mill') once stood. The great barns on the north side of the farmhouse, with their tarred weatherboarding, remind me of barns of similar shape and construction (except for the use of Weald Stone in these at Abinger) that I have seen on Canvey Island in the Thames Estuary where Dutch influence was also very strong.

Abinger Hammer is associated, in rather sad circumstances, with Bishop Samuel Wilberforce, the son of the Wilberforce who freed the slaves. If you walk out to Evershed's Roughs to the north-east of the village you will find a granite cross bearing simply the initials 'S.W.', an impression of a bishop's crook and the date 1873. Here it was that Bishop Wilberforce fell from his horse whilst riding to Holmbury. His death robbed his country of a potential Archbishop of Canterbury, and the bishop himself of the chance of fulfilling his ambition to see the inside of Wotton House, home of the Evelyn family. The bishop was nicknamed 'Soapy Sam', and when he was asked how this came about he used to reply that it was because he was continuously getting into hot water!

We cannot leave Abinger Hammer without referring to the famous watercress beds in the neighbourhood. 'Gomshall Cress' is widely known for its unique flavour, and Grim's Kitchen continues to serve watercress teas as it has done for as long as I can remember. I have a soft spot for Grim's kitchen for a very personal reason. I had arranged to take the girl who eventually became my wife to Grim's Kitchen for a watercress tea, more years ago now than I care to remember. However, when we arrived there the place was closed; we never had our watercress tea after all—but I found a wonderful wife. Not many marriages begin in a kitchen, but a good many seem to end up there! There is more than the acknowledged nutritional relationship between watercress and iron—these watercress beds at Abinger Hammer occupy the sites of the original hammer ponds, although the requirements of watercress are such that pure spring water from artesian wells is used rather than river water from the Tillingbourne. Nevertheless the flat valley terrain supplies the level land needed for the laying out of the beds which are much admired by passers-by on the Dorking-Guildford road.

At this point, strictly speaking, we leave the Tillingbourne, or rather it takes its leave of us. For the Tillingbourne merely utilizes the wide valley between the North Downs and the Lower Greensand, it did not create it. As the Tillingbourne valley turns off to the south the road itself heads directly for Dorking through Wotton Hatch and Westcott.

The church of Wotton Hatch cannot be missed; it stands, as it has stood for 900 years, on a little knoll below the road on the north side, with all the withdrawn dignity of its age, and deep contentment with its incomparable setting below the escarpment of Ranmore Common and the White Downs. But where is the village? There is an inn on the road, and very attractive it is, but an inn alone does not make a village. I have never solved this mystery, but I suspect it must have something to do with the Evelyn family, who lived for many generations at nearby Wotton House. It was John Evelyn the diarist who perhaps gave us a clue when he described in one of his books the many streams and ponds that once existed around Wotton House, and around which were located the many powder mills built by his ancestors, but he says that these were later drained and filled in. Possibly the village died when the powder industry died, and it may have been located in the Valley of the Tillingbourne; in this case the church would have been quite a distance from the village, but this is not an uncommon feature in Surrey villages. We must file this away, among other such mysteries in the folder headed 'Isolated churches —Unsolved Mysteries'. As an epitaph on the Evelyn family it is perhaps poetic justice that Wotton House, the seat of the family that first introduced gunpowder into Britain, now houses the Fire Service College. As for the famous diary, perhaps a more-remembered legacy of this talented family than gunpowder, this is safely lodged at Christchurch College, Oxford. The most enduring legacy of all, however, are the woodlands of Leith Hill and the surrounding district, which owe their origin to John Evelyn's passion for planting trees in the barren sandy heaths round his home.

From the (relative) heights of Wotton Hatch the road plunges down a dark sunken lane, passing on the right hand side the Rookery—one-time home of the Malthus family and birthplace of the famous Reverend Thomas Malthus, but now converted into luxury flats—crosses the Pippbrook, and continues up the other side of the valley to Westcott. We have just crossed a watershed. The Tillingbourne drains to the Wey, the Pippbrook to the Mole. But the impatient motorist is probably too busy worrying about the slow-moving lorry up front, that is forcing a stream of traffic to crawl up Coast Hill (how inappropriate a name) in bottom gear, to give a thought to the fact that this hill marks the boundary not only of the Dorking Urban District but between one river system and another.

One is so accustomed to associate Westcott with its dovecote on the village green that it comes as rather a surprise to learn that this was erected only a few decades ago to commemorate the ending of the First World War. If Wotton Hatch is a church without a village, then Westcott is, or was until the last century, a village without a church. The present very attractive church was built in 1852 on Westcott Heath, the distinctive lych gate being added in 1890. But if the village lacked a church for so long it certainly did not lack a vigorous community life. I have been collecting newspaper cuttings of Surrey miscellania for many years now, and I have before me as I write an article in the local paper about some old characters of Westcott village. There was the 'Sabbatical Milkman', for instance, who lived in the village some eighty years ago. He earned this title because he would never allow his horse to work on Sundays but would deliver the milk himself with a yoke attached to his shoulders. Another old village character was Old Morris who used to drive round in a donkey cart collecting laundry. The village had a band; an annual fair which dated back to Domesday times; and a curious traditional method of punishing wrong-doers called 'Rough Music'. The villagers would gather outside the culprit's home and make a cacophonous noise with saucepans, kettles or any other suitable object. In those days every villager grew his own vine, for the soil round about was congenial to the growth of grapes, but later they turned to the growing of peppermint. It is in keeping with the image of a lively local community that the vicar of Westcott, the Reverend Salzmann, known locally as 'The Cricketing Parson', was captain of the local cricket side for most of the thirty years he spent as vicar here until his death in 1944. If evidence were needed that the village is still a thriving place, and not merely a dormitory of its larger neighbour Dorking, it may be found in the presence here of the Surrey County office of the National Farmers Union.

The town of Dorking lies almost exactly in the centre of Surrey, roughly equidistant from its north and south boundaries and, although the distances are about twice as great, from the east and west boundaries. Of all the market towns of Surrey, Dorking is the one I would unhesitatingly choose as most typical of the genre—except for one noticeable omission: it has no town hall comparable in antiquity with those of Godalming or Reigate. Yet Dorking has very much the air of a town. It is a railway junction, an important crossing-place of major roads, an urban district in its own right, and it has a church that, with its magnificent steeple soaring 210 feet high (a memorial to the Bishop Wilberforce who fell at Abinger), has no more pretensions to being a village church than Wotton House has to being a cottage. And it has decorations right across the High Street at Christmas time—a sure sign of civic pride and mature urbanity! A few other towns in Surrey also qualify for admission to this select little league; towns like Godalming, Guildford and Woking come to mind, but other towns that might well have been rivals to Dorking drop out of the running—winding coloured bulbs round the lamp posts simply will not do!

Dorking for me is not so much a town as a view. For in what other town in Surrey can you do your shopping in the market place and enjoy at the same time such uninterrupted views of Box Hill and Ranmore Common as, in other parts of the kingdom, one might travel far to see. Nothing delights me more about my own home town of Caterham than to enjoy the tree-covered slopes of the valley whilst walking in the town centre, but the fortunate people of Dorking enjoy every day a view twice as impressive in its scope and twice as intriguing in its changing colours and moods with the different seasons and times of day. As for the town itself, I like best the contrast between the wide High Street and the nar-

*The High Street, Old Oxted*
*In Old Shere*

row West Street; the raised footpath at the west end of the High
Street, which, for some reason that I have never properly under-
stood, rouses in me a feeling of pleasure associated vaguely with
the seaside, holidays and fishing villages in the South-west; and
the very attractive façade of South Street curving up the hillside
and suggesting a Jane Austenish air of elegant town life. Surely
there were some 'Assembly Rooms' here at one time, where the
gentility from the surrounding countryside would gather, the
men to show off their latest carriages, and the women their couture
—and their eligible daughters.

Dorking's life as a market town began in the twelfth century
when the 7th Earl of Warenne received a charter from Edward I.
Today the market still flourishes in the centre of Dorking, although
it is now mainly devoted to fruit, vegetables and fish, the livestock
market, which was at one time held in the High Street (hence its
width at the east end), having come to an end in 1926. Today only
the hitching posts outside the 'White Horse' remain—as many a
motorist who has backed over-hastily into a convenient parking
space has cause to remember. This spot is probably the historic
heart of Dorking. The 'White Horse' is itself over 400 years old,
and the site was first occupied at least as far back as 1278. Dorking
was an important staging post on the old Stane Street, and if you
project the lines of Stane Street northwards from near Holmwood
(where the route becomes conjectural) and southwards from where
it reappears in the Mole Valley, you will find that the lines cross
about where the 'White Horse' now stands. Maybe it is not fanci-
ful, therefore, to regard the history of this historic site as dating
back yet another 1,000 years beyond 1278.

The town is surrounded by places with unusual names. There is
Cotmandene for instance. This is an open space south of the High
Street where for many centuries a fair has been held on the eve,
and day, of the Feast of the Ascension, and where cricket was
played for over 200 years; at one time the ground was almost as
famous as the Oval is today. The name Cotmandene sounds old
and Saxonish, and the antiquity of the site was indeed proved
when an Iron Age urn was unearthed here some years ago. Then
there is the Nower, an open space complete with a copy of the
Greek Temple of Venus, built in 1844 and donated to the town by
Lieutenant Colonel R. W. Barclay of the well-known brewery

12

'Jack the Smith', Abinger Hammer

family. The streets to the south of Dorking, as many a rambler knows, climb steeply up the side of the valley towards the Glory Wood, from which glorious views are obtained of the town below dominating the Mole Gap beyond. One can readily understand why the Romans directed their main road from the South Coast to London straight to this natural corridor, and why Dorking was destined in any event to become an important traffic nexus and administrative centre.

Dorking is unique among Surrey towns in having given its name to a breed of poultry and that Dorking breed is unique because it has five claws. 'A Dorking Cock Proper' makes a very appropriate top-piece to the town's coat of arms, and the sign of the cock greets every traveller entering Dorking by road. The local town guide comments: "it is no wonder that the local inhabitants have acquired the pet name of Dorking 'Chicks', and that a native of the town proudly claims his right to be known as a 'Five Clawed 'Un'."

Of all the buildings in and around Dorking, perhaps the best known was Deepdene. There it stood above the bypass that bears its name, and thanks to which it lay more exposed to the gaze of every passing motorist than any other great house in Surrey. It was truly a product of the Age of Grandeur—the Blenheim of Surrey. The first Deepdene was built in the Palladian style by the Hon. Charles Howard in 1652, and it must have looked very different from the building which succeeded it, for Aubrey, after a visit there in 1673, spoke of its "pleasant and delightful solitude", and he went on to say: "The house is not made for grandeur but retirement, neat and elegant." Thomas Hope changed all that in 1806 when he came into possession of the property. He set about turning this elegant little retreat into one of the great houses of Surrey. He spared no expense in adding wings to the old building and transforming the surrounding gardens with statuary. His was the Deepdene in which Disraeli stayed whilst writing his *Conings-by*, which William IV and Queen Adelaide and King Edward VII visited in great state—and which was occupied by departments of the Southern Region of British Rail during and after the war. I knew the building had been up for sale for some time, but still it was a shock the other day to see this grand ghost of the past reduced to a mere pile of rubble. Passing the site that same evening

I noticed that the old timbers and other burnable debris had been set alight, and the pile was still glowing, the whole forming an eerie and Turner-like silhouette framed against a dull leaden evening sky. Deepdene died in glory that night. Perhaps it was better so. Deepdene was too grand in every way for this age of mini-everything. Yet still there is a sadness at such a parting. As William Morris said: "Every time one of them (historic buildings) disappears it is a national misfortune, for while most other mistakes we make may be remedied, the destruction of an ancient building is irremediable." Now there is an ultra modern building on the site. It is fine in its way. . . but it is not the Deepdene we knew.

Music lovers associate Dorking primarily with its famous son, Dr Vaughan Williams, and with the Leith Hill Music Festival, with which he and his family were so closely connected ever since it started. The festival was not born at Dorking, but in the little village hall of Abinger one summer evening in 1904, when a dozen people met together and decided to launch a choral competition. They elected Miss Margaret Vaughan Williams as their secretary. On 10th May 1905 Dr Vaughan Williams conducted the first evening concert in Dorking, and so began his long connection with the town. Choirs came from villages within a ten-mile radius, and by 1922 the annual festival had become so popular that it had become necessary to extend it over three days. A larger and more permanent home was now needed, and in 1931 the festival moved from the Drill Hall to the newly opened Dorking Halls.

In 1953 Dr Vaughan Williams resigned as conductor and became President of the Leith Hill Festival. To Dorking he gave his services as a conductor and patron of the arts, but his music he gave to the nation—and in 1944 the family home, Leith Hill Place, as well. He loved this part of Surrey as only a man of great sensitivity could, and I never hear the haunting music he wrote for the old ballad "Greensleeves" without thinking of the lovely Valley of the Tillingbourne, in which, surely, he found his inspiration.

# 16

# ALONG THE VALE OF HOLMESDALE
## FROM BOX HILL TO OXTED

If you stand on Box Hill, or indeed any of the vantage points eastwards of Box Hill, such as Pebblecoombe, Colley Hill, Godstone Hill or Titsey Hill, and look southwards towards the Weald, you will see a broad valley, excellently farmed and with many prosperous villages and towns, and in the distance the ridge of the Lower Greensand. This is the historic and beautiful Vale of Holmesdale. Even if the wash-down of chalk from the Downs, and sand from the Greensand Ridge, onto the Gault Clay at the foot of the escarpment had not produced a rich and fertile soil and some of the finest farms in the county, there can still be no doubt that this natural east-west corridor would have been an important line of communication and settlement. Strung like pearls on a necklace are a succession of towns and villages; at every major gap in the chalk ridge, a town and, at the lesser gaps and where the prosperous agriculture of the Vale required it, a village. Each parish stretches from the Chalk right down to the heavy clay of the Weald so as to include a variety of soils. Unlikely as it may seem, for instance, Headley, at the top of the chalk escarpment, is part of the rural district of Dorking and Horley. And for the whole of its length the Vale is sheltered not only from the north winds, but also from the flowing tide of urban development, by the magnificent chalk escarpment which rears itself from the flat valley floor with dramatic suddenness. Sometimes it is clothed in green springing downland turf, with here and there gashes of white where the chalk lies exposed, or great white wounds where a quarry has taken a deep bite into the chalk; and sometimes it is covered with trees from top to bottom.

As seen from the Vale, the chalk escarpment is one of Britain's great natural features. From the point of view of the people of the Vale it has the advantage, not shared by its Siamese sister the South Downs (the two were part of the great Wealden Dome in geological time), that it faces southwards and therefore does not rob the Vale of its sunshine early in the afternoon. The southern edge of the Vale is marked by the Lower Greensand Ridge, which is smoother and generally lower than the North Downs (except in the Leith Hill area) and has soils of a more sandy texture that give rise to heathlands and commons. Like the chalk Downs, the Lower Greensand ridge was affected by the same Wealden uplift, or tilting, and thus has its escarpment on the south side, with its dip slope on the north towards the Vale of Holmesdale. In places the Greensand escarpment is even more dramatic than that of the Chalk (although less extensive); it is not always realized for instance that Leith Hill, at 967 feet, is so much higher than Box Hill (600 feet). The main road along the Vale of Holmesdale keeps closer to the Lower Greensand than to the Chalk, because it was there, where the sands gave way to the impervious Gault Clay, that the springs broke surface and water was plentiful. Thus the necklace of settlements along the Vale is exactly comparable, in geological terms, to the line of villages along the northern edge of the Chalk where it joins the London Clay.

Between Dorking and Reigate lie the three 'Bs', Brockham Green, Betchworth and Buckland. The first two lie slightly to the south of the main road, but Buckland sits right astride it, with the ancient church on one side and Buckland's curious towered tithe barn, shaped exactly like a church, on the other. Brockham Green, for me, is cricket on a summer's evening, a huge bonfire on 5th November (it vies with Edenbridge and Lewes), and in the winter, carols round the illuminated Christmas tree on the green. It has a church, cruciform-shaped like a miniature cathedral, which sits on the green as if it owned it. W. G. Grace played cricket on the green, and when he was at the crease the church windows were hardly safe; the last time I watched cricket there a well-hit ball signalled its own boundary on the side of a parked car. Brockham Green has the inevitable pump, old-world houses, and as perfect a backcloth, in the wooded slopes of the North Downs, as any village in Surrey. But why is it that Brockham Green and Betchworth, unlike Buckland, lie off the main road? Perhaps the explanation has something to do with the River Mole, for both villages lie on the river (the name Brockham is usually associated with badgers, which used to abound in the river banks nearby, but it may equally well denote simply 'the settlement by the brook'), which by now has gathered together most of its Wealden tributaries in preparation for the assault on the chalk wall. Crossing the Mole was never easy, for it was given to violent floods at times, and bridges were few—often fords, like Flanchford nearby, had to be used; many of the footpaths around Brockham are raised for protection against the floods. Perhaps the village grew up where there was a convenient crossing place. In recent years a new footbridge has been built parallel with the ancient road bridge—it is of ferro concrete and tubular steel and presents a hideous contrast to the old pack-horse type of bridge inherited from the past. My sympathies are with those villagers who show their disgust at the new monstrosity by continuing to walk across the old bridge. We have too few Brockham Greens in Surrey to be able to afford such mistakes as this.

Brockham Green may be an old settlement (there was a settlement here at Domesday), but ecclesiastically speaking it is a mere infant. The church dates only from 1847. But neighbouring Betchworth makes up for it with a church dating back before Domesday to the time of Edward the Confessor. It is beautiful in itself, and it possesses some remarkable treasures, including an old chest, hewn out of a solid piece of oak and reputed to be 1,000 years old, with wood as hard as the iron bands that bind it. That Betchworth was at one time a place of greater importance than Brockham is evidenced by the fact that, to the puzzlement of many motorists along the Reigate-Dorking road, it has given its name to places the other side of Brockham Green, places like Betchworth Park and Betchworth Castle. The latter is today merely a ruin beside the Mole in the grounds of Betchworth Park Golf Course. When it was built in 1449 by Sir Thomas Browne, he clearly selected the site for its commanding position at the entrance to the Mole Gap; however, the castle was never tested in war and was demolished in 1700. The name is perpetuated in the old Castle Mill a short distance down the River Mole, the last water mill to utilize the power of the Mole before it crosses the Chalk—

it is also the largest and finest. I have a particular affection for this old mill because we have had an original oil painting of it hanging over our lounge fireplace for many years, and the placid waters of its mill pond are as real to me now as if I had lived in the mill itself. A painting of the mill hangs outside the Watermill Restaurant on the main Reigate-Dorking road, but it is a pity that so few of those who drive past realize that by walking down the rough track beside the restaurant they can see for themselves one of the finest water mills in Surrey. In J. Hillier's fascinating book *Old Surrey Water-mills* only Shalford Mill of all the hundred or so water mills that were at work at some time in Surrey has more page references than Castle Mill, Dorking.

It would seem that Betchworth and Brockham Green were either substantial villages in the fifteenth century, or exceedingly unfortunate ones, for Thomas Morsted of Aglond Moor, Betchworth, left in his will "33/4d. to be disposed among 100 poor in Bechesworth and Brokham, to each 4d." He also left 16d. to Betchworth Church "for the reparation and amendment of the Chapel in the said Church in which my farder and moder ben buried". He did more—he also had a small brass inscription placed on the south wall of the side chapel: "Here lies Thomas Morsted and Alianon his wife, upon whose souls may God have mercy." The brass is still there, but happily it would be difficult today to find a hundred really poor families in Betchworth and Brockham Green.

And so we come to Reigate, which, with its near neighbour Redhill, is the largest town in the Vale of Holmesdale and presumably feels justified therefore in taking as the borough motto the ancient couplet of Camden's:

> The Vale of Holmsdall
> Never wonne ne never shall.

Reigate is old and has the dignity and slight reserve of age; Redhill is a Victorian upstart, ugly, brash, thrusting and vigorous, the offspring of the Brighton Road and of the Brighton Railway, opened in 1841, which its dignified neighbour had refused to admit. Before the alternative road to Brighton was built in the 1820s, branching off the old Merstham to Reigate Road at Gatton Park, the area that is now the town of Redhill was just a rural backwater of Reigate with a few farms, some cottages and a tannery. The town took its name from the reddish colour of the sand hereabouts. Redhill grew rapidly, sustained by its two arteries, and soon its population passed that of Reigate. Yet the borough still derives its name, and all its urban attractiveness, from Reigate. Apart from the Old Town Hall I like best of all in Reigate the classic groups of buildings on both sides of West Street, and, as a close third, the row of cottages along Flanchford Road, sitting like a line of spectators with their backs to the sun watching the cricket on the green opposite. Redhill has nothing to match these and their setting or if it has I have yet to discover it.

Until it was closed recently, Reigate was approached through a tunnel. I well remember the excitement, as a child, of negotiating Reigate tunnel (there was two-way traffic in those days), and then emerging right in the centre of the town within a stone's throw of the Old Town Hall. The only remote parallel I can recall is the entrance into Guildford Station by railway from the south, where you pass through a long tunnel and emerge right in the centre of Guildford. After passing through a seemingly endless succession of London streets, and then the semi-suburbia of Banstead and Burgh Heath, we made the steep descent of Reigate Hill with its wonderful views across the Weald and even a hint of the sea in the distance, and then, as if to confirm the fact that we had at last broken out of London's web, we found ourselves in Reigate—unmistakably a town in its own right—a country town in the country—a true town of Surrey—now we really were on our way to the sea. Even now, over thirty-five years later, I can never pass the Old Town Hall without reliving again in some small way that first thrill of youth. I even annoy my family on occasion by purposely taking the congested High Street rather than the bypass along London Road, just because I like to see the Old Town Hall. A town, and individual buildings in a town, can be as integral a part of our lives as the people we have met and the friendships we have made.

Most of the towns commanding important gaps in the chalk wall had their castles; Farnham, Guildford, Betchworth, Reigate and Blechingley all had castles. Reigate Castle was built by the early great Norman family, the Warennes, who figure as prominently in the early history of this part of Surrey as Bishop Odo seems to do in so many other parts of southern England. For several centuries their castle dominated the surrounding district, and the people of the town lived within the protection of its walls. Yet the relationship was an uneasy one, for the Norman landlords exercised a strong and often a tyrannical control over their domains. It is all the more curious, therefore, that a legend should have grown up that a group of barons met in the caves under Reigate Castle to frame the Magna Carta. Was it ever likely that a man who could greet the royal justices, when they came to demand by what right he held his franchises, by flourishing his sword and exclaiming "Here is my warranty! My ancestors who came with William the Bastard conquered their lands with the sword, and with the sword will I defend them," should have sided with the barons at Runnymede? Yet still adults and children come, year after year, to see the cave where this unlikely incident is supposed to have taken place. The castle represents in fact a period of tyranny, whilst the Old Town Hall, erected about 1728, represents the growth of municipal justice. When Reigate came to celebrate its centenary in 1963 with a great pageant, it fittingly chose first the castle and then the Old Town Hall as the two backcloths against which the history of the borough was portrayed.

Reigate is the only place in Surrey that can boast not one windmill but two. In the mid-eighteenth century the town had no less than twenty windmills in the vicinity and was then an important centre of the oatmeal trade, but today there are only nine windmills left standing in the whole of Surrey. The windmill on Wray Common is in an excellent state of preservation, and it is well worth pulling off the Gatton Park Road for a few yards to see it at close quarters; the mill is at present used as a private residence. The other windmill, on Reigate Heath and visible across the valley, has also been well restored, having been fitted out with new sails some years ago. The mill has the unique distinction of being used as a church during the summer, and when I was last there a group of musicians was just arriving for a concert of Bach music—there was just room for the cello under the huge cross-beams that support the mill. The mill is owned by the Reigate Heath Golf Club and is leased to the parish as a church. To complete this odd combination, the mill stands on the site of both an old chapel and also a gallows (hence the name Galley Hill). Where else but in Britain would a mill owned by a golf club and built on the site of a gallows be used for a church and a concert of Bach! At a luncheon recently I met a corn merchant whose old established family business was at Reigate, and he was bemoaning the passing of an era, a change symbolized by the pensioning off of these two fine windmills. Today a small corn merchant is more likely to be selling bird seed, dog biscuits or lawn grass, than corn for flour or poultry. The mills still stand, but the age that brought them into being has gone.

Many centuries ago, long before even the windmill age, some enterprising Roman discovered that the soil near Redhill had remarkable cleansing qualities. Perhaps he was one of the servants living in the Roman villa situated at the foot of White Hill near Caterham. Before long the servants, whose task it was to trample the master's togas in a great vat to get them clean, were adding a little of this substance to assist the process and help remove the grease. Later this same substance was used for removing the grease from raw wool, and thus it came to be called 'fuller's earth' (fulling being the process of cleaning wool). For several hundred years fuller's earth from the Redhill area was used in the English wool trade and became so important that its export was forbidden in case other countries should thereby benefit, to the detriment of the English wool industry. Fuller's earth is still used in the textile industry, but has to some extent been replaced by substitutes. However many new uses have been found for fuller's earth, and it is now employed in the bleaching and purifying of oils, in pottery glazing and in the manufacture of cosmetics and water paints. Fuller's earth occurs in its natural form only very rarely, and the product is exported from Redhill to places all over the world.

On a lighter note, I always enjoy the story of Thomas Fuller, author of *Worthies of England*, who, when asked to suggest an epitaph for himself, offered the words: "Here lies Fuller's Earth."

Unfortunately there is a price to be paid. The fuller's earth companies have removed vast quantities of the substance from the north side of the Nutfield Ridge and have recently begun to excavate on the south side of the main Redhill to Godstone road. It may not be long before the road is left on a narrow isthmus with deep excavations on either side, a common sight in the chalk country of Swanscombe and Northfleet but unknown in Surrey. Near Nutfield also is a large factory belching out white smoke and introducing a foreign air of industrialization to the otherwise rural scene. We have come a long way from the days when the Romans trampled their vats in the villa at the foot of White Hill.

Perhaps this part of the Vale of Holmesdale is doomed anyway. The desecration began after the war, when the London County Council decided to place one of its two Surrey out-county estates (to rehouse Londoners for whom accommodation could not be found within the county boundary) adjacent to the old-world village of Merstham. It was a curious choice of location and was presumably dictated by the need to find a site conveniently situated for those who wished to remain in close contact with friends and relatives in London—the very opposite pattern of thinking from that which inspired the choice of sites for the New Towns. However, the decision was taken, and the affluent stock-brokers of Rockshaw Road gradually saw an estate housing some thousands of people spreading across the countryside their terraces had hitherto overlooked, although if they wished they could raise their sights and enjoy the view of the fuller's earth factory on Nutfield ridge. The estate, admittedly, is well tucked away; probably few of the motorists who pass through Merstham, and comment on the attractiveness of the village—especially the cul-de-sac so aptly named Quality Street—realize that this large estate exists just the other side of the railway. The poor rich people of Rockshaw Road, having adjusted themselves to the presence of the estate, now have another huge adjustment to make. For their road has now become the site of one of the largest motorway interchanges in England—another Almondsbury. Here the new Brighton Motorway, after crossing the Old Brighton Road at Merstham on an enormous fly-over, crosses the new South Orbital Road in a flurry of clover-leaf interconnections at several levels. I have a friend who is one of the engineers on the new Brighton Motorway; I do not grudge him the engineer's delight he takes in selecting a finely graded route, nor am I too concerned about the rash of 'For Sale' notices springing up along Rockshaw Road once again (the stock-brokers can no doubt find other attractive sites along the Pilgrims Way), but I do grieve for the passing of a lovely quiet valley at the foothills of the Downs, and for the irreplaceable loss of yet another small fragment of England's diminishing countryside.

An odd feature about Merstham is that what is now the cul-de-sac called Quality Street, was at one time the old road to Croydon, the present road past the 'Jolliffe Arms' being built in 1807. The old road left Merstham at the south end, along what is now School Hill, and meandered its way to Reigate through the intriguingly named Battlebridge. Thus the alignment of Merstham has been completely altered. One now has to negotiate a chicane through the village, trying hard not to overrun the pavement by the sharp turn at the northern end. Quality Street acquired its name as a joke that stuck. Seymour Hicks, the famous actor, and his wife, Ellaline Terriss, were living in the fifteenth-century Old Forge House in the early years of this century and at the time they were appearing in the play *Quality Street*—and so it was by this happy chance that such a lovely backwater acquired so apt a title.

The ridge road from Redhill to Godstone used to be called 'the Forgotten Road' by some of the local people because, although only a narrow road, it had to carry an increasingly heavy stream of traffic. But others resisted the idea of the road being widened, fearing this would destroy the beauty of the villages along its length. Instead they favoured the building of a major new parallel road on the other side of the valley. The battle between the 'improvers' and the 'preservers' raged fast and furious, at heart the basic problem of how to adapt to the needs of modern living whilst preserving the heritage of the past. This was but a local skirmish in the war that is continually going on in all the countries of the developed world. As events have turned out both solutions have been adopted simultaneously! The old ridge road is being widened in many places, whilst the new South Orbital Road is being built along the other side of the valley. But at least the villages should be saved.

The queen of the ridge road villages is Blechingley—or is it Bletchingley? There is always confusion as to the correct spelling, but the local historian Uvedale Lambert has pointed out that the 't' was never included in old documents before 1582, and I have seen an old milestone at Tylers Green near Godstone dated 1744 which contains the words "Blechingley and Rygate Road". I will therefore side with the ancients and, despite the Post Office, omit the 't'. There seems to have been a vogue for adding 't's' around the eighteenth century, for Mitcham also acquired its 't' at that time. But it is the village that matters, not its name. Blechingley is perhaps the most precious pearl on the necklace, and one that should surely be preserved at all costs. Fortunately, the village has a wide main street—an indication of its importance in times past. It was once a borough and possessed a castle; it is also said to have had seven churches, and many inns, including four that have since disappeared completely. In the 1870s the village had such a lawless reputation that it was put out of bounds to the soldiers in the new Guards Depot at Caterham! The finest of Blechingley's inns is the 'White Hart', part of which dates back to the sixteenth century and probably earlier still; in the forecourt the North Downs Morris Dancers are sometimes to be seen dancing on a summer's evening, the vigour, if not the accuracy, of their dancing, growing with each round of ale. Blechingley Church is very impressive and full of interest, although the vast monument to Sir Robert Clayton, Lord Mayor of London, who died in 1707, and his wife, seems somehow less impressive when one discovers that it was executed, fulsome dedication and all, whilst Sir Robert was still alive—he was apparently taking no chances that posterity would render him the honour that was his due. But my favourite spots in Blechingley are King Charles Cottage, now a delightful little restaurant where they serve meals fit for a king, and Church Walk, the little side lane or 'twitten' to use a Surrey word (although this was in fact the main street of the village at one time), that runs between the church and the Nutfield Road. This is a beautiful little fragment of Tudor England, marvellously well preserved, and, as the plaque indicates, safeguarded for all time.

Since leaving the Borough of Reigate, we have been in the rural district of Godstone. This area stretches far to the south of the 'Forgotten Road' almost as far as East Grinstead, and it is a further sign of the importance of the Vale of Holmesdale that a village located at the extreme northern edge of this extensive area should give its name to the rural district. Its name, however, is about all Godstone gives, for the headquarters of the Rural District are located not at Godstone but at Oxted. Godstone, like Dorking or Reigate, was fore-ordained by geography to exist, and if geography had been a little kinder in making the gap through the Chalk more marked it would inevitably have developed into a town rather than a village. The Romans selected the Godstone Gap for their road from Lewes to London, but later the Merstham Gap became more important and Reigate and Redhill prospered more than Godstone. As to the road along the Vale of Holmesdale, it takes a curious dog-leg route through Godstone village, and I have often speculated as to the reason for this. If one traces the continuation of the Reigate to Godstone road eastwards through Godstone village it passes Godstone Church (which lies about half a mile from Godstone village) as a track and would if continued on from there join the Westerham Road near Tandridge. Since Godstone Church was built there have been changes in the road and settlement pattern of the district, and the church has been left isolated.

In times past, before the Black Death devastated the area, there were two villages, a lesser one round Godstone Green and the principal one where Godstone Church now stands. This latter was called in Saxon 'Wolcnestede', and at Domesday 'Walkingstead' (modernized spelling), signifying the homestead where cloth was 'walked' or trampled in vats—no doubt with fuller's earth added, another very interesting reference to the existence of this local industry at that time. It may be that as the need arose for a good road to carry the iron from the Felbridge ironworks to London so the Saxon village declined, and the even older one at Godstone Green, through which the Romans had routed their Brighton to London road, grew in importance. The 'White Hart' at Godstone, like its namesake at Blechingley is a very old and picturesque inn. It was first mentioned in the time of Richard II, a few decades after the Black Death, and it may well have been at about this time that Godstone Green superseded Walkingstead. Godstone became a centre for the leather trade, as were other villages in the Vale, and for a short time in the early seventeenth century the powder factories owned by John Evelyn were located in Godstone. It is a strange coincidence that two of the greatest diarists in the English language came from two adjacent Surrey villages, for the Pepys family came from neighbouring Tandridge. Godstone still has no less than seven ponds, a legacy from its 'industrial' past which contributes not a little to its present attractiveness. Under a great sarsen stone in the churchyard at Godstone Church, as if to keep his restless spirit in check, lies the body of Walker Miles, a founder of rambling clubs and a great countryman. With its green, its old cottages and its village pond, Godstone still merits Cobbett's description (and he was not over-given to praise) ' a beautiful village", although it is best seen at other times than when the Eastbourne Road is choked bumper to bumper with cars heading for the coast, whilst a queue of cars waits on the Blechingley Road for an opportunity to negotiate the dog-leg. As I write I have before me a newspaper cutting showing a photograph of Godstone at the turn of the century; there is one horse and carriage, a man, three boys wearing *Oliver*-type peaked caps, and a dog lying asleep in the middle of the road outside the 'White Hart'. Pervading all is a sense of quiet and peace that Godstone is unlikely ever to enjoy again, unless of course someone decides to build new roads bypassing the village.

The last, and in some respects the most distinctive, pearl on the Holmesdale necklace is Old Oxted. Situated on the side of a steep hill, the village looks as though it has stepped out of some Cornish pastoral scene—one half expects the sea to be there at the bottom of the hill, beyond a little harbour. The cottages of Old Oxted have miniature causeways leading to front doors painted in bright colours like their Cornish counterparts and placed at right angles to the street. And at the top of the hill lies the 'Old Bell' inn, the oldest and most attractive building in the village. Until recently Old Oxted had no by-pass and the main east-west road south of London went straight through. Any mother wheeling her pram down the High Street took her life, or rather lives, in her hands. As elsewhere there were the 'improvers' and the 'preservers'. The former said that Old Oxted must have its own by-pass, but the latter said, "No, leave it alone; wait until the South Orbital Road has been built on the other side of the valley." As elsewhere both solutions have been adopted simultaneously. A new miniature by-pass has been built for Old Oxted, while work is going on along the line of the South Orbital Road. Mothers now walk their charges safely down Old Oxted High Street while traffic thunders past only a short distance away.

It is easy to be cynical about New Oxted, with its aping of the Tudor image, but one has to admit that the total effect is very pleasing, particularly along Station Road West. But—and this is a big but—whoever planned Oxted so that its main shopping street is neatly bisected by a railway line? It is surely the most odd example of 'non-planning' in the whole of Surrey. And as if this were not enough, New Oxted has another glaring example of non-planning—the new gasholder right in the centre of the town. I asked a local shopkeeper how the people of Oxted permitted such an eyesore to be erected, and he said that it was because the alternative proposals would have added an extra few pence to the rates and added: "We are so used to it now that we no longer notice it." What an indictment! I still find it incredible that a community could prefer to allow such an attractive little town, in such an incomparable setting below the North Downs, to be blighted by this monstrosity—just to save a few pence on the rates. Even if it is not always visible from the town itself, seen from the viewpoint above Titsey Hill it is a hideous disfiguring eyesore— a sad advertisement of Man's inhumanity to Nature.

The two Oxteds merge almost imperceptibly into Limpsfield and Hurst Green to form a rapidly growing urban area. Hurst Green is a twentieth-century Redhill—a creation of the railway that brought Dr Beeching himself, and many thousands of other commuters, through the North Downs in a long tunnel to deposit them in the Weald—the advance guard of what could become a tidal wave of commuters flowing southwards to coalesce with the waves ponding back from places like Dormansland, Edenbridge and East Grinstead. The Oxted railway line is the only one through the Surrey chalk that plunges boldly under the high escarpment rather than utilizing a natural gap. It is therefore doubly dangerous in terms of its impact on the countryside below the chalk. For where there is a natural gap there is inevitably a town—the railway confirms and reinforces the natural pattern but does not change it. But where the railway flaunts Nature and tunnels through the wall, it emerges in quiet undeveloped countryside, and immediately starts its work of transformation. Hence Hurst Green and Dormansland constitute one of the greatest threats to this part of rural Surrey.

Limpsfield stands a little aloof from the urban invasion taking place around it. The village has managed to retain much of its old-world atmosphere, and the Norman church of St Peter has one of the best-maintained churchyards in Surrey—a fitting resting place for the body of the composer Frederick Delius. Beatrice Harrison

*Moated manor house, Crowhurst Place*

*Wealden oak and Horsham stone, Brewer Street*

not only brought the body of Delius to Limpsfield (he died in France but had signified his wish to be buried in an English churchyard), but with her cello she encouraged a nightingale to sing at Limpsfield—and so marked a milestone in the development of broadcasting in Britain.

The village has many of those little touches of the unexpected that people look for when they park the car and stroll through the High Street: a beautifully carved facia board over an outhouse by a garage, a clock set into a barn wall at Detillens, and a fashion shop with the title 'Weeds and Tweeds'. Limpsfield is a favourite location for preparatory schools, as indeed is the whole of the Vale of Holmesdale. I tell my young niece in school there how lucky she is, but I suppose she won't realize it for herself until she grows up, marries a mining engineer and has to live in Wigan! Above the village on the east side lies Limpsfield Common, a wild-looking spot of sandy heathland and woods, where Major Baden-Powell and the flamboyant Colonel Cody are said to have flown man-lifting kites; it is approached by a steep hill protected by traffic lights (another reminder of the increasing urbanization of this corner of Surrey) and protecting a small mansion of classic pro-portions which lies snugly in the hollow of the hill as if each was made for the other. I always regard this hill as marking the end of the Vale of Holmesdale. Here on one side of the road lies the remarkable row of old stone cottages called Wolf's Row, with a miniature battlemented house sandwiched in the midst of them; whilst on the other side lies the mansion I have just referred to. Together these represent the two nations within a nation, the squire and the yeoman, who for centuries sustained a quiet and deeply satisfying way of life in this lovely Vale of Holmesdale, a way of life that must have seemed as changeless and enduring as the timeless beauty of the Vale itself—until the traffic lights came.

13

*The church-like barn at Buckland*
*On the battlefield, Ockley Green*

# 17

# LINGFIELD, AND THE EAST SURREY WEALD

The village of Outwood, at nearly 400 feet, is the highest in the East Surrey Weald, and it acts as a watershed for the surrounding countryside, the rivers to the east flowing into the Medway and those to the west flowing into the Mole and thence into the Thames.

Such a spot just shouts for a windmill—and Outwood, until a few years ago, had two—known as 'The Cat and the Kitten'. The original post mill, erected in 1665, was owned by two brothers in the mid-nineteenth century, but they fell out and one of them erected a rival mill immediately alongside in 1860. This was a tall smock mill (if, like me at one time, you can never remember which is which, a useful tip is that a smock mill is shaped like a miller's smock, tall and round), and presumably the aggrieved brother literally hoped to take the wind out of the other's sails! However he could not have done such a good job of construction, for the smock mill fell into disrepair and eventually collapsed in a high wind a few years ago. So the 'Kitten' died before the 'Cat' and Outwood now has only one mill—but what a fine specimen it is! It is the oldest working windmill in England and has been very well restored and maintained by the present owners who warmly welcome visitors. I once took a party of a hundred children there. Although it was a little harrowing trying to keep 200 tiny hands out of the cog-wheels whilst the great sails were being hand-turned, or making sure the children who were helping to turn the sails did not forget to let go as they went up (the owner's niece had done so and fell crashing to the ground as the sail passed the vertical—a piece of news I learned within minutes of arriving at the mill and which did not exactly help my peace of mind), it was nevertheless a most interesting experience. The children climbed to the top of the mill and strained their eyes in the direction of London as if trying to see the glow in the sky as the people of Outwood had done in that autumn of 1666, during the Great Fire of London, only a year after the mill had been built. The present owners have added a miniature zoo and a rural museum to interest visitors, and many thousands of people go there at fine summer weekends. I am sure the occupiers of other interesting rural sites located at a convenient afternoon's drive from London and the bigger towns of Surrey might well consider providing similar facilities and so help to meet a real and growing need. There is a great interest in rural life, past and present, among townspeople, probably greater than most people who live in the country realize.

The road to Outwood from Blechingley is as quiet and un-spoiled a rural backwater as one could wish—or at least it was until natural gas was discovered there two or three years ago. This area around South Godstone is the only place in England, apart, I believe, from a site in the Cleveland Hills, where natural gas has been discovered and tapped on the land. A tall 95-foot drilling rig was erected here two years ago, and one had visions of a new industrial city being established one day in the East Surrey Weald. However, after a company had spent £2 million in sinking five exploratory wells in this area, the drilling rigs were removed, and nothing further has happened. Enough natural gas was discovered to supply a small town for at least six years, but apparently the company decided that it was not worth exploiting commercially. So the road to Outwood has relapsed into its erstwhile peace and seclusion, although whilst the concrete drilling pad inside its wire perimeter still remains it is a slightly uneasy peace.

Outwood lies midway between two important roads: the London to Brighton Road via Redhill and Horley, and the London to Eastbourne road via Godstone and East Grinstead. To those in the know, and who have the time to stand and stare, the by-road from Caterham, through Blechingley, Outwood, Turners Hill and Lindfield is a beautiful secondary route to Brighton—but I had better keep my peace or this route will soon become as crowded as the rest. Finding uncrowded by-roads is the game of the age—just as finding little-used footpaths was a generation ago. The Eastbourne Road follows the course of the more easterly of the two Roman roads through the Surrey Weald, the London-Brighton Way, or, as it is sometimes called, the London-Portslade Way. The old Roman road goes straight over Tilburstow Hill, passing the significantly named Stansted (Stanstreet) House, a name which gave an early clue to the existence of this road, and is joined by the modern road again just beyond South Godstone. It then runs along the course of the present road to a point beyond Blindley Heath, where it suddenly changes direction (Roman roads rarely change alignment on low ground) and heads straight for Brighton. Thus what is now the Eastbourne Road was in Roman times the Brighton Road. It is puzzling, as was mentioned earlier that the Romans did not utilize the Merstham Gap through the North Downs but chose the Godstone Gap instead—possibly they wanted to avoid the wet lands of the upper Mole and at the same time they wanted the road to serve the ironworks then in existence south of East Grinstead. It is remarkable that the existence of this road was not finally established until the 1930s, thanks to the persistence of one or two archaeologists, in particular Mr I. D. Margary and Major James Dunning. Mr Margary traced the courses of Roman roads through the Weald as assiduously as an ornithologist traces the course of migrating birds. His book *Roman Ways in the Weald* has justly been called "A classic work".

The road across Blindley Heath always rouses in me vague images of prizefighters, highwaymen and foul deeds. The road runs along a causeway that must surely be the original built, at goodness knows what cost in human effort, by the Romans. Past the little cricket field the road crosses the upper waters of the River Eden; but a greater contrast than that river's name and this benighted heath, called by Stevenson in 1808 "this foul pasture", it would be difficult to find.

Beyond Blindley Heath, near the appropriately named New Chapel, is one of Surrey's most unusual buildings—the Mormon Temple built in the years 1952–5. I and my family are among the diminishing number of non-Mormons who have seen the inside of this building. For this is a temple, and the Mormons invited visitors to inspect the building before it was dedicated on 7th September 1955—since that date only members of the Mormon faith have been able to enter the building. They wanted non-Mormons to see the inside because, as a young Mormon explained to me at the time, they did not want the public to think that because it was closed to non-Mormons there was anything mysterious or 'cranky' about what was going on inside. This temple is not a regular place of worship in the sense that a normal church is, but a particularly sacred place used for specially important ceremonial purposes, including the baptisms for the dead (the Mormons believe that the living can act as proxies obtaining the admission into the Kingdom of those who have died, hence the great interest taken by all Mormons in their ancestors). One of the unusual features of the interior of the temple was the space devoted to the filing of thousands of genealogical and other records. The interior is luxuriously furnished in polished wood of many kinds and deep pile carpets everywhere. The most outstanding memory I have is of the great baptismal font. Supported on the backs of twelve oxen representing the Twelve Tribes of Israel, and executed in shining metal, the huge font is equipped for total immersion and is placed in a deep glass-and-tile compartment. A miniature bridge provides access to the font, whilst the opposite wall is covered with a huge mural of the original baptism scene in the River Jordon. The Baptism Room is magnificent yet vaguely terrifying. The chromium-plating and glass, giving the place a near-clinical atmosphere, was reminiscent more of an operating theatre than of the traditional font in a village church. My 2-year-old son provided a much-needed touch of humanity when he said, in a very loud voice: "Look Mummy—Moos." Other rooms in the temple include the lecture theatres, equipped with tiered seats and fold-away cinema screens, and changing and robing rooms beautifully decorated and furnished—yet nowhere do I recall having seen a cross, an altar, or a Bible. This magnificent building, reputed to have cost £600,000, was paid for by the 15,000 or so active members of the Mormon Faith in Britain, the money being found by tithing. This is one lesson at least we have to learn from the tiny band of Mormons and their bright new temple at Lingfield. The grounds are beautifully maintained, and you are certain to hear an American accent if you mingle with the many visitors, who come to the site on any sunny afternoon.

The extreme south-east corner of the Surrey Weald is dominated by Lingfield, with over 7,000 people the largest village in Surrey (slightly larger than Cranleigh which is running it a close second). Lingfield has always been something of an enigma to me. It does not lie on the main Eastbourne Road but slightly off it, nor does it lie on an east-west road of any significance. Even the old Roman road, with its sudden change of direction, bypassed the village; and still today there is no 'A' road through Lingfield. The village indeed has a railway—but the station is half a mile away. There is no industry of any importance. Yet, despite this string of disadvantages, Lingfield has thrived and now has the air of a little town, with a racecourse of its own, many fine houses, and a growing residential 'suburb' at Dormansland near the railway a mile and a half away. The growth of the new Lingfield has not destroyed the beauty of the old. The precinct by the church (which is very large and has been called the 'Westminster Abbey of Surrey') is one of Surrey's loveliest groups of old timbered houses. I remember it particularly because I was once a member of a group of men visiting Lingfield to try to persuade them to start a Men's Society of their own there. We met in the old Star Inn, a nice touch—the church has acquired the old sixteenth-century inn and with it something of its air of conviviality. At Lindfield where the church has acquired an old public house in the main street, I believe the inn sign still hangs outside. Sometimes, of course, the boot is on the other foot, and at Capel the inn was at one time the vicarage! The other old building of note in Lingfield is the miniscule village 'cage' or lock-up which stands by an old oak by an old pond. Eric Parker, observant as usual, noted that the floor of the cage was higher by two steps than the ground outside and you had to throw your prisoner upstairs—a most perilous business: "It ought to have been built so that you could take him by the left leg and throw him downstairs like a Christian." The last prisoner occupied the cage in 1882, and it has subsequently been used as a museum specializing in 'village crime'!

From Lingfield a road ambles and rambles northwards, to Crowhurst and Tandridge. Crowhurst is a tiny hamlet with an old row of single-storey cottages, a church on a hill-top and a great yew tree said to be 11 yards in girth; a poor wizened old thing it is, trussed up in chains as if to prevent it rushing out and poisoning all the cattle in the neighbourhood; in every breeze it creaks and moans in protest. It is said to be 1,500 years old, but surely cannot last much longer thanks to the showman who hollowed out the interior a century or more ago and installed a table and chairs to seat a dozen people; the door he placed in the side of the tree is still there. Crowhurst is also renowned for its iron tombstone, the only one in Surrey. But the real jewel of Crowhurst lies half a mile or so to the south of the church—Crowhurst Place. Here is an incredibly beautiful moated Tudor mansion which can hardly have changed since Henry VIII used to stay here on his way to see Anne Boleyn at Hever Castle. It is unfortunate that the house lies out of view from the road down a private drive, and not everyone has an author's ready-made excuse for intruding on another's privacy.

Tandridge is a tiny village, altogether too small to have given its name to the whole Hundred, stretching from Farleigh in the north right down to the Surrey-Sussex border. Here indeed is a mystery. For Tandridge today has only a tiny huddle of cottages and a church and a road that wanders quietly to nowhere. However, there are one or two clues to the possibility that centuries ago Tandridge was a place of some importance. For instance, the road up from Lingfield follows the line of Tandridge Parish, an extraordinary-shaped area stretching ten miles long and in places only a quarter of a mile wide . . . and the parish in turn seems to be related to the ancient trackway that used to run southwards from Tandridge parallel with the old Roman road but on the east side of it. So Tandridge was once on a road that went somewhere! And there is another clue. On the lay-by off the Godstone to Oxted road a plinth has recently been erected bearing these words: "On this hill, the Hundred's knoll (known later as 'Undersnow'), the Saxon tythingmen from the surrounding villages of the Hundred of Tandridge met as the first local government and court in the Godstone Rural District." It would seem therefore that Tandridge was centrally placed, and in the days when transport was a major difficulty this was a great advantage. It must have been a strange collection of individuals, that group of parish councillors (the parishes in those days were called 'tithings') sitting on a knoll near Tandridge at the foot of the chalk escarpment, or perhaps in a barn of some kind. There is a touch of sympathy in the text on the plaque erected by the local authority, a kind of fellow-feeling. The Godstone Rural District Council are to be warmly commended for their initiative. Such local history markers as this are all too rare in this most historical of countries, whereas in the United States, whose history often begins when our history books virtually close, they are now very numerous and add greatly to the interest of a journey across the continent. Perhaps the problem here is precisely the super-abundance of places of historical significance; if every such place were identified hardly a yard of roadway would be without its historical marker. The solution may be, as in the United States, to place these markers in lay-bys, especially where road straightening has left cut-off loops of road here and there, so that the public have time and opportunity to read the inscription.

A few days ago, as I write, I was discussing the churches of Surrey with the Bishop of Southwark, the Right Reverend Mervyn Stockwood, when he recalled that a few months previously he was taking a service in Tandridge Church and suddenly he noticed something strange about the stained-glass window at the back of the church. It was a nativity scene, and gathered round the crib were the familiar figures, dressed in the eastern style, and in the centre was Joseph. He was dressed, like the others, in eastern robes, but to the Bishop's amazement he was raising a straw boater to the Holy Child. I could scarcely credit such an extraordinary anachronism, and as soon as I had the opportunity I went to see for myself. Lo and behold—there it was, just as the Bishop had said. It is a remarkable example of Victorian rustic obeisance defying all chronological logic! But Tandridge Church is worth going to see (if indeed you can see anything; as the Bishop had warned me, it is about the darkest church in Surrey) for other reasons than this. Like Newdigate Church it has magnificent thirteenth-century oak beams supporting the spire in typical lattice-work construction, and outside the church is another great yew, also reputed to be over 1,500 years old, and said to have existed even before there was a Christian church on the site. The evidence for this is that the foundations of the Saxon church on the site were so arranged as to avoid disturbing the roots of the tree.

We now recross the Outwood-Smallfield spur to the Brighton Road. Today the country below Redhill has become a long ribbon of industrial development beside the Redhill-Horley road. This is no territory in which to linger; yet just the other side of the railway is some lovely rural countryside. As you look out of the train

window on the east side you are deep in the Surrey Weald, but as
you look out of the other side you might as well be in London.
Only in one isolated spot does the tide of industrial development
flow across the railway, an exception which is the more regrettable as it diminishes the effectiveness of the railway embankment
as a breakwater. Overlooking the landscape on the eastern side are
one or two impressive mansions occupying commanding sites on
the south-facing slopes of the Greensand Ridge, which has been
called "the best sun-trap in England".

Dull though it now is in its course through the Surrey Weald,
the Brighton Road has seen some stirring times in the past. In 1823
William Cobbett noted that there were "hundreds of men and
horses constantly at work to make pleasant and quick travelling
for the Jews and jobbers". However, the hey-dey of the coach was
short-lived. In 1841 the London to Brighton Railway was opened
and the journey was being completed in one hour and forty-five
minutes for 4s. 6d. second class. Cheap transportation was at last
available to the masses. The coast was at London's back door. The
railway soon had such heavy traffic that the two level crossings
in Horley had become inconvenient and a bridge was built to
carry the Balcombe Road over the railway. Today 700 trains a
day pass through Horley, and about a third of them stop at
Horley Station. About 5,000 people use the station every day
either coming or going. Horley changed in a generation from a
tiny village occupying a clearing in the wood, and owned by the
now-insignificant village of Horne (hence its name), to a town.
The original village, like most of those lying on the Weald,
perched on a little 'island' of stone—in this case Horsham Stone,
surrounded on all sides by Wealden Clay. As the town grew, so it
had to spread onto the surrounding claylands—and onto the
ancient Horley Common. The area lacked landscape appeal, and
clay is seldom a popular subsoil for residential development because of drainage difficulties. And so Horley developed a late
Victorian rash of uninteresting and dull villas. Its fate, indeed, had
already been sealed a century or more before, when Dr Russell first
popularised sea bathing and Horley, instead of being an island lost
in the Weald, became a stopping place half way between London
and the sea. Like Lingfield, Horley once had a racecourse, but
when Gatwick airport was built and then enlarged to take the

larger aircraft coming into use, the racecourse was swallowed up
and so also was the old London to Brighton road. One of the
curiosities of Surrey is the old four-lane highway to Brighton just
beyond Horley which appears to be exactly as before except that
there are signs advising the motorist: "No Through Road." The
Brighton Road now does a wide loop right round the airport and
brings motorists to the combined rail/road terminal building, the
first of its kind in Britain. Today about 3,000,000 passengers use
the terminal annually. There is a spectators' enclosure on the roof
providing a magnificent view of aircraft coming and going.
It all seems very far away from the pre-war days when Gatwick
was used by aircraft little bigger than the Tiger Moth. The old
circular control tower can still be seen south of the new Terminal
Building: such is the pace of modern development that it was
obsolescent almost as soon as it was built. A fine medium-distance
view of Gatwick Airport can be had from the little-known Russ
Hill just south of Charlwood.

From the Air Age we pass in a trice to the time of King Alfred.
In the fourteenth century the whole of this district was known as
Thunderfield-in-the-Forest. Where is this place, 'Thunderfield',
that gave its name to so large an area? You will not find it on a
small scale map, for there is little to see now except the old moat—
but it lies about a mile east of Horley by the River Mole: this is
perhaps the oldest visible evidence of Man's handiwork in the
whole district, save for the remains of the old Roman road.
Thunderfield Castle dates probably from the time of King Alfred
and has been identified with the Dunresfield Castle mentioned in
King Alfred's will. The name, being derived from the Saxon God
of War, Thor, supports the identification.[1] But why was it built
and when was it destroyed? Here is an unsolved enigma, one of
the many that still draw people to interest themselves in local
history, and long may it remain so.

The River Mole's main purpose in life is to drain that area of the
Weald which lies between the Wey on the west and the Eden on
the east, and this task it completes in the first fifteen miles of its

[1] I recently came across a reference in one of Evelyn's letters (1675) which
suggests a possible alternative origin of the name: "In the cart-roads where the
rains have gullied is frequently found that kind of Pyrites which the country
people call 'Thunderstones'."

length. For the remainder of its forty-two miles the river has one compelling objective—to reach the Thames. But first it has to negotiate the North Downs. As it flows northwards through the Surrey Weald it gathers together its many tributaries—the Stanford Brook, the Deanoak Brook, the Gad Brook and the Tanners Brook—as if girding its loins for the supreme effort of negotiating the awesome bluff of the North Downs.

West of the Brighton Road lies one of the main iron-working areas of the Surrey Weald, and buried among the woods and copses that are all that remain of one-time forests of this still-remote and forgotten corner of the county are the three fascinating villages of Charlwood, Newdigate and Leigh. The whole area is criss-crossed with lanes that wander aimlessly between the villages, shadow-boxing with obstacles that have long since disappeared. Although very few of the churches in the Weald were mentioned in the Domesday Book, that at Charlwood was not only mentioned but was built of stone—a rare distinction at that time. Possibly its importance lay in its association with the iron industry. It was thought at one time (and many books on Surrey still repeat this assertion) that iron working in the Surrey Weald began in the sixteenth century, but a court case dated 1371 shows that iron was worked here much earlier than that. A certain John Neel was fined for digging up the highway and removing loads of earth at a spot near Hookwood, just east of Charlwood; but he claimed that it was only a path over a certain waste parcel "in which was a mine of iron". It is also perhaps significant that in 1936 an old iron bloomery site, with fragments of pottery of the fourteenth and fifteenth centuries, was found at Thunderfield Castle, whilst an iron cannon ball, about the size of an orange, was found in a nearby garden. Thus the iron industry in the Surrey Weald must date at least from the fourteenth century, and almost certainly earlier still. Charlwood Church, apart from being one of the earliest stone churches in the district, has another distinction. In 1858 the Reverend Thomas Burningham discovered that there were murals on the south wall of the church. These were carefully uncovered and revealed a series of paintings depicting the history of St Margaret. They have again been renovated in recent years and in my opinion are far superior in execution to those of Chaldon Church. The Charlwood horses in particular are most graceful

animals, and about as far from the crude demons of Chaldon as
one could imagine; the subject matter, also, is more attractive than
the hell-fire and brimstone of Chaldon. Charlwood, indeed, is not
a hell-fire and brimstone sort of place—rather it has a friendly and
genial air. A lively sense of the past pervades every corner of this
charming village, and its fascinating history has been recorded in
detail in one of the best books of local history in Surrey, Ruth
Sewill's and Elizabeth Lane's *The Free Men of Charlwood*. No one
dare be patronizing about the Women's Institute if they can
produce local historians of this calibre!

Newdigate lies deep in the Weald and, like the other two villages, is never seen *en passant*; you are unlikely to see this village
*en route* to another place, you have to be headed in that direction
to see it. To this fact perhaps we owe the village's remarkable
state of preservation and the absence of disfiguring modern
development. The whole parish of 4,732 acres lies on thick
Wealden clay which so discolours the waters of the Mole that it is
surprising no one has coined the phrase the 'murky Mole'. But the
Mole gets her own back occasionally by flooding, despite the fact
that the river is usually flowing in a deeply incised valley. A
pleasant tradition says that the name of the village is derived from
the words '*En eau de gat*' or 'by watery roads', but, since an old
spelling of the village is Newoodigate, it is more likely that the
true origin is 'on Ewood gate', that is, on the road to Ewood, a
neighbouring hamlet where the ironworks were situated. We
tend to forget in this macadamized age how difficult the roads
must have been in past centuries; an old record relating to the
roads around Horley speaks of "ruts four feet deep and a long line
of carts broken down". It has indeed been suggested by some
authorities, with half a tongue in cheek, that one of the reasons
why these three iron villages were specifically excluded from
restrictions on timber cutting in Elizabethan ordinances, was that
the roads were so bad that even if the trees were cut down they
couldn't be transported anywhere! The turnpikes led to some
improvement in the main roads, but they left the side roads unim-
proved—indeed the extra traffic churned them up even more.
When a local paper conducted a series of interviews among residents of these three villages some years ago they asked the oldest
inhabitants what the most significant changes had been, and the

most often quoted comment was the improvement in the roads. Many recollected the terrible state of the country lanes in their childhood days; the mud in winter and the rough flints in summer. At Charlwood and Crowhurst there are stone causeways, or 'causies', laid to facilitate movement over the wet clay during the winter. The one at Crowhurst stretches a mile, from the church to Crowhurst Place, and was built in 1631 by John Gainsford, who decided, at the age of 76, that he would walk in the wet to church no more; so he built a stone-flagged causeway, the previous path having been, as the parish registers inform us, "a loathsom durtie way every stepp".

The pride of Newdigate, which is reflected in the excellent way in which it is maintained, is the lovely twelfth-century church of St Peter. It has long been known as the 'Hunter's Church' because it is believed to have been built originally by the Earl of Warenne, who owned most of the land around here, for the use of the lords and knights whilst out hunting deer in the forest. It stands on a hill, a vital landmark in the wooded country of the Weald, and has a timber tower of open lattice timber construction, the beams seeming altogether too massive for the tower's modest proportions.

Just north of Newdigate is Iwood, or Ewood, where was situated in 1575 a flourishing ironworks occupied by one Robert Reynolds. He lived in the mansion house, and, in addition to the ironworks, furnace forge and hammer, he also owned a water mill for grinding corn and a brewhouse—no doubt ironmaking was hot work! When an Act was passed in 1558 to prevent the excessive felling of timber, Newdigate was among the parishes exempted, and one of the reasons, apart from that mentioned above, is said to have been that the woods in this area were well managed and coppiced. Another, and probably more likely explanation, is that the furnace at Ewood had come into the ownership of the Crown in settlement of a debt. A later Act also exempted Newdigate for similar reasons. However the iron industry eventually died out, and with it went much of the district's prosperity. The old hammer pond at Ewood fell into disuse and was eventually drained in 1860. The mid-nineteenth century was a difficult period for this forgotten corner of Surrey. Men earned about 10s. per week, children left school at 12 or before, and the fees at Newdigate School were 2d. per week. No wonder the rector noted in the parish records: "the people of the parish are desperately poor." We are perhaps prone to overlook the hardship and poverty that so often lay behind the attractive cottage exterior on the village green. Not, of course, that poverty of possessions can always be equated with poverty of spirit—often it is very much the reverse. But once isolation has been broken down and the young people see other ways of life, material poverty can breed a resentful spirit and a breakdown of moral fibre. Fortunately, Newdigate is not just a picture-book village living only on its past associations. It has some modern industry, including the Schermuly Pistol Rocket factory (for which remoteness is a positive virtue) located at Parkgate near the old iron works, as well as aquatic nurseries at Beam Brook (for which the surface water is a positive virtue), and both of these take their place, along with agriculture, in utilizing local resources. It also has a fine modern school where the fees are even less than 2d. per week— they are nothing—and where Newdigate mothers wait outside in their gleaming new sports cars to collect their children.

The third of the forest villages of the Upper Mole is Leigh, or rather 'Lye' as it should be pronounced and as it was spelt in a deed of 1530. This form of pronunciation is said to be unusual, but 'Ardingly' is pronounced the same way; it means simply a clearing in the forest, and appears again in Cranleigh and Horley. The 1530 deed records the sale of Leigh Place Estate to Edward Shelley, an ancestor of the poet Percy Bysshe Shelley. Like many other Wealden houses, Leigh Place, reputed to date from the twelfth century, has a moat in which have been found from time to time a varied collection of curios, including coins, cannon balls, and a seventeenth-century silver porringer. The building's curious windows and turrets were added in an early nineteenth-century renovation, the whole effect, however, is one of great tranquillity and charm.

As for the village of Leigh it is one of the prettiest in Surrey, with several timbered and tile-hung cottages, so typical of the county, clustered round the village green. Many of them, like other Wealden cottages, have roses in abundance trailing over them, for there is no finer place in the whole country for the cultivation of roses. Some of the buildings in Leigh, like the half-timbered structure known as the 'Priest's House' and the church of St Bartholomew, also have the characteristic Horsham Slab stone roofs, which seem over the centuries to have coalesced into one great slab of stone. Only the stout Wealden oaks could be relied upon to support the tremendous weight of such a roof. As one would expect of a Wealden church, the woodwork of St Bartholomew's is of excellent quality, and the church has a fine shingled broach spire dating from 1890, a rare heritage of beauty from that architecturally barren period. Like its two sister villages, Leigh possessed its own ironworks. This was situated on eight acres of land called Burgett and Grove Lands, a lease of which had been obtained in 1551 by George and Christopher Darrell, iron-masters. The trees were felled rapidly, and by 1635 a court case refers to the great oak and beech woods that had 'formerly' existed at Shellwood, Westwood, Leigh Green and Dawes Green. Where the tenants had once fed their swine among the trees ('pannage', as it was called in Domesday) they were now pasturing cattle. This had happened despite the fact that Leigh, along with Charlwood and Newdigate, had been exempted from the Eliza-bethan restrictions on tree felling because of its 'well-managed' woodlands. It was from this period that the Weald changed from a forest with grassy clearings, to a pasture with scattered coppices and woods; but still the roads wander from village to village as if trying to find their way through the inpenetrable forest. There is indeed much about the Weald that is only explicable if one can see what was, rather than what is—and there is no part of the Weald of which this is more true than the East Surrey Weald from Leigh to Lingfield.

# 18

# LEITH HILL, LITTLE SWITZERLAND AND OCKLEY

If Box Hill is the queen of the North Downs, then Leith Hill is her consort. Leith Hill, as befits a consort, tends to take a less prominent position, is less easy of access, is deferentially swathed in bracken and common trees rather than the unique box, and is considerably taller. Whereas Box Hill is so typically a product of the chalk country, which represents a large part of southern England, Leith Hill is a product of the much less widely distributed Lower Greensand country, with its pinewoods and thick undergrowth, its magnificent rhododendrons and its less dramatic escarpment. Leith Hill is the highest point in the south of England, and it is traditional to repeat Evelyn's famous assertion in his diary that "from it may be discerned twelve or thirteen counties on a serene day". I must confess that I have never achieved this feat, although I have seen St Paul's Cathedral, and I have seen the sun glistening on the sea through the gap in the South Downs, and these are reward enough for the climb.

Leith Hill is the Jungfrau of what is often called 'Little Switzerland', a range of hills stretching from Blackheath near Albury, through Pitch Hill and Holmbury Hill to Anstiebury in the east, and which the geologists have rather picturesquely christened 'The Hungry Greensand' to distinguish it from the more fertile Greensand country immediately to the north in the Vale of Holmesdale. Infertile it may be, but this beautiful countryside has satisfied a deep spiritual hunger in countless numbers of people, for many of whom it represents some of the finest walking country south of London. "Be sure you give plenty of space to the Leith Hill area," said my wife when we were discussing progress on the book, and I knew she was reflecting a widespread affection for a

*St Bartholomew's Church, Leigh*

piece of countryside that Matthew Arnold once described as "inexhaustible in beauty".

Even without its tower, Leith Hill would still be a fine viewpoint and natural feature; yet there is no denying that it would lose something. Let no one say that a landscape untouched by man is necessarily better than one that carries his signature. The tower makes the hill personal to us in a special way, just as the symmetrical clump of trees on Chanctonbury Ring (where Man and Nature have joined forces) does on the other side of the Weald. I took a group of children to Leith Hill a few years ago, and after tea at the hotel just at the foot of the Hill we all scrambled up the steep side of the escarpment to the tower and then up the staircase to the viewing platform at the top. Watching the children's excited faces, I was taken back in a flash to the day before the war when I first stood on this spot listening to our guide telling the story of the tower. How it came to be built by Squire Richard Hull of Leith Hill Place in 1766 to provide a panoramic view over the Weald (and—who knows? to satisfy a whim to own a mountain? For I believe that hills over 1,000 feet high are technically called mountains); how he died six years later and, to the scandalization of the neighbourhood, was buried, according to the terms of his will, underneath the tower (where it is said they pitched his body in head first muttering: "Why didn't he want to be buried like a Christian?"); how the local people avoided the tower after this and left it to the smugglers who abounded in the district; how in 1864 the tower was re-opened and refurbished, and thenceforth became the landmark and popular visiting place it is today. I listened with more than ordinary interest because Dr Hull, a distant relative of the Squire of Leith Hill Place, was the churchwarden of our parish church at Streatham where we lived at the time. I can remember now how Dr Hull would stride up and down the aisle directing people to their seats, with his arms folded neatly behind his back—a touch perhaps of his ancestor's eccentricity.

Like the tower itself, Leith Hill Place has played a key part in the history of Little Switzerland—or rather its owners have. What men they were! After the Hulls came the Wedgwoods. In 1847 Josiah Wedgwood, a descendant of the founder of the pottery firm, bought the mansion and gave up active participation in the family pottery business to potter contentedly in the gardens and

14

*The water mill, Elstead*

environs of Leith Hill Place. Not that he was allowed much peace to potter, for he had married the sister of Charles Darwin, and the celebrated scientist was constantly demanding the co-operation of his family in various experiments. In one of these the worm casts found on a measured piece of ground had to be collected, dried and weighed, over the course of a whole year; this showed that the earthworms of Leith Hill Place ejected about $7\frac{1}{2}$ tons of earth per acre per annum—but what earthly use this piece of information is I do not know. It was through the Wedgwoods that another great family came to Leith Hill Place—the Vaughan Williams. A daughter of Josiah Wedgwood married the Reverend A. Vaughan Williams, and after his death in 1878 she lived at Leith Hill Place until she died in 1937 at the age of 94. Her elder son, Hervey, lived there until his death in 1944, when the Vaughan Williams family handed the property to the National Trust. After so long an association with the Wedgwoods it is fitting to record that the house still contains many beautiful examples of Wedgwood ware, including some valuable Blue Jasper, and these are on display for the enjoyment of visitors who come to look over the house.

However we associate Little Switzerland not so much with people as with the landscape. Little Switzerland is walking country *par excellence*. There are few fences or hedges and many footpaths; a high proportion of the area is common land and much of it is owned by the National Trust. There is such a plethora of paths that it is very easy to lose one's way; more than once I have been hopelessly lost at Leith Hill, there are so many sudden changes in topography vegetation and relief (I once saw the area described aptly as "a nest of valleys") that even the short walk from Leith Hill to Friday Street can take the best part of an afternoon. But map and compass are forgotten as you swing at last down the lane into Friday Street, the scent of woodsmoke in the nostrils, and the anticipation of toasted teacakes reviving the flagging spirits. This is Friday Street as I prefer to think of it, although to most people it is no doubt looking for a space to park round the lake, or a frustrating search for an empty lay-by along narrow lanes never intended for such heavy traffic.

Walking across Leith Hill was not such a pleasant experience during the war. I remember trying to negotiate the many obstructions, such as 'W.O. Keep Out' notices, backed up by the copious use of barbed wire, whilst the tower itself was bolted and barred and blazoned with signs declaring, "Danger. Land Mines. Keep Off." The whole area was taken over by the army, and the woods provided convenient camouflage for huge ammunition dumps. Our family has sad cause to remember these. My wife's uncle was a scientist at the Abinger offshoot of the Royal Observatory at the time, and one terrible night in May 1942 some of the ammunition dumps exploded causing great havoc and danger to the people of Abinger, all of whom had to be evacuated for a time. He has sent me this graphic description of the incident:

A heavy explosion scattered burning debris amongst surrounding ammunition, causing the fire to spread. The whole dump became involved with several heavy explosions and a continuous barrage of small ones, over a period of several hours. Corrugated-iron ammunition cupolas rocketed high into the sky, shells whistled through the air and away into the distance, and windows were broken as far away as Dorking shops.

Although, surprisingly, no one was hurt at the time, my wife's aunt was in pregnancy when the explosions occurred, and the shock of the whole experience brought on a premature birth which caused her death. Thus tragedy lurked, even at such a place as Leith Hill—and the irony is that the rest of the family all thought they were perfectly safe in such a remote spot. The enemy also left his mark even here, however, for in 1944 a flying bomb destroyed the parish church of St James, Abinger; it was rebuilt in 1951 in its original style.

It was the isolation of the Abinger area that led to its being chosen in 1924 as the location for the small but important branch of the Royal Observatory responsible for carrying out magnetic observations. Somewhere had to be found reasonably close to London, yet removed as far as possible from railway lines that could upset the delicate magnetic readings that the observatory was mainly established to record. For fifteen years, from 1940 to 1955 when the task was transferred to Herstmonceux, the six 'pips' of Greenwich time signal came from Abinger. Eventually even Abinger was found to be too near London and in 1957 the observatory was moved to a spot near Hartland in North Devon;

we quite frequently visit our relations there, and a wild and remote spot it is too.

But enough of ordnance and observatories! These are essentially foreign to the quiet spirit of Leith Hill, which belongs more naturally to Charles Darwin and his patient observation of the earthworms. We have visited Friday Street, but there are other lovely villages and hamlets in the area. Like Coldharbour, for instance, clinging to the steep escarpment below Leith Hill, big enough for a church, a pub, a cricket pitch (the highest in Surrey), but not much else. Like all the villages of Little Switzerland, Coldharbour was up to its neck in smuggling. Mr W. H. Chouler, an authority on the Leith Hill area, reports Mr Hervey Vaughan Williams as saying that he could remember as a boy speaking to a very old man in the village who could himself recall as a boy being awakened in the middle of the night to hold open a gate to let a train of smugglers through. When the local people happened to discover some contraband hidden by the smugglers (sometimes in a hole dug in the soft Leith Hill sand) their custom was to place a chalk cross on a few of the items and when the smugglers returned they would leave these items as a thanks offering for the discovery not being reported. Even Leith Hill Place itself was probably used by the smugglers, since the workmen installing electric light there some years ago discovered a cunningly concealed hiding place. Holmwood and Holmbury St Mary were also deeply involved in smuggling, but the three villages were like the three wise monkeys—they heard nothing, saw nothing and said nothing.

The wild country of Little Switzerland attracted other wild characters in addition to the smugglers. Holmwood Common was for centuries the refuge of homeless and lawless men, and was a favourite haunt of highwaymen, whilst sheep stealing and poaching were almost a staple industry over the whole area and provided a steady flow of recruits for the local gibbets, like the one at the top of the hill above Shere. As late as 1805 the roads around Dorking were so frequented by highwaymen that a wholesale greengrocers' cart journeying from Horsham to London had protection from a man armed with a blunderbuss who sat at the back of the cart. Gypsies also added a colourful and dubious element to the local population. But perhaps the most colourful of all were the 'broom squires', those odd characters who ostensibly made a living by collecting the broom on the local commons and selling it, but who made more on the side than they did in the centre; Baring-Gould has captured something of their wild character in his book *Broom Squire*.

It was only with the establishment of rural police, the building of better and more open roads and, above all, the increase in population in the area, that the lawless elements in the community began to disappear and in their place came people from the opposite extreme of society—affluent city folk. They built their fine houses among the woods and heaths of Little Switzerland, and in a generation or two the whole district changed character. The affluent few were followed soon afterwards by the less affluent walkers, hikers and cyclists, led by such dedicated guides as Walker Miles (in whose memory the direction indicator on Leith Hill Tower was donated) and S. P. B. Mais. Where are the rambling and cycling clubs today? Before the war it was a common sight to see the cycling clubs heading for the countryside in the morning, perhaps seventy of them at a time, riding two abreast, and then returning in the evening with huge limp bundles of bluebells lying across their saddlebags. Where are they now? Perhaps the young people are riding minis instead—but at least the bluebells are left in peace.

The hills of Little Switzerland were natural fortresses, and in times gone by they were fortified and used as places of refuge when necessary. Stone querns used for grinding corn have been discovered at Hascombe Camp and Holmbury Camp dating from 150 B.C. to the fifth century A.D. A curious legacy of this one-time role of the hilltops was their division among the various parishes in the district. Wotton, Ockley and other local parishes, some even as far away as Ockham, possessed small outlying portions of land round Holmbury until 1879, when the boundaries were revised, and the explanation is almost certainly that these represented 'bolt holes' to which the people could flee in the event of serious danger in far-off days.

If you stand on Leith Hill and look across the Weald it seems to comprise one vast forest, almost as it must have looked 2,000 years ago. This is, of course, an illusion, and it is due to the preservation of so many narrow strips of woodland or 'shaws' between the fields and villages, and because in the Weald there are so many oaks and other mature trees in the hedgerows. One geographer has painstakingly worked out that only 12 per cent of the surface area of the Weald Clay in Surrey is in fact covered with trees. However, this is a substantial proportion, and anyone who knows the Weald could not have been surprised a few years ago when a puma was reported to be roaming about the district—search parties were formed but the animal was never caught.

Cutting right across this difficult country, and heading for the gap in the chalk downs at Dorking, is Stane Street, the most important of the Roman roads in Surrey. There is no missing Stane Street because, unlike so many of the Roman roads in the Weald, it is still used as a road over much of its length, and a dead straight road is such a rarity in the Weald that it stands out like a sore thumb. I have always been particularly fascinated by the stretch of Stane Street that runs through Ockley (where it is called simply Stone Street or, at one time, Brandy and Silk Street because of the activities of the smugglers). The road runs dead straight for about three miles, pointing towards Holmwood, and then the modern road veers away suddenly to the east, leaving the Roman road to continue across country as a cart-track. I always wanted as a child to get out of the car at that spot and to follow the road across the fields, fondly imagining that I had only to disturb a little topsoil to unearth a Roman coin or vase. No doubt, I would have been very disappointed. The Surrey Archaeological Society have recognized the tremendous interest people have in the Roman roads by uncovering about 120 feet of Stane Street in Redlands Wood near Holmwood and restoring it to its original condition.

Ockley is one of the most beautiful and intriguing villages in the Surrey Weald. Like most of them, it has a wide village green, the widest in fact of any village in Surrey, a well which at Ockley is covered by a very attractive stone-pillared canopy rather like that at Cranleigh, and magnificent views of Leith Hill and the Lower Greensand escarpment away to the north. But it is the spacious green that is the dominating feature of Ockley—it is big enough to be a battlefield, which is exactly what history says it was. The Battle of Ockley took place in the year A.D. 851 and was fought between the invading Danes marching westwards from Canterbury towards the heartland of southern England and the West Saxons under King Ethelwulf who were advancing up Stane Street to head them off. According to the *Anglo-Saxon Chronicle* the Danes were soundly defeated, and by sunset there were none of the enemy left on the battlefield to bury their numerous dead. That is the bare record of history. But did it really happen here? Historians seem to be uncertain. The *Chronicle* gives the location of the battle as "At Aclea among the Suthridge". It is true that Ockley was known by this name in the ninth and tenth centuries, but there were also other villages in Surrey with this name. There are some people who suggest that the battle took place near Leith Hill, and this indeed would seem a more likely location to me than the flat featureless forest of the Weald. In the meantime the Old Schoolhouse Restaurant at Ockley gives its clients not only a superb meal but also a little map showing crossed cutlasses at Ockley Green (and the date A.D. 852 which seems to be at conflict with the *Chronicle*), and I for one hope that it will continue to do both for a long time yet.

We are now in the border country between Surrey and Sussex, a country of extensive woods, lakes and streams, the latter flowing, like the stream through Ockley village, southwards to join the Arun. In Tudor times this was one of the great sporting preserves of England, and much of it still is. Some time ago I tried to get to Vachery Pond but found my way barred by large warning notices declaring that the area was a game reserve and that entry was forbidden under the Armed Trespass Act, and ending with the decidedly unpleasant peremptory order: "So Keep Off". Surely it is possible to inform the public that an area is a game reserve without using the language of an Irish absentee landlord to his rebellious tenantry! Seeing this notice put me in mind of the old limerick:

> Here lies the body of William Day
> Who died asserting his right of way,
> He was right, dead right, as he strolled along
> But he's just as dead as if he'd been wrong.

Back in Tudor times the king himself would often go hunting in his Royal Deer Forest here, and, in addition to the deer, there would be some wild boar and wild cats (Cobbett himself records having seen a wild cat near Farnham in the eighteenth century) to provide occasional sport and an element of danger. One Edward de la Hale gave an endowment to Okewood Chapel in the middle of the Royal Deer Forest because, so legend says, his son was providentially saved from being mauled by a wild boar. Few people lived in this wild and remote district, but the huntsmen would occasionally meet a gang of woodcutters busy in the woods. They were rough illiterate men who probably showed signs of their prolonged absence from 'civilization'; perhaps the rich seigneurs had a twinge of conscience. At any rate they built a chapel at Okewood, deep in the forest, primarily for the use of these men, but also, like those of Charlwood and Newdigate, for their own use whilst out hunting. That was in 1290, and there it stands still "embosomed in a wooded ghyll and shut off from the world by a mass of oak trees and undergrowth". I was there one frosty Boxing Day morning, when there wasn't another soul around, and to my amazement the little church was beautifully warm and gaily decorated with holly, and from the noticeboard I saw that there were several services being held over Christmas. It delighted me that this wonderful old church had not survived merely as a museum of the past but still had a vigorous life of its own. If Ockley claims to be the loneliest village in Surrey (because its bus services to other villages and towns are so poor—being on the main A29 it is not isolated in any other sense) then Okewood Church must without doubt be the loneliest church in the county. Soon it will inevitably be 'discovered', and they will have to build a car park and make space to turn the cars round at the bottom of the gill. I for one hope they will put the car park in the woods out of sight of the church and forbid cars to pass except at the times of services—let other visitors walk the last few hundred yards and so ensure that Okewood Church remains, in the words of a former Vicar there: "one of the most unique and certainly one of the most attractive churches in the British Isles".

In my hurry to get to Ockley I have neglected its neighbour on the eastern side (and nearer in fact to Ockley station than Ockley itself is)—the village of Capel. Instead of turning off the Dorking–Worthing Road at Beare Green we continue straight ahead. As for Beare Green, it is a hamlet, clustered round a lovely cricket green, which has been ruined beyond repair by one of the worst examples of Victorian rural vandalism in Surrey—a line of ugly dolls' houses, each identical with its neighbour and equidistant from it, a deadly symmetry in a setting that demands irregularity of shape and design and some attempt at least to capture the informality of any typical village whose buildings span the centuries. These houses might conceivably belong to a town, but to a village never! I understand they are planning to build another 350 houses there, with schools, shops and a church. It is the best thing they can do, and I will not shed a tear—only I hope they don't build another 350 dolls' houses equidistantly spaced!

Capel, like so many Surrey villages, is a victim of the motor car. One octogenarian villager a few years ago was reported in the local paper as saying that she could remember as a school girl playing marbles in the main road on her way to school. The road was then made of rough flints and the children wore heavy nailed boots. Today if you played marbles on the A24 you would quickly earn yourself a marble headstone. Just crossing the road today is difficult enough, especially on a Sunday. Mrs Hooker, the octogenarian lady, recalled that on Sundays the road used to be so quiet that if any vehicle came along the villagers would rush out to see what it was. It raised so much dust that its arrival and departure could hardly pass unnoticed in any event—in this respect at least perhaps we have made some progress!

Capel is something of a musical village. Not only has it a choral society of its own—which was one of the founder members of the Leith Hill Festival back in 1905 and has won many musical honours since then—but it has connections with two leading families in the musical world. These are the Bax family, at one time famous for their clandestine Quaker membership and their associations with George Fox, and from whom Sir Arnold Bax, Master of the Queen's Music was descended, and the Broadwoods of Lyne House, the well-known manufacturers of pianos who still own much of Capel and its surroundings.

Most Surrey villages have their crop of stories and legends, and Capel is no exception. I like particularly the one attached to Smith's Charity. Smith was an alderman who would go about the countryside dressed as a tramp and a gypsy, and he would mete out his charitable giving according to the measure of charity he himself received. Thus if a village received him kindly he left an annual gift of bread for the poor, but if he was whipped from the place his gift was a whip. Capel's charity was bread (now changed to fuel which is more needed by the poor than bread); but Charlwood's (uncharacteristically I feel) was a whip! Another Capel story centres on the churchyard—or rather on an old yew which stands by the entrance to it. It is said that if you walk round the tree one hundred times at midnight a ghost will appear. Perhaps it will be the ghost of one "Alce Clark" whose grave lies a few feet away, its headstone adorned with the skull and crossbones. Was it a female smuggler's grave (the 'i' being omitted in error) and does her ghost walk out of irritation at the inaccuracy? There are many old nooks and crannys around Capel and a sprinkling of the old timbered houses so characteristic of the Weald, houses that have been there so long that the very timbers seem to have taken root. At Temple Elfold, whose name commemorates its association with the Knights Templars, may be seen in a wall some ancient 'bee boles' which are very rare in England. Another interesting reminder of the monastic origins of this estate is the rectangular pond in the garden—a common feature of monastic properties. It is the discovery of such rare survivals of the past, in hidden-away corners of the Surrey Weald, that makes it for many people the most exciting part of the county still left to explore.

# 19

# CRANLEIGH, AND THE FOLD COUNTRY

Of all the winding Wealden ways the road from Ockley to Cranleigh via Ewhurst is surely the most contorted. It probably owes this characteristic to the depth of the clay hereabouts. Cobbett travelled along this road, in the reverse direction, and he wrote that the first three miles from Ewhurst:

> was the deepest clay that ever I saw, to the best of my recollection. I was warned of the difficulty of getting along, but I was not to be frightened at the sound of clay. Wagons, too, had been dragged along the lanes by some means or another; and where a wagon could go my horse could go. It took me, however, a good hour and a half to get along these three miles. Now mind this is the real Weald where the clay is bottomless; where there is no stone of any sort underneath.

Today the surface is excellent, but you still follow the contortions that generations of travellers took in trying to find a sure footing in the 'bottomless' clay. You arrive at Cranleigh robbed of all sense of direction—but the richer for having passed through two attractive and contrasting villages, Forest Green and Ewhurst.

Forest Green is not only geographically in the centre of the Surrey Weald, but it typifies the Wealden forest village better than any other. After passing through many shaws and copses *en route* you suddenly light upon this broad clearing in the forest, with its old-world inn 'The Parrot' (even prettier at night when festooned with coloured lights than during the day), the houses of many varying shapes and ages clustered round the green and its cricket pitch. I went there on the same Boxing Day morning as I had visited Okewood Church, a frosty sunny morning following a light fall of snow. We had come especially to see the Christmas meeting of the Surrey Union Hunt, and it seemed that the inhabitants of all the villages for miles around had come with the same idea. It was a perfect Christmas-card scene. The huntsmen in their red coats were sitting astride their horses whilst the hunt servants carried round steaming hot mince pies and glasses of whisky, while the other riders in black riding habits and bowlers kept a respectful distance.

Then the Master of Foxhounds arrived, with his pack weaving and scurrying at his horse's heels. Forest Green, for one day in 365, was suddenly a metropolis of milling crowds. Then came the sound of the horn, the cry, "Hunt's On", and the hounds went streaking off towards Leith Hill with the riders in hot pursuit, including the little girl who took a fall before she had gone a hundred yards but bravely remounted at once. It might have been a cameo of England a century ago—were it not for the traffic jam of cars blocking the road in each direction for half a mile. I was so caught up with the animation of the whole proceedings that I almost forgot my innate dislike of blood sports. I only wish we could have the hunt without the fox or the pursuit without the kill.

For the other 364 days of the year it is a wonderfully quiet and peaceful place, is Forest Green. When the match is over the first lights begin appearing around the green the players walk across to 'The Parrot' and the whole place is still. In and around this village centuries ago was sung a folk song that had a lovely melody: today we know it as the carol "O Little Town of Bethlehem", and it is attributed to Forest Green in the hymn books. The words seem to fit the village as well as the tune fits the words, and now whenever I pass through the village, as I do quite frequently, I am humming to myself "O little town of Forest Green, How still we see thee lie . . .".

So I hum my way to Ewhurst, another quaint little village, but without a village green (this is at Ewhurst Green a little further south). It has a most attractive church, and a pleasing air of detachment which may survive a little longer despite its proximity to Cranleigh.

Cranleigh vies with Lingfield not only for the title of the largest village in Surrey but for my personal title of the most enigmatic of Surrey villages. On a mere 'B' road, with no industry to speak of, about ten miles from the nearest convenient commuter station at Guildford, and surrounded by farming country of rather low fertility and many woodlands and commons, Cranleigh has grown rapidly in recent years and is approaching its planned population of 11,000, thanks to new housing developments like that at Park Mead. Cranleigh has not even attained the dignity of being a Rural District Council but is part of the huge administrative district of Hambledon Rural District Council covering over 100 square miles and with its offices in Guildford, outside its own area. Yet despite all this, when you enter Cranleigh you feel at once that this is a place of some consequence; you take in the tree-lined main street with its fine new shopping and pedestrian precinct (surely the most successful blend of traditional and modern architecture in Surrey today), its cinema, its magnificent public school, its cricket green—even its gasholder—and you know you are in a community whose achievement of Urban District Council cannot be long delayed.

I ascribe Cranleigh's progress to two factors. Its geographical position, unpromising as it may seem at first sight, gives Cranleigh some important benefits. It lies near the Bramley branch of the River Wey, and when the Wey-Arun Canal was built the village gained from its proximity to it. Then when the railway from Guildford to Horsham was built in 1865 Cranleigh was the main station *en route* and benefited a great deal as a result. The line was closed a few years ago by Dr Beeching (and the station site was put to good use as part of the new shopping precinct mentioned earlier), but this has not made a great difference since the services in recent years were not very frequent and most people travelled by car to Guildford. The village is about ten miles from the three nearest towns, Guildford, Dorking and Horsham, and it is thus well placed to serve as a regional centre for its own surrounding district—it is significant that Cranleigh was the first place in Britain to have its own village hospital (in 1859). The other factor, supplementing the advantages of geography, concerns the people rather than the place. For you don't have to be long in Cranleigh to realize that there is an extraordinarily well-developed community spirit in the town. Despite its lack of official civic status Cranleigh has its own Chamber of Trade that publishes a Guide to

Cranleigh as good as, if not better than, most of those produced by much larger and more affluent communities. Even the Hambledon Rural District possesses no Guide to the Rural District and makes do with a map and a page of text on the back. The community spirit expresses itself in many ways, in the cricket pitch on Cranleigh Common; in the magnificent new swimming pool now being built; in the attitude of the energetic and much-loved Rector of Cranleigh, who told me, "It often worries me that I can now walk along the High Street and see people whom I do not recognize," (and he has a parish of about 10,000 people!); and in the regular 'Welcome to Cranleigh' evenings arranged for new-comers; but it owes its survival, above all, simply to the fact that Cranleigh has not yet outgrown its village closeness. To quote Cranleigh Guide: "Although Cranleigh has grown so much, and is growing faster every year, it is still miraculously a village." When Frank Swinnerton, who has lived in a lovely old cottage by Cranleigh Green for many years, published his recent book, *Reflections from a Village* he apparently had no hesitation in choosing that title. It is true that he calls his closing chapter "Passing of a Village", but one notices that he himself remains to the end a true Cranleigh man, and continues, in the face of all the evidence, to talk of "our village". I have lived in two Surrey villages that have become towns, Banstead and Caterham Valley, and in each case some attempt has been made to retain the title 'village', but if it is used it is always in a faintly self-conscious manner. At Cranleigh everyone still talks of the 'village', and never the 'town'.

The tall crane perched atop the fountain in Cranleigh's High Street gives the clue to the name of the village. The name Cranley (when the railway came to the village in 1865 the spelling was changed to avoid confusion with Crawley) was derived from the craneries situated at Baynards and Vachery. As we have already seen, this part of the Weald was one of the king's favourite hunt-ing grounds in Tudor times and before, and the cranes were bred for the royal palate; it is said that William Rufus once objected because a crane had been set before him half cooked. The great lake at Vachery is still one of the largest (and most difficult to locate—I once motored all round it trying to catch a glimpse, but in vain) in Surrey, and it provided the water needed to maintain the water level in the Wey-Arun Canal in the early nineteenth century.

The rest of Cranleigh's history is very much a replica of that for other Wealden villages; the setting up of an iron furnace during Surrey's second 'Iron Age'; the building of the turnpike road in 1794 which is commemorated by a tall obelisk in the village showing the mileage to Windsor in one direction and to Brighton in the other (a reminder that the turnpike was built at the suggestion of the Prince Regent who, like Prince George before him, had found the unmetalled road across the Weald from the 'bridge-head' at Godalming well nigh impassable); the opening of the railway in 1865 (after which it was no longer necessary for the mail to be brought from Guildford in a small cart drawn by two mastiffs—a form of transport still persisting here, although it had been banned in London twenty-five years before); and in recent years the growth of a commuter population. Cranleigh's public school, however, is of special interest. It was founded in 1863, two years before the railway arrived, and was intended originally for the education of farmers' sons. From its original twenty-six boys the school has grown to over 500, and since 1898 has been recognized as a public school. It is still predominantly a boarding school, although it now has a few day boys. Typical of Cranleigh's community spirit, which has communicated itself to the school, is the emphasis upon community service which has now partly replaced the fagging system. Another rather unusual feature of Cranleigh among public schools is its interest in agriculture; the school has its own farm, and boys interested in agriculture can learn in their spare time.

Disused railways have a fascination for me equalled only by disused canals, mines or quarries. The old Guildford to Horsham line through Cranleigh is for me one of the most poignant of Surrey's has-beens. Go to Baynards Station, built almost exclusively for the convenience of the masters and servants of Baynards and Vachery, and there you will see a station three short years along the road to dereliction: grass growing along the track, bric-a-brac littering the station platform and the name-plate missing from the twin uprights—some souvenir hunter's booty no doubt. The great gates of adjacent Baynards Park are closed and padlocked. The master no longer rides down the magnificent tree-lined drive to catch the morning train to London. What is to be done with these disused railway tracks? At Cranleigh the local authorities have opted for what seems to me the worst of all possible solutions—they are dumping refuse in a cutting! Surely there is a magnificent opportunity here for some imaginative change of use. Why not develop the track from Guildford, or at least Wonersh, to Cranleigh as a linear playground for young people, with a cycling track, paths for walkers, nature walks, adventure playgrounds, and well-sited kiosks for refreshments. Where the canal runs nearby there could be water-sporting centres linked to the linear park. Is it too visionary for the Space Age? At least it is a more imaginative suggestion than dumping refuse, which seems almost an insult to the enterprise of those who built the line a century ago.

Near Cranleigh is Shamley Green, an attractive village with the double distinction of having no less than three churches, and of being omitted from many maps of Surrey including Eric Parker's. The village has a Tanyard Farm where a tannery existed in 1840, the hides being soaked in pits kept supplied with water from the well on the farm.

Equidistant from Shamley Green, Blackheath and Albury, lies one of the oldest and most mysterious of Surrey's historic sites— the Roman Temple at Farley Heath. A minor Roman road leaves Stane Street at Rowhook and proceeds in a straight line due north-west towards St Martha's Chapel and the Guildford Gap. According to the maps it appears to have stopped short at the high ground of Farley Heath, where there was a Roman Temple, but it must surely have continued the short distance further to link Stane Street both with the Roman road from Midhurst to London and the east-west route through the Valley of the Tillingbourne. This road must have fallen into complete disuse following the departure of the Romans for it does not form any part of the present road pattern and cuts right across all the existing roads and footpaths so that its very existence was unsuspected until quite recently. What was the temple at Farley Heath like? Why was it built on this high barren heath? Why was it not built on Stane Street itself? We shall probably never know the answers to these questions, and maybe that is as well—an unsolved mystery is more exciting than a solved one which is why I think *The Mystery of Edwin Drood* is the most intriguing of all Charles Dickens' novels.

The country lying west of the Bramley Wey (sometimes called

*Leigh Place, ancestral home of the Shelley Family*
**Pump and priest's house, Leigh**

the 'Old River' to distinguish it from the Wey-Arun canal, which ran parallel for part of its distance) is the Fold Country, so called after the three villages, and many farmhouses, with the suffix 'fold' —which means a clearing or pasture in the forest. The three villages are Alfold, Dunsfold and Chiddingfold. In these remote villages could be found in the last century people who had seen the "Pharisees", or Faerie Folk, and had watched their moonlight dancing. W. Graham Robertson, who wrote the Chiddingfold Pageant Plays, wrote in 1931: "I once called to console with an old neighbour who had lost his son, and found him sitting in his smock frock—he was one of the last to wear this beautiful garment—beside his cottage door. 'I knew he was going,' he said to me very quietly. 'You see, he trod upon the Blue Flower.' I suppose I looked enquiry, for he went on: 'Ah, you don't know? No, likely not. There do grow a little blue flower in the harvest fields and the man who treads on it dies within the year. So I've just been sitting and waiting.'"

These three villages were at one time centres for the local wool and iron industry—and above all for glass-making, particularly at Chiddingfold. Utterly unlikely as it may seem today, Chiddingfold in the thirteenth century was the chief glass-making centre in England. In fact it is likely that the first glass manufactured in England was made in these Surrey glassworks. A deed of A.D. 1226 speaks of a grant of 20 acres of land near Chiddingfold to "Lawrence Vitrarius (glassmaker)", whilst from the records of Westminster Abbey we know that this same glassmaker supplied glass, both white and coloured, for the construction of the abbey.

In a very interesting article in the *Surrey County Journal*, a magazine that was published during the seven years from 1952 to 1959 (and after a decade or so has been succeeded by the flourishing Surrey County Magazine), John Clegg has described the history of early glassmaking in Surrey. He suggests that Chiddingfold was chosen mainly because there was a plentiful supply of bracken in the district, the ash from the burnt bracken being used as a source of potash for a flux in the process. The local sands, rich in silica, were also particularly suitable for glassmaking. Plentiful supplies of timber for fuel, and streams for driving machinery, were also available. No less than twenty sites have been identified

15

*The Mormon Temple, Newchapel*

in this corner of Surrey, and names like Glasshouse Copse, Glasshouse Field and Ovenhouse Field can still be traced.

The industry was still existing at Chiddingfold in the middle
of the sixteenth century since Charnock's *Breviary* of 1557 contains the following piece of verse (which is of greater historical
interest than geographical accuracy since the author incorrectly
places Chiddingfold in Sussex):

> As for glassmakers they be scant in this land
> Yet one there is as I doe understand
> And in Sussex is now his habitation
> At Chiddingfold he works of his occupation.

The industry appears to have gone into decline about the middle of
the sixteenth century, for in 1567 Jean Carré, a glassmaker of
Flemish origin living in London, petitioned for a licence to make
Venetian glass in London, and it was stated at the enquiry that
only small articles and rough goods were being made at that time
at Chiddingfold, and no window glass at all. Carré obtained his
licence to make window glass, but seems to have run into
difficulties in obtaining fuel in London, and he eventually set up
his glass works in the well-wooded corner of Surrey that he had
so disdained earlier. Chiddingfold in its hey-day must have been
a glassmaking centre of some importance because there is a map
dated 1556 in the Palazzo Vecchio at Florence which shows only
two place names in Surrey—Guildford and Chiddingfold! Jean
Carré died in 1572 and was buried at Alfold Church, where there
is an inscription on a copper tablet fixed to a slab of Sussex marble
which reads: "This slab of Sussex Marble marks the probable site
of the grave of Jean Carré, a noted worker in the ancient local
glass industry, who died May 27th. 1572 and was buried in this
churchyard." Three years later, in 1575, the immigrant glass-
makers left the district, and, although the industry continued a
little longer, it had died out completely by the middle of the
seventeenth century. This is usually attributed to the shortage of
fuel, but the indefatigable Surrey historian, E. N. Hughes, who
has personally located many of the one-time glassmaking sites,
has suggested that it was the proclamation of 1615 prohibiting the
use of timber for fuel (to safeguard supplies of ships' timbers for
the navy), and not actual physical shortage, that was primarily

responsible. Aubrey says that in Elizabeth's reign eleven glass furnaces were closed because the local people objected to them.

Is there no more tangible reminder of this ancient industry than a mere place-name or two? Indeed there is. In Chiddingfold Church is a lancet window made from fragments of ancient glass picked up from the rubbish heaps beside the old furnaces. In Chiddingfold Village, a few doors from 'The Crown', is a house which was once the home of the glassmaking family of Peyto; it can be recognized by the ancient hawthorn tree which stands in front of it surrounded by a low brick wall. This tree is said to be one of the oldest in England for as early as 1503 it was mentioned as an ancient landmark, even at that time. However one must accept these traditions with a great deal of caution, and I remember Eric Parker's wise remarks when speaking of the ancient oak at Tilford:

> These historic oaks make difficult problems. Wherever you find a great tree, local legend gathers around it. Queen Elizabeth dined under it or shot a stag under it; Charles II climbed in it; Wesley preached under it; it is the boundary of the parish; it was the boundary of the Abbeyland eight hundred years ago. But was it always, then, the greatest tree for miles around? Eight hundred years ago, may there not have stood another tree near where it stands today, as large or even larger? Surely the traditions of one great tree pass, when the tree falls, to its nearest great neighbour; but they pass so seldom, and so slowly, that the villagers hardly note the change. Three generations are born and die, and no villager living has seen the older great oak; the younger, slighter tree succeeds to its glories.

Another tangible reminder of a different kind is the excellent model in the Haslemere Educational Museum; this depicts in a most lifelike manner one of the old glassworks at Chiddingfold. During the 1914–18 war the residents of Cranleigh had yet more tangible reminder close to hand. Road stone was scarce, and so the old slag heaps remaining from the glassworks of Chiddingfold were used as quarries for material with which to repair the roads. Older Cranleigh residents can still remember the newly repaired roads glittering in the sun—a unique and beautiful memorial spanning in a flash 400 years of history.

But Chiddingfold is not to be dismissed in a word—glass—any

more than Abinger Hammer is merely iron or Ockley merely a
battle. Each village has its history, but it has its present too. Each
is a village with its own distinctive character and vigorous life.
Chiddingfold is the arch-type of a nucleated village with its
central green and round it the church, inn and shops, with roads
radiating from it in several directions. Abinger Hammer is nucleated, but without a green—Ockley has a green but is not nucleated·
—it is an almost perfect example of a linear village, straggling as it
does for over a mile along Stane Street, with roads running off the
trunk like irregularly spaced boughs. Chiddingfold also had an
iron industry, and an 'underground' clothing industry. In the
Middle Ages the clothing industry was confined to the towns
(such as Godalming and Farnham) and was forbidden in the
villages. However, we know from court records, in which individuals were accused of carrying on an illicit cloth trade, that the
manufacture of cloth was being carried on not only in Chiddingfold but in the neighbouring villages of Wonersh, Shalford, Ash
and Shere as well. Glass, iron and wool all depend upon local
supplies of raw material, and because of the bad communications
of the Weald this dependence on local resources has always been a
feature of the villages south of the Greensand. And it is a feature
of Chiddingfold still. Wholly in character is the local factory
making walking sticks which has existed there for over 100 years.
The making of walking sticks is in fact quite a feature of Wealden
villages and there are other centres at Holmwood and Witley.
Today, of course, industry takes second place at Chiddingfold to
residential development; like Haslemere and Hindhead, Chiddingfold has grown in popularity as an attractive place in which to live
within fairly convenient commuter distance from London. Already
residential development has spread across the busy Portsmouth
Road onto the western side, and before long Chiddingfold will have
a twin village there, as Hindhead has Grayshott and Haslemere, Shottermill. When Chiddingfold has lost its charm I suppose the commuters will move on to Dunsfold and Alfold—and
the damage will have been magnified (if you will forgive the pun)
three fold. I fully realize that people must have somewhere to live.
But I believe that villages like Chiddingfold have such a character
that they belong not to a favoured few but to everyone, and that
their character should be preserved and passed on to future

generations. Let residential development take place in the villages that belong to a lesser order of beauty, and let the Chiddingfolds of Surrey be saved from any development of a type and scale that could destroy their unique and irreplacable character.

# 20

# HINDHEAD AND FARNHAM, THE DEVIL'S PUNCH
# BOWL AND THE DEVIL'S JUMPS

Surrey surprises with its unexpected hills. Box Hill indeed you
expect, since it is part of the long chain of hills that comprise the
North Downs. But Chobham Ridges, Tilburstow Hill, the Devil's
Jumps, Crooksbury Hill ("As high as Crooksbury Hill" is an old
Surrey saying) and even Wimbledon Common, surprise and delight. However, the part of Surrey which possesses this quality
most abundantly, and which continues to surprise me even after so
many years familiarity, is the Devil's Punch Bowl and the country
around Hindhead. Surrey may come in like a lamb at the Thames-
side meadows of Runnymede, but she goes out like a lion at
Hindhead.

Climbing the long spur from Milford, and then rounding the
rim of the saucer to look straight down into the great combe of
the Punchbowl—this is an experience reminiscent more of North
Wales than of Southern England. Indeed I always connect in my
mind the Devil's Punch Bowl with the Horseshoe Pass between
Llangollen and Ruthin, and the reason in not simply that my
father's old Ford car broke down in a very similar position on
both hills (which events had a somewhat traumatic effect on my
young mind), but that in shape and scenery they are remarkably
similar; the main difference being that when you top the ridge of
the Horseshoe Pass you have a fine view across Denbighshire, at
Hindhead there is no such reward. Instead you find yourself in
that rather uninspiring half-way house for coaches which is the
town of Hindhead, and then follows the slow descent to Petersfield without a single view. The escarpment at Hindhead, it will
be noted, faces northwards, so that, geologically at least, the Punch

Bowl belongs to the South Downs rather than the North. Standing on his Punch Bowl, in fact, the Devil could look across Sussex
to his Dyke just behind Brighton. The wise motorist is the one
who parks his car at the car park thoughtfully provided at the top
of the Punch Bowl and then scrambles up Gibbet Hill to enjoy
the magnificent view towards Haslemere and Shottermill. He will
be standing 895 feet above sea level, or 900 if he stands on the
Celtic Cross there, near the spot where once stood the gibbet that
earned Hindhead so evil a reputation in days gone by. Those were
the days when few people valued natural or 'wild' landscape for
its own sake—how otherwise could anyone describe Hindhead as
"certainly the most villainous spot that God ever made", as
William Cobbett did? He no doubt had in mind the infertility of
the soil in these parts, but others who had passed this way may
have associated his words more with the murderers hanging from
the gibbet and the creaking of their lifeless bodies, eerie in the
night's silence. Like so many others before them they would have
hurried along the Old Portsmouth Road, oblivious of the wonderful views on either side (before it was re-routed along the more
protected inner rim of the Punch Bowl, in 1826, the road used to
run along the crest), hoping only that the undergrowth beside the
road did not harbour any desperardos. All travellers on the
Portsmouth Road knew of the dreadful crime committed in 1786,
when three ruffians had set upon a lone sailor and left him dead
and naked, only to be caught themselves soon afterwards and sent
to the gibbet erected on the scene of their crime. One wonders
who was the more deterred by the gibbet and its gruesome load,
would-be ruffians or law-abiding travellers! It seems out of proportion at first sight that this far-off crime should have cast its
shadow over the history of this region for so long. Yet there is a
reason. In an age when common people were travelling more
widely, the gibbet at Hindhead, and the crime it recalled, came to
symbolize the dangers that beset the traveller on high open heathland and common, of which Hindhead is so typical. The stone
obelisk on Gibbet Hill, the chains that were used to hang the
prisoners exhibited in the entrance hall lounge of the Royal Huts
Hotel, and the lonely sailor's grave in Thursley Churchyard with
its inscription:

No dear relation, or still dearer friend,
Weeps my hard lot, or miserable end;
Yet o'er my sad remains, (my name unknown,)
A generous Public have inscrib'd this Stone.

—they all commemorate not merely an isolated incident that took place upon Gibbet Hill, but the dangers and anxieties that every long-distance journey entailed in an age before the internal combustion engine made the vehicles more dangerous than the roads.

Perhaps I have been a little hard on Hindhead itself. During the busy summer season it is still the coaching station it has been for centuries, conveniently situated as it is about half way between London and the coast and at the top of a long hill that taxes modern vehicles only a little less than it did horse-drawn ones; but rows of fifty-two-seaters drawn up outside the self-service cafe will never have the romantic appeal of the four-in-hand waiting outside an old coaching inn. However, at other times of the year Hindhead can be a delightful place. Bernard Shaw, Conan Doyle (one can still see the letters 'C.D.' incorporated in the iron gates of 'Undershaw'), Professor Tyndall and other famous people have made their home there, and many slightly lesser mortals too, among whom were some cousins of mine whose back garden opened directly on to the Punch Bowl. Instead of taking the dog for a walk round the block, they pass through the garden gate and find themselves among the pinewoods, bracken and heather, and what Charles Dickens called "undulations shapely and uncouth", of the Punch Bowl; who would not be tempted to sup with the Devil in such a parlour? Charles Dickens obviously knew the spot well, to judge from this description in *Nicholas Nickleby*:

They walked upon the rim of the Devil's Punch Bowl, and Smike listened with greedy interest as Nicholas read the inscription on the stone, which, reared upon that wild spot, tells of a foul and treacherous murder committed there by night. The grass on which they stood had been dyed with gore and the blood of the murdered man had run down drop by drop into the hollow which gives the place its name. "The Devil's Punchbowl", thought Nicholas, as he looked into the void, "never had better liquor than that."

Hindhead has a near neighbour at Grayshott, a residential area of surprising extent, but as this lies in Hampshire we will turn our attention to Hindhead's other neighbour—Haslemere. Haslemere was once a pocket borough and sent two members to Parliament before it was dissolved in 1832, when a wit of the district wrote:

> Toll, toll: these Boroughs ne'er will be
> By us through life forgotten;
> Nor will their patrons when they lie,
> Just like their Boroughs, rotten.

Haslemere, despite its electoral demotion, is still the capital of the south-west corner of Surrey, as Lingfield is the capital of the south-east corner, and it has an urban atmosphere about it that Lingfield lacks. The Old Market House in the centre of the town, the long High Street with its pollarded lime trees, its half-timbered houses and several imposing buildings, the Georgian Hotel, the Rex Cinema and the museum; they all contribute to Haslemere's urban personality.

Like many other Wealden settlements, Haslemere does not enter recorded history until after the Domesday Book, the first mention in fact being 1180, when the village appeared as an ecclesiastical offshoot of Chiddingfold—itself for so long an ecclesiastical offshoot of Godalming. By the time of Elizabeth, however, Haslemere had lost its offshoot status and had acquired its own charter— and its own industries, the traditional Wealden industries of iron, cloth, leather and papermaking. These industries gradually declined, and although for a while a new industry took their place, silk manufacture, which employed some 200 people in the disused ironworks in the year 1809, this too eventually succumbed, and the town relapsed into the obscurity that characterized most parts of the Weald during the long sleep between the exhaustion of its iron and timber resources and the realization that there was another as yet unexploited resource—landscape and natural beauty. The romantic movement of the mid-nineteenth century brought Tennyson, Pinero, George Eliot and many other famous people, to Haslemere, whilst the new railway, opened in 1859, enabled hundreds of people of more modest means to follow, literally, in their train. Modern Haslemere is a modern miracle—a town that is very largely a commuter town, yet one that has a highly developed community and cultural life of its own and is certainly no mere dormitory appendage of some larger neighbour. A glance at its full social calendar and rich cultural life, including its annual music festival, that does for this part of Surrey what the Leith Hill Festival does for the eastern part, will confirm that it is no mere dormitory. Perhaps the secret is that the influx of new commuters has been slow enough, and the existing core of the community well enough established, for each new wave to be absorbed without difficulty. Compare this, for instance, with Hurst Green, Redhill or the Clandons. Haslemere is that rare achievement—a town, the greater part of whose male working population is exhaled forty-five miles away every morning and inhaled again every evening, yet continues breathing normally and healthily; there is surely a lesson here for town planners everywhere.

Haslemere's Educational Museum calls for special mention since it has pioneered a new conception of the role of museums in small country towns. Founded in 1894 by Sir Joseph Hutchinson, it was moved to its present site (from where the U.D.C. offices now stand) in 1926. Under its first curator, E. W. Swanton, O.B.E., who served in that capacity for over fifty years, the museum has helped to open windows in the minds of children—and adults for that matter—over a wide area round Haslemere; windows opening into the realms of geology, botany, zoology, archaeology and history (we have already referred to the model of a glassworks at Chiddingfold in the museum). The museum is full of pleasant surprises, but the most delightful of all is to look out of the windows at the back of the building and see nothing but fields and woods—and this from a building in the middle of Haslemere's High Street! It is encouraging to find an institution like this that is almost entirely maintained by private subscription—another indication of Haslemere's lively civic pride and local awareness.

As befits the home for many years of Sir Robert Hunter, one of the founders of the National Trust, the Haslemere and Hindhead districts contain a large area of land owned by the Trust, including the Devil's Punch Bowl itself, Blackdown across the border in Sussex, and Frensham Great Pond. Maybe the local residents who got together in 1906 to acquire the manorial rights to the Punch Bowl, were mindful as much of the desirability of preserving the seclusion and privacy of their own properties as of the national well-being, but the net result is the same—these lands are preserved from violation for all time. One shudders to think what the area might look like today if the National Trust had not stood guard over them until Town and Country Planning became an effective force—can there be much doubt that some at least of the extensive residential development that spread southwards from Hindhead into Grayshott would by now have been located on the crest of the rim of the Punch Bowl? The nation owes these men of Haslemere an immeasurable debt.

From Haslemere, in the extreme south-west corner, we now set out to explore the Surrey border country—the country of the Upper Wey. This is an area of great scenic beauty and immense variety, of heaths and commons, arid sands and sedgy ponds, the quiet meadows of the youthful Wey and the sudden hills of Kettlebury and the Devil's Jumps that pierce the plain and startle the eye. Descending northwards from Gibbet Hill we find our-selves at Thursley, or 'Thor's Ley', a name which reminds us, if Ockley had not already done so, of the association of the Danes with Surrey. Thor, it will be remembered, was the Scandinavian God of War (we dedicate one of the days of the week to him, which I suppose is about the right proportion since we seem to have been at war for about a seventh of our life-span as a nation), and legend has it that he made war upon the Devil who annoyed him by jumping from hill to hill. One day Thor caught the Devil in the act and bowled him over with a stone; they say you can still see the stone on the Jumps. With such a warlike name it is perhaps fitting that Thursley was at one time a major centre of the Wealden iron industry, a new ironworks having been opened here as late as 1610. On Thursley Common can still be seen the pits from which the ironstone was extracted, and the hammer ponds still exist along the stripling tributary of the Wey. It was the presence of ponds like these—including the Frensham Ponds, which were at the end of the eighteenth century supplying carp to the London markets in considerable quantities—in this otherwise arid and infertile sandy country, that gave Marshall an idea. "Might not large tracts of this worthless land be profitably covered with deep water, not merely as a source of fish but to water the dry lands that lie lower?" he suggested. He may have been an expert agriculturalist, but his geological knowledge seems to have been on the thin side. These ponds exist in this sandy heathland mainly because of the presence below the surface of a hard impervious material called 'pan', generally clay or ironstone, which effectively prevents the escape of surface water. Frensham, Black Lake, Elstead Pond and Woolmer Pond are all of this kind. To have attempted to flood large areas of Thursley Common or Tilford Common would have been like trying to store water in a colander. Stevenson, writing of the soils of this part of Surrey a few years later (1809), described them in rather picturesque language as "barren sand, soft, deaf and duffey (spongey)". Between Thursley and Churt, however, there is a corridor of land which is very fertile and which was successfully exploited by David Lloyd George for fruit growing.

And so we come to the flat valley of the Upper Wey, and to the village of Elstead with its interesting and lovely old bridge across the river (typical of several others along the Wey between Farnham and Godalming) and its water mill that dates back to Domesday times. The history of Elstead Mill is a microcosm of the history of the district itself, for it was used at different times not only for flour milling but for malting, fulling, paper-making, worsted fringe manufacture, and today for the generating of electricity—only the iron industry was missing. It is a tall handsome building of red brick with a slightly incongruous, yet pleasing, cupola on the roof.

The village of Milford lies to the east of Elstead, but it has been robbed of whatever beauty it once possessed by the motor car; Milford is like a hand pressed flat on a table, the thumb is the Godalming Bypass, the index finger the old Portsmouth Road to Godalming, and the other three fingers roads to Littlehampton, Bognor and Portsmouth. As Eric Parker said in his 1950 edition (it probably did not apply in 1908 when his book was first published) "Milford on a summer Saturday is less a village than a road". The dead hand of five major roads has throttled this village. This Milford has no Haven.

Tucked away a little to the south of Milford is Hambledon, a village that might pass altogether unnoticed were it not for the fact that it has lent its name to the huge rural district of Hambledon which covers over 100 square miles of country between Farnham and Cranleigh. Like Tandridge it just happened to be about in the centre of an amorphous district, and so they called the administrative area by its name. How many people in Surrey have ever heard of the village outside those who live within a few miles radius? I asked a Surrey friend recently if he had heard of the village, and his immediate reply was "Ah the famous cricketing village"—but he was wrong, that lies across the border in Hampshire. Of course there are no administrative offices in Hambledon, these are in Guildford. From 1st April 1974 the Rural District was renamed 'Waverley'.

From Milford we 'thumb' our way northwards along the Godalming Bypass to the turn-off for Compton, the first of the three beautiful villages in the valley below the Hog's Back.

The villages of this valley are as ancient as the Great White Way itself; for the road through the valley was an alternative road to that along the crest. The drovers no doubt preferred the Hog's Back route with its wide grassy verges, but individual travellers probably preferred the more sheltered and homely route through the valley, and appreciated the opportunity of a drink at one of the inns there, or a night's lodging—and if it was windy or wet the valley must have seemed a better proposition than the exposed Hog's Back. Furthermore, the valley was a convenient route back to the hilltop track for those who had made the detour to Waverley Abbey *en route*. Travelling along the valley at night recently I was surprised and pleased to discover that one is completely unaware of the heavy traffic along the top of the Hog's Back—at no point did I see any headlights. Mercifully the road must lie just sufficiently below the crest itself for the headlights to be hidden. So one proceeds in quiet solitude along the valley, untroubled by the existence of those two lines of traffic, hurtling towards each other like tracer bullets, just over the horizon.

Compton, which has an old-world calm all its own, must at one time have been the most important of the three villages along the valley. I happened to see Camden's *Britannia* map of Surrey the other day, and noticed that Compton was shown even though the scale was very small (this was at the end of the sixteenth century). I know a little of Compton because I once had a friend whose first appointment as a pastor in the Congregational Church was to the Compton district, and on my visits to him I gained some impression of its peacefulness and charm—and a sense of remoteness that even the presence of the Godalming Bypass a few hundred yards away has not altogether dispelled. Most young ministers cut their ecclesiastical teeth on a large slum parish, but my friend had the singular fortune to cut his in the gentle countryside, and among the cultured and warm-hearted people, of Compton. Compton Church has some fascinating and unique treasures, including a double chancel and the only two storeyed sanctuary in England, together with a wooden Norman screen fencing off the upper sanctuary which is claimed to be the oldest in England. Notice also the tiles made by the people of Compton surrounding the door of the cemetery chapel, a fitting tribute to the famous, if now rather *passé*, artist G. F. Watts, who lies buried a few yards away. The chapel is built of hard chalk known locally as 'clunch'—the ancient keep of Guildford Castle is built of the same material. Compton's art gallery and chapel are visited by thousands of people every year.

The next village along the valley is Puttenham, built on sloping ground so that the cottages, like those of Oxted, are approached by outside steps of brick or stone. From here a first-class road climbs the steep face of the escarpment, continuing as a minor road down the other side to the village of Wanborough. The Hog's Back is so steep-sided that I remember as a child being puzzled that roads (and presumably cars) could actually climb its sides. Today the impact is slightly diminished by the new road bridge which has just been completed along the Hog's Back at this point so that the cross traffic now passes under the main road. "Puttenham lyes upon a fine gravel", wrote Aubrey, "and on an ascent, from where is a good prospect of the country, and is remarkable for its situation, the wholesomeness of its most beneficial air, and other desirable advantages, to render life easy and pleasant." The third village in this enchanted vale is Seale, completing a trinity of beauty and charm that might today have suffered the fate of Ash and Tongham, only a mile or two further north, had it not been for the interposition of the Hog's Back to stem the urban tide.

We now stand at the outskirts of Farnham, but before entering the town we will, with the travellers of old who were seeking a roof for the night and a friendly welcome from the monks, take a detour to Waverley Abbey, one of the most romantic and significant of Surrey's historic sites. The abbey was the first to be founded by the Cistercians in Britain. They were a strict monastic order whose adherents lived a simple life and needed few possessions, but whose skill and hard work made them, paradoxically, rich and successful. The sister of Tintern Abbey in the Wye Valley, Waverley was the grandmother of seven others and was thus one of the most influential abbeys in the order. As with other Cistercian abbeys, the site of Waverley was deliberately chosen for its isolation, although it is doubtful if they would have chosen the location they did had they known how susceptible it was to flooding; more than once the buildings were completely under water and had to be evacuated. The monks of Waverley certainly paid a high price for their adherence to the rule of their order that the abbey should be built by a stream and "remote from the conversation of men". The abbey flourished for several centuries, and in 1270 it is reported to have provided hospitality to the Bishop of Winchester and no less than 7,066 guests! However, its proximity to London made it an early target for Thomas Cromwell in 1536, and he quickly harried his quarry to ground, the dissolution of the monastery taking place later that year. Waverley Abbey then became a quarry in another sense as the local inhabitants, led by Sir William More (who was rebuilding Loseley at the time), helped themselves to stone from the buildings. Today most of the original structure above ground has disappeared, leaving only some beautiful vaulting and a few heaps of stone where the walls of the abbey once stood. If Sir Walter Scott had not immortalized the name, perhaps Waverley Abbey would by now have suffered the fate of Merton Priory.

Farnham fulfils so many functions that it is difficult to decide which is its major one. It forms the southern edge of that sprawling urban and industrial area that occupies both sides of the Surrey-Hampshire border from Frimley through Ash and Aldershot to Farnham. As befits the birthplace of that great traveller, William Cobbett, Farnham is also the nexus of several important routes, including the London Road via Bagshot, the London Road via Guildford, and the east-west road along the North Downs. And, thirdly, it is the major market town and administrative centre for a large area of Surrey and a sizeable part of Hampshire across the border. In appearance and tradition Farnham is so obviously a country town that I have elected to regard its third role as its most distinctive, and it is for this reason that it appears in Part Three of this Portrait—it could just as logically have appeared in either of the other two. Because it lies at the very apex of the 'half spear-head' of the chalk country, at the point where the Low Country, the Chalk and the Weald all meet, Farnham, alone of all the towns in Surrey, could equally appropriately wear all three 'hats'.

There is nothing *nouveau riche* or bourgeois about Farnham. Red brick it may be, but it is the red brick of Hampton Court not of Rugby. The town wears the mantle of authority, and carries itself with the natural grace and dignity of a fourteenth earl. This authority derives in part from its regional status as the capital of the south-west corner of Surrey, but even more from its role as the traditional seat of the bishops of Winchester and its possession of a large and strategically important castle. Like so many other ecclesiastical and fortress towns, Farnham has a beguiling assembly of architectural styles spanning the centuries, but it has a larger proportion of genuine eighteenth-century architecture than any other town in Surrey. Castle Street is without doubt the most magnificent entrance to any town in the county, although, regrettably, probably few people approach Farnham from this direction. The road drops steeply down from the hills to the north of Farnham, skirts the castle walls and Farnham Park and then suddenly you find yourself right in the centre of Farnham—in its finest street in fact. None of the dreary suburbia that is the price you have to pay for the beauties of central Guildford, Dorking or Reigate. Let Farnham preserve this jewel in its crown at all costs, for it is utterly irreplaceable and as vital a part of the spirit of Farnham, and indeed of Surrey, as Caernarvon Castle is to the Welsh or Castle Rock to Scotland.

Farnham Castle was the home of the Bishops of Winchester for over 1,000 years, ever since the Saxon king Ethelbald gave the land to Saint Swithun, although it is now of course part of the Diocese of Guildford. It may seem strange to us today that a castle should also serve as a bishop's palace, but in the Middle Ages, when Bishops were often Chancellors of England, this was not unusual. The castle keep was built by the Normans, but the magnificent entrance tower, embattled and built of the red brick so characteristic of Farnham's buildings (and which has led to Farnham being christened 'The Red Town') is better-known to most people—it

*By-water of the Wey near Waverley Abbey*

was built by Bishop Fox at the end of the fifteenth century. The castle changed hands several times during the Civil War and suffered some damage, but it survived this ordeal, only to be partially demolished by order of Parliament in the time of Cromwell.

Farnham is the centre of an industry which is found nowhere else in Surrey—hop gardens. They can be seen on either side of the road as one descends from the Hog's Back towards Farnham. Years before I saw the Kentish hopfields I had been intrigued by these few hop gardens and often wondered how they came to exist so far from 'home'. They represent, in fact, the dying remnant of what was once a far more extensive industry in the district. How it first came to Farnham nobody knows, although there is some evidence of the existence of hop gardens at places along the Vale of Holmesdale, and its extension westwards, which has led to the suggestion that the growing of hops spread through the valley until it arrived at Farnham. However, it seems more likely that the industry was established directly at Farnham because the soil conditions were suitable, there were south-facing slopes, and plentiful supplies of copse timber for poles were near at hand. The local farmers found such a lucrative market for their small timber that they had a saying: "The underwood will buy the horse, the wood the saddle." The hop plant (which comes from the same family as the stinging nettle) was established in England during the Reformation, and this gave rise to the couplet:

Hops, Reformation, baize and beer,
Came into England all in a year.

However, the industry does not appear in the records of the Farnham district until the early seventeenth century. By 1726 it had begun to have a marked effect upon the landscape, as a contemporary observer, J. K. Lawrence, noted: "the noble plantations of hops at Farnham, where for regularity and exactness they appear like woods and groves cut into vistas . . . are a wonderful sight.' In 1886 the acreage of hops in the Farnham district reached its peak level of 3,837 acres (out of 70,127 in England and Wales as a whole), but thence onwards, with the decline in beer drinking and the increasing public preference for light beers, the acreage steadily declined, and today there are only a few hundred acres of hops left. No longer can one see the notoriously insanitary camps
16

*The Devil's Punch Bowl, Hindhead*

erected for the migrant hop-pickers, vagrants, Irish women and children and ne'er-do-wells of all kinds, numbering, at the height of the industry's prosperity in this corner of Surrey, no less than 6,000 workers. Religious missions were established to cater for their souls, but one cynic at the time remarked that the water these poor people had to drink was so foul that it would save lives if they stopped drinking it altogether and took to beer instead! The cholera claimed as many victims as the Devil, and the well-intentioned missionaries were kept busy. All this, happily, is a thing of the past, but one or two vestiges of this once-great industry, in addition to the few lonely hop fields that every motorist sees as he descends from the Hog's Back, still lingered on. For example, there were the breweries which continued to flourish in Farnham, although they drew their hop supplies from other areas. Until quite recently one could walk into a Farnham greengrocers and buy a small quantity of local-grown hops for home brewing, and still, I believe, the school holidays in the Alton-Farnham area are traditionally fixed with regard to the hop-picking season so as to allow the children to participate.

At Farnham we stand at the very edge of Surrey, in fact the town is truly a border town and looks as much to Alton and Winchester as it does to Guildford. It has been said that Surrey "is like a plain shawl with a beautiful border"—if so (which I would dispute) then the Farnham district is certainly an exquisite part of the border.

We have yet one more place left to visit before we take our leave of Surrey. I have purposely left it to the last. When leaving for a time a place you love very much you instinctively seek out some spot which most intimately symbolizes the essence of that place. So now we take this last pilgrimage of farewell, passing through Farnham, across the Wey, up the steep hill the other side, across Farnham Common and on to Frensham Great Pond. This sandy heath, with its pine trees and its bracken and its many paths and riding tracks scarred across its desert-like surface, and its great pond with its water-fowl, this wild stretch of common, represents what is most characteristic of Surrey's scenery. Yes, Surrey has magnificent chalk scenery, but so also have Kent and Hampshire and other counties. But Surrey alone has such magnificent heaths and commons, from Wimbledon, buried deep in the Metropolis itself, to Chobham, Pirbright, Banstead, Limpsfield, Leith Hill, Hindhead and the great swathe of country from Cranleigh to Farnham. They are wild and raw and unkempt, and one can roam at will over hundreds of square miles; they mean broad open skies, the smell of pinewoods and the friendly aloneness (that is not the same as loneliness) of the countryside to tens of thousands of Surrey people, accustomed, in their working hours, to the dark alleys between tall buildings, the stink of petrol and exhaust gases and the crushing loneliness of a crowd.

Yet all this may be gone tomorrow. Even here at Frensham Common groups of houses stand here and there, utterly alien in the landscape, portending what the future might hold. The Surrey County Council has nominated Frensham as the second of the new Country Parks in Surrey (the other is at Box Hill), and this wise move will ensure that adequate provision is made for the people who wish to come and enjoy this area. Surrey is an embattled county fighting for its survival—and Frensham Common is as much in the front line as Wimbledon Common. Sails speckle the waters of the Great Pond—and we do not object, for when the yachtsmen have gone, and their boats lie quietly asleep in their cradles, the water fowl return to claim their own, and during the long winter months they are left alone to enjoy their domain. Here it was that Julian Huxley studied the courting habits to the Great Crested Grebe and so added a chapter of knowledge of post-Darwinism—but that of course was before they drained the pond to prevent its being a landmark to German bombers. However if urban fingers creep out from Farnham to grasp this 'worthless land', and other areas like it in Surrey, we must protest. For it is not Frensham Common alone that is at stake, but the very future of Surrey as a place of beauty in which people are proud and happy to live. At a deeper level still, what is at stake is the full development of the human spirit, for, as William Wordsworth expressed it: "When the eye is starved of beauty the soul languishes." Surrey people are dimly aware that their county is a test-bench where the *modus vivendi* is being forged that can enable Man to enjoy his natural environment without destroying it in the process. Upon a solution to this problem being found depends the happiness, and the chance for a full life, of millions of Surrey people yet unborn. Unless an answer is found the portrait of Surrey will be changed, like the picture of Dorian Gray, into a progressively hideous disfigurement of a once beautiful face. I have every confidence that this will not happen; I believe that with the Ministry of Housing and Local Government together with our own County Planning Department, the Countryside Commission and the National Trust, all alert to the dangers, and as anxious as anybody to avert them, Surrey will not be allowed to disappear beneath an urban tidal wave that sweeps all before it, but will direct such growth as is inescapable into those channels where it can do least harm to the landscape. This may mean a restriction of personal choice for the common good, and if this book has helped to make the acceptance of such restrictions more acceptable it will have achieved one of its objects. Whether it has achieved its other object, to awaken in every Surreyman's breast a fresh appreciation of his county's beauty, the reader alone must be the judge.

# INDEX